How You and Your Computer Think Alike—and Don't: An Exploration into the Nature of Mind

How You and Your Computer Think Alike—and Don't: An Exploration into the Nature of Mind

Steven Cushing, Ph.D.

ISBN 978-0-557-40710-1

Published by Pond Place Press, Boston

*To all sentient beings,
biological and
—perhaps someday?—
mechanical*

Preface

This book has its roots in a course I developed and taught to demonstrate to non-technical undergraduates how traditional philosophical problems of knowledge, cognition, language, and human nature can be investigated with computer-related concepts and techniques. The students were primarily humanities and social studies majors for whom that course would be the only conceptual exposure to computers they would ever expect to have. The book draws on material from computation theory, artificial intelligence, and logic programming, with emphasis on three key notions: (1) that mental phenomena are real, (2) that they can be studied experimentally, and (3) that they can be modeled insightfully in computational—i.e., information-processing—terms. The first of these notions presents a challenge to *behaviorism*, the view that the mind is an epiphenomenon that cannot or need not be understood. The second presents a challenge to *phenomenology*, the view that the mind is real but can be understood only through introspection. The third notion provides a means for investigating the claims embodied in those two challenges; it is not a claim that computation is all there is to mind.

Exploring these notions takes the form of a series of expeditions that begin with mental exercises or experiments that anyone can do on their own. Though simple in concept, each exercise illustrates a basic fact or principle drawn from one of the disciplines generally recognized as having contributed substantially to the development of cognitive science: computer science, philosophy, psychology, artificial intelligence, and linguistics. In teaching, I conduct each experiment in class and then have the students themselves conduct it as a homework assignment, with their friends or families as subjects. Feel free to do that here, as I describe each exercise in turn and then draw out its implications for the computation/cognition connection.

Acknowledgements

Outlines of the course that eventually became this book were published in the proceedings of two conferences at which I presented them: *Behavior Research Methods, Instruments, & Computers* (**21(2)**:155-159) and *Computers and the Humanities* (**25**:275-280). I would like to thank the organizers of those conferences and the editors of those proceedings for giving me the opportunity to explore these ideas in those venues. Many thanks also go to the participants in those conferences and to the students who took that course for the helpful, thought-provoking feedback they graciously provided along the way. Special thanks go to the staff of The Computer Loft in Allston, Massachusetts, for technical assistance with obsolete equipment. Most importantly, I thank Meera, Maya, Muntu, Maitri, and Suzanne for inspiration and diversion that was indispensible in helping me to endure the always tedious process of bringing a manuscript through to completion.

Expeditions

1. Reckoning: Functions and Algorithms

I begin by conducting a "mind-reading" demonstration, in which I correctly guess, for each of the students, a number that the student has chosen. After telling them to choose a number from one to ten, I instruct the students to perform various arithmetic operations, after which they are asked what result has been obtained. I then tell them, always correctly, what the number was that they originally chose. To their credit, the students generally do not believe that I have actually read their minds—nor do most of their friends, when they do the exercise as a homework assignment. However, they are always at a loss to explain how I might have determined their numbers, their best guess usually being "some kind of mathematical trick." The "trick," in fact, is simple algebra, in which I apply to the symbol x the same operations that I instruct the students to apply to their chosen numbers. The final expression, when combined with each of their results, becomes a simple equation that is easily solved mentally for x.

As an example, consider the steps in (1), which illustrates the process for one choice by me of arithmetic operations and for a student who has chosen the number 6.

(1)	Instructions to Students	Sample Student's Results	Mental Calculation
	1. Choose a number.	6	x
	2. Add 1.	$6 + 1 = 7$	$x + 1$
	3. Multiply the result by itself.	$7 * 7 = 49$	$(x + 1)^2 = x^2 + 2x + 1$
	4. Subtract the square of the original number.	$49 - 36 = 13$	$2x + 1$
	5. Tell me your current result.	13	$2x + 1 = 13$
	6. Your original number is 6.		$x = 6$

No matter what numbers the students choose, my mental calculation will parallel theirs exactly, as long as they follow my instructions correctly. When the student in the example adds one to the chosen number 6, the resulting 6 plus 1 becomes 7, but for me it is just $x + 1$.

When the student multiplies that *7* by itself, the *7* times *7* becomes *49*, but my $x + 1$ times $x + 1$ becomes $x^2 + 2x + 1$, as (2) shows, where each "piece" of each x + 1 is multiplied by each "piece" of the other.

$$(2) \quad (x+1) * (x+1) \quad = \quad (x * x) + (x * 1) + (1 * x) + (1 * 1)$$
$$= \quad x^2 + x + x + 1$$
$$= \quad x^2 + 2x + 1$$

As is common in computer usage, I use "*" for "times" in (2). Subtracting the square of the original number *6* from *49* leaves the student with *49 - 36* which becomes *13*, while I am left with *2x + 1*, having subtracted the x^2 from my result in (2). By the time the student reaches the final result *13*, I have obtained the necessarily equivalent result *2x + 1*, so I just solve the equation that equates these results for the "unknown" *x* in the usual way by performing the same operations on both sides of the equation, as (3) illustrates.

$$(3) \quad 2x + 1 \qquad = \quad 13$$
$$2x + 1 - 1 \qquad = \quad 13 - 1$$
$$2x \qquad = \quad 12$$
$$(1/2) * 2x \qquad = \quad (1/2) * 12$$
$$x \qquad = \quad 6$$

Two further variants of this exercise are illustrated in (4) and (5).

(4)	**Instructions to Students**	**Sample Student's Results**	**Mental Calculation**
	1. Choose a number.	6	x
	2. Add 1.	6 + 1 = 7	x + 1
	3. Multiply the result by itself.	7 * 7 = 49	$(x + 1)^2 = x^2 + 2x + 1$
	4. Subtract the square of the original number.	49 - 36 = 13	2x + 1
	5. Subtract the double of the original number.	13 - 12 = 1	1
	6. Your final result is 1.		1

(5) Instructions to Students	Sample Student's Results	Mental Calculation
1. Choose a number.	6	x
2. Add 1.	6 + 1 = 7	x + 1
3. Multiply the result by itself.	7 * 7 = 49	$(x + 1)^2 = x^2 + 2x + 1$
4. Subtract the square of the original number.	49 - 36 = 13	2x + 1
5. Subtract 1.	13 - 1 = 12	2x
6. Take half the current result.	6	(1/2) * (2x) = x
7. You now have your original number.		x

In (4), I get all students to reach the same final result by having them subtract twice the original number in a new step 5 after subtracting its square in step 4. In (5), I get the students back to their original chosen numbers by having them subtract *1* in a new step 5. This leaves them with twice their original number, after which I have them take half of that in a new step 6. Variants (4) and (5) differ from (1) in that I still end up knowing something about the students' final results without ever having to ask them for any information. In (4) I know their results, which are the same for all of them, while in (5) I know only that they have all returned to their original starting points.

Despite its simplicity, this exercise succeeds in illustrating the most fundamental concept of computer science, namely, the *formal character of algorithms*. An *algorithm* is a step-by-step procedure (i) that always produces a definite result in a finite number of steps, and (ii) that can be applied to all entities of the appropriate sort (in this case, numbers) depending only on the general form of the symbols that express the algorithm without regard to what those symbols refer to. This property of *formality* is what makes it possible for humans to implement algorithms as computer programs and for computers to produce humanly significant results by blindly manipulating symbols in accordance with fixed rules. The steps in the right-hand Mental Calculation columns of (1), (4), and (5) are simple examples of algorithms, each providing a general procedure that parallels the specific calculations for specific values in the respective left-hand columns and taking only the forms of numbers into account. For example, the number *13* in step 4 is of interest there not for its own sake, but because it can be expressed in the form *2x + 1* for some previously chosen number *x*. The number *49* in step 3 is of interest only because it is a perfect square, that is, of the form x^2. Not every number has this form, if we restrict the values of *x* to whole numbers. That will be the case throughout this expedition.

Arithmetic expresses the *particular* properties of individual numbers, for example, the fact that only the number *49* has the property of being the square of *7*. In contrast, algebra expresses the *universal* properties of numbers in general, for example, the fact that every number *x* has the property that $(x + 1)^2 = x^2 + 2x + 1$. Computer programmers make use of such universal properties when they write programs that manipulate the forms of numbers, much as I did in (1), (4), and (5). They don't need to have any knowledge at all of what particular numbers turn out to be referred to, when the programs they write are actually run.

One especially interesting universal property of numbers is the distributive law of multiplication over addition, stated in its two versions in (6).

(6) (a)   x * (y + z)   =   (x * y) + (x * z)

    (b)   (y + z) * x   =   (y * x) + (z * x)

This law says that if you multiply a number *x* by the result of adding two other numbers *y* and *z*, you will get the same final result as if you multiply each of the numbers first by *x* to get *x * y* and *x * z* (or *y * x* and *z * x*, depending on the order of the multiplications—the result is the same in either case) and then add those two results. It is this law that underlies mental calculation techniques such as that of multiplying *18* by *23* by splitting *23* into two parts, *20* and *3*, and then multiplying *18* by each part separately and adding those results, as (7) shows.

(7)   18 * 23   =   18 * (20 + 3)

             =   (18 * 20) + (18 * 3)

             =   360 + 54

             =   414

This is also the law that underlies (2), in which I broke *x + 1* into *x* and *1* for the purpose of multiplication. However, in that case, it implicitly operated three times, first breaking up the first *x + 1* by

(6)(b), with the second $x + 1$ treated as a single unit, and then breaking up the second $x + 1$ by two occurrences of (6)(a), as (8) shows.

$$\begin{aligned}
(8) \ (x + 1) * (x + 1) &= [x * (x + 1)] + [1 * (x + 1)] & \text{[by (6)(b)]} \\
&= (x * x) + (x * 1) + [1 * (x + 1)] & \text{[by (6)(a)]} \\
&= (x * x) + (x * 1) + (1 * x) + (1 * 1) & \text{[by (6)(a)]} \\
&= x^2 \ + \ \ x \ \ + \ \ x \ \ + \ \ 1 \\
&= x^2 \ + \ \ 2x \ + \ \ 1
\end{aligned}$$

This law is especially interesting because it raises the question of the non-symmetry of $+$ and $*$ in ordinary arithmetic. In other words, if there is a distributive law of multiplication over addition, why shouldn't there be a distributive law of addition over multiplication? Mathematicians call that sort of thing a *dual* law. Such a law would be as (9) states, which is identical to (6) except that the "+" and "*" have been interchanged.

$$\begin{aligned}
(9) \quad (a) \quad & x + (y * z) & = \quad & (x + y) * (x + z) \\
(b) \quad & (y * z) + x & = \quad & (y + x) * (z + x)
\end{aligned}$$

The answer to this question is, of course, that numbers just don't behave that way, as (10) illustrates.

$$\begin{aligned}
(10) \quad & 2 + (3 * 4) & = \quad & 2 + 12 \ = \ 14 \\
& \text{but} \\
& (2 + 3) * (2 + 4) & = \quad & 5 * 6 \ \ = \ 30
\end{aligned}$$

In other words, the particular fact in (10) that *14* is not the same as *30* is enough to invalidate (9) as a universal law, which would have to apply to all numbers. Since (9) requires that the two calculations in (10) must have the same results, the fact that they do not disproves (9), disqualifying it from being a law.

However, there are mathematical structures—that is, ways of dealing with numbers—for which the analogs of both (6) and (9) do hold, and some of these are very useful in computer applications. To make things a bit simpler, focus, just for the time being, on a smaller collection of numbers, say, the numbers in (11), rather than on the full collection of all numbers.

(11)   1, 2, 3, 4, 6, 9, 12, 18, 36

Quite aside from how they have been ordered in (11), these numbers have a *natural ordering* in terms of their relative sizes, as the diagram shown in Figure 1 illustrates. Such diagrams, called *Hasse diagrams*, were first introduced in the early years of the last century by the number theorist, Helmut Hasse, to illustrate methods of solving equations. Each number in (11) is represented by a *node* or *vertex* in Figure 1, and each number's vertex is connected by an *arc* or *edge* to the vertex of the next smaller number below it, if there is one. For example, *1* is immediately below *2*, which is immediately below *3*, and so on. However, we can also order the numbers in (11) in a different way, in terms of their *divisibility*, that is, in terms of which numbers divide evenly into which other numbers. Viewed in this way, the numbers in (11) turn out to be ordered very differently, as the Hasse diagram shown in Figure 2 illustrates. In this figure, each number's node appears below and connected to just those numbers that the number divides evenly into.

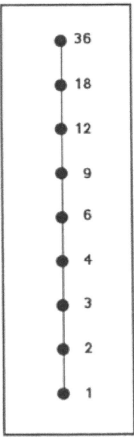

Fig. 1: Hasse Diagram for the Natural Ordering of (11)

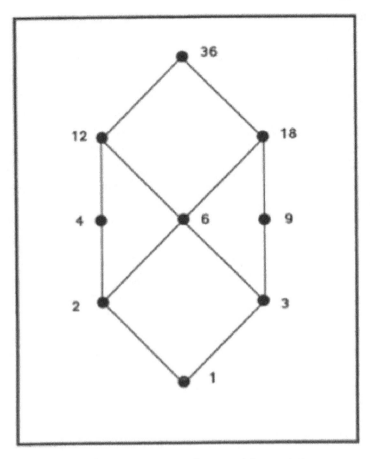

Fig. 2: Hasse Diagram for Divisibility in (11)

Each of these figures provides a visual representation of what mathematicians call a *partially ordered set* or *poset*, that is, a collection of objects—in this case the numbers in (11)—that are ordered with respect to each other in some way. The poset represented in Figure 1 is also said to be *linearly ordered*, because the numbers end up being ordered in a straight line. This contrasts with the more complicated geometry of Figure 2. Figure 1's poset is also said to be *totally ordered*, because no matter which two numbers we might choose, we can always reach one from the other on some path moving only upward from below. That is not the case in Figure 2. For example, we can get from *2* to *18* in Figure 2 by taking two upward steps along the diagonal that connects *2* with *18*, passing *6* along the way. However, we cannot get from *12* to *18* along any path in Figure 2 by taking only upward steps, as we can do in Figure 1.

The posets that the two figures represent contain the same numbers (11), but they provide different orderings for those numbers. Figure 1 reflects the usual sequential ordering of numbers, whereas Figure 2 reflects their ordering in relation to divisibility. Figure 2 can also be characterized in terms of two operations that reflect divisibility. Now put aside, for a moment, the arithmetic of addition and multiplication and view the numbers in (11) in terms of the poset in Figure 2. There is nothing inherent in the symbols "+" and "*" themselves that requires us to use them with the meanings that we usually give them, or that prohibits us from using them in some other way. The usual meanings of these symbols are historical accidents, the result of a decision by someone at some time to use these symbols in that way. The symbol "+" could just as well have been used to represent not the sum, but the *least common multiple* of two numbers—that is, the smallest number that both numbers divide evenly into—and the symbol "*" could just as well have been used to mean not the product, but the *greatest common divisor* of two numbers—that is, the largest number that divides evenly into both numbers. For example, in terms of this alternate usage of these symbols in reference to the poset of Figure 2, the value of *2 * 3* will be *1*, because *1* is the largest number that divides evenly into both *2* and *3*, and the value of *2 + 3* will be *6*, because *6* is the smallest number that both *2* and *3* divide evenly into. Similarly, the value of *12 * 18* will be *6*, because *6* is the largest number that divides evenly into both *12* and *18*, and the value of *12 + 18* will be *36*, because *36* is the smallest number that both *12* and *18* divide evenly into.

In a computer setting, what we just did here is referred to as *overloading*, that is, giving more than one meaning to an operation symbol, depending on the kinds of objects we are using the operations with, or on the ways those objects might behave in relation to each other. In relation to the numbers with their usual ordering in Figure 1, we gave the symbols "+" and "*" the meanings addition and multiplication, respectively, but in relation to the numbers in their divisibility ordering in Figure 2, we could just as well give the same symbols the meanings least common multiple and greatest common divisor, respectively. Overloading of symbols takes a little getting used to, but it turns out to be a very convenient technique and produces interesting results, as we are about to see. A computer gets used to it immediately, just by being programmed to do so. Overloading of symbols is really no stranger than the fact that an ordinary word can have more than one meaning; for example, the English word, *trunk*, can mean a storage box, a tree's stem, or an elephant's nose, depending on the context in which we are using it and what we are using it for. Of course, we need to take care, just as we do with words, to overload symbols only in contexts in which the meanings we intend for them will be clear, and to use them in those contexts strictly in accordance with those intended meanings.

What is interesting about this particular bit of overloading is the fact that, unlike addition and multiplication, which satisfy the distributive law (6) but not its dual distributive law (9), least common multiple (denoted here by "+") and greatest common divisor (denoted here by "*") turn out to satisfy both of the distributive laws (6) and (9), as (12) and (13) illustrate.

(12)   for the distributive law (6):

$$2 * (3 + 4) \qquad = \qquad 2 * 12 \qquad = \qquad 2$$

and

$$(2 * 3) + (2 * 4) \qquad = \qquad 1 + 2 \qquad = \qquad 2$$

(13)   for the distributive law (9):

$$2 + (3 * 4) \qquad = \qquad 2 + 1 \qquad = \qquad 2$$

and

$$(2 + 3) * (2 + 4) \qquad = \qquad 6 * 4 \qquad = \qquad 2$$

For (12), the smallest number that both *3* and *4* divide evenly into is *12*, and the largest number that divides evenly into both *2* and *12* is *2;* meanwhile, the largest number that divides evenly into both *2* and *3* is *1*, the largest number that divides evenly into both *2* and *4* is *2*, and the smallest number that both *1* and *2* divide evenly into is *2*. For (13), the largest number that divides evenly into both *3* and *4* is *1*, and the smallest number that both *2* and *1* divide evenly into is *2*; meanwhile, the smallest number that both *2* and *3* divide evenly into is *6*, the smallest number that both *2* and *4* divide evenly into is *4*, and the largest number that divides evenly into both *6* and *4* is *2*. In fact, no matter how we choose particular numbers from (11), the laws in (6) and (9) will always work with these new meanings for "+" and "*", so both (6) and (9) turn out to be universal laws for these new operations, even though (9) is not a universal law for addition and multiplication.

The poset in Figure 2 is an example of what mathematicians call a *distributive lattice*, a mathematical structure that appears very often in computer science. It is said to be *distributive* because it satisfies both of the distributive laws (6) and (9). It is said to be a *lattice* because, no matter which two nodes might be chosen, the paths up or down from them will always eventually have a unique node where they first touch. This contrasts, for example, with the poset that is represented by the Hasse diagram in Figure 3.

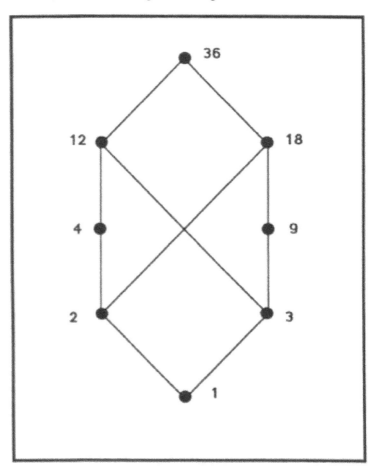

Fig. 3: A Poset that is NOT a Lattice

This diagram does not represent a lattice because paths up from nodes *2* and *3* can first cross either at *12* or at *18*, rather than only at one unique node, and paths down from nodes *12* and *18* can first cross either at *2* or at *3*, rather than only at one unique node. This is because the intersecting point at the middle of the diagram, which would correspond to the node of *6* in Figure 2, is not occupied by any node in Figure 3, but is merely a point at which two lines cross. You can imagine one of the two intersecting lines from *2* to *18* or from *3* to *12* to be jumping slightly over the other in three dimensions, but in two dimensions we have to draw them so that they seem to intersect, even though there is no node at that point. The poset in Figure 3 provides a perfectly legitimate ordering of the numbers in (11) with *6* removed, and this way of ordering those numbers might very well be useful in solving some problem. However, it is an ordering that lacks a key property of lattices and thus would not be appropriate for problems that require a lattice structure.[1]

The poset of Figure 1 *is* a distributive lattice, but not for addition and multiplication; rather, as a lattice, it reflects the operations *maximum* and *minimum*, that is, the operations that provide the larger or smaller, respectively, of two numbers. The poset qualifies as a lattice, because the paths down from any two numbers will always first touch uniquely at the node that represents the smaller of the two numbers, their minimum, and the paths up from any two numbers will always first touch uniquely at the node that represents the larger of the two numbers, their maximum. We can see that it is distributive by overloading "+" and "*" to mean maximum and minimum, respectively, as illustrated in (14) and (15).

(14)   for the distributive law (6):

$$2 * (3 + 4) \qquad = \qquad 2 * 4 \qquad = \qquad 2$$

and

$$(2 * 3) + (2 * 4) \qquad = \qquad 2 + 2 \qquad = \qquad 2$$

(15)   for the distributive law (9):

$$2 + (3 * 4) \qquad = \qquad 2 + 3 \qquad = \qquad 3$$

and

---

[1] *Suggested excursion:* Figure 3 shows a poset that is not a lattice. Try to construct a lattice that is not distributive. In other words, figure out what it would take for a poset to be a lattice without being a distributive lattice. (*Hint:* Try putting a node between *6* and *36* in Figure 2. Then test the distributive laws. Remember that the resulting diagram no longer represents divisibility. What, if anything, does it represent?)

$$(2+3) * (2+4) \qquad = \qquad 3 * 4 \qquad = \qquad 3$$

For (14), the maximum of *3* and *4* is *4* and the minimum of *2* and *4* is *2*; meanwhile, the minimum of *2* and *3* is *2*, the minimum of *2* and *4* is *2*, and the maximum of *2* and *2* is *2*. For (15), the minimum of *3* and *4* is *3*, and the maximum of *2* and *3* is *3*; meanwhile, the maximum of *2* and *3* is *3*, the maximum of *2* and *4* is *4*, and the minimum of *3* and *4* is *3*. In fact, as we noted for greatest common divisor and least common multiple in relation to numbers chosen from Figure 2, minimum and maximum also satisfy both (6) and (9), no matter how we might choose numbers from the lattice in Figure 1.

Of course, the lattices that are really of most interest are not those of Figures 1 and 2, but the infinite lattices that include all numbers, of which those figures are just portions. It is possible, but unlikely, that anyone would ever really be interested only in the numbers in (11), which we focused on here temporarily just to simplify the explanations. Figure 1 represents only a small portion of the lattice of all numbers with the usual ordering, which is shown more extensively in Figure 4, and Figure 2 represents only a small portion of the lattice of all numbers with the divisibility ordering, which is shown more extensively in Figure 5.

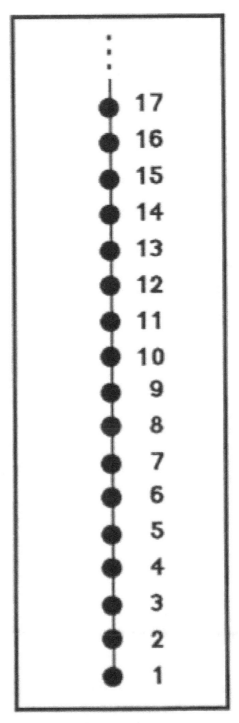

Fig. 4: Lattice of All Whole Numbers with the Natural Ordering

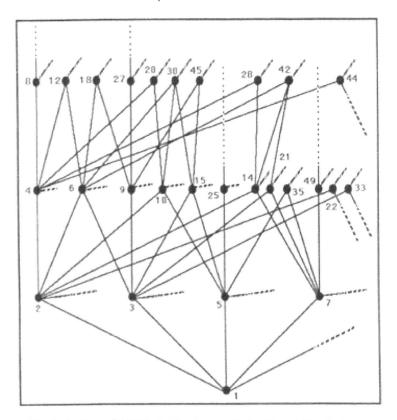

Fig. 5: Lattice of All Whole Numbers with the Divisibility Ordering

Technically, the numbers in these figures are referred to as the *natural numbers*, the *positive whole numbers*, or the *positive integers*. Other sorts of numbers, such as *negatives* and *fractions*—as well as other sorts of non-number abstract objects—can be "constructed" from these numbers, or defined in relation to them, in ways that we will examine on Expedition 2. However, mathematicians always refer to the branch of mathematics that deals with the numbers in these figures—that is, the positive whole numbers—as *number theory*, so we will continue to refer to them here simply as numbers in the interest of intuitive clarity.

Notice what numbers appear just above the *1* in Figure 5. Each of these is what mathematicians call a *prime* number, a number that has exactly two distinct divisors, itself and *1*. Students often feel and, in fact, sometimes insist, that *1* should be considered prime, because it also has no divisors other than itself and *1*. However, *1* itself *is 1*. The primes are the numbers that appear at the first level of the divisibility lattice, but *1* appears at the zero[th] level, that is, at the very bottom. This is the ground floor in the European system for numbering building levels, or the basement in the American system. Since *1* lives in a very different place from the primes in the lattice that is defined by divisibility, it really is a different kind of animal.

We can express every number above the first level in Figure 5 uniquely—that is, in only one way—as a product of some selection of numbers from that first level. This is illustrated in (16), where "***" is now used again to mean ordinary multiplication.

(16)   unique factorizations:

4	=	2 * 2
6	=	2 * 3
8	=	2 * 2 * 2
9	=	3 * 3
10	=	2 * 5
12	=	2 * 2 * 3
14	=	2 * 7
15	=	3 * 5

This fact, known as the *Fundamental Theorem of Arithmetic*, is usually stated by saying that every positive whole number except *1* can be expressed uniquely as the product of prime factors. It has important applications in computer security and cryptography as the basis of sophisticated coding and decoding techniques. If we were to alter the definition of *prime* to include *1* among the numbers that we consider to be prime, then this uniqueness would be destroyed, as illustrated in (17), along with the simplicity of the theorem's formulation.

(17)   non-unique factorizations:

4	=	2 * 2 = 2 * 2 * 1 = 2 * 2 * 1 * 1 = 2 * 2 * 1 * 1 * 1 ....
6	=	2 * 3 = 2 * 3 * 1 = 2 * 3 * 1 * 1 = 2 * 3 * 1 * 1 * 1 ....
8	=	2 * 2 * 2 = 2 * 2 * 2 * 1 = 2 * 2 * 2* 1 * 1 ....
9	=	9 = 3 * 3 = 3 * 3 * 1 = 3 * 3 * 1 * 1 = 3 * 3 * 1 * 1 * 1
10	=	2 * 5 = 2 * 5 * 1 = 2 * 5 * 1 * 1 = 2 * 5 * 1 * 1 * 1 ....

Numbers whose factorizations consist of one prime—that is, numbers that are themselves prime—are at the first level of the lattice; numbers that are the product of two primes are at the second level of the lattice; numbers that are the product of three primes are at the third level of the lattice; and so on. The only number that appears at the zero[th] level of the lattice is *1* and, consistently with this pattern, it is the only number there is that consists of no primes at all.

Figure 5 shows how all numbers except *1* can be obtained from the primes by multiplication. Figure 4 shows how all numbers except *1* can be obtained by starting at *1* and "climbing the ladder" of the natural ordering some number of steps, one step at a time. It turns out that this latter notion is really all there is to numbers, because everything else about them, such as addition, multiplication, and other operations on numbers, can all be defined in terms of this step-by-step climbing. This climbing process, called *recursion*, occurs as a facility in many programming languages. As Figure 4 shows, every number has exactly one successor number, the number immediately above it in the natural ordering, and every number except *1* is the successor number of exactly one number, the number immediately below it in the natural ordering. In other words, *1* is the unique starting point that every other number can be reached from in some number of successor steps. If it is known that *1* has some interesting property, and if it is also known that the successor of every number that has that property also has that property, then we can conclude that every number that there is has that property, because every number can be reached from *1* through a sequence of successor steps. This key feature of whole numbers is called the *principal of mathematical induction* and is what makes recursion work, as we will now see.

The notion of successor can be used to define all other operations on numbers. Any number *x* has a successor, the number that is immediately above *x* in the natural ordering, that is, in the ordering in Figure 4. We can denote that successor by the symbol "*successor(x)*". Similarly, for any particular numbers *x* and *y*, we can denote the results of the addition and multiplication, respectively, of *x* and *y* by the symbols "*sum(x,y)*" and "*product(x,y)*". This is often referred to as *prefix notation*, because the name of the operation appears before the symbols for the numbers, in contrast to the *infix notation* that we used earlier, in which the symbol for the operation appears between the symbols for the numbers. Universal principles, such as the distributive laws, tend to be easier to read and understand when formulated in infix notation, while recursive definitions tend to be clearer when formulated in prefix notation, but the two notations are exactly equivalent in terms of what they are able to express.

We can easily translate any statement in either notation into an equivalent statement in the other.[2]

Given these new symbols, the operation of addition can be defined in terms of the notion of successor, as (18) indicates.

(18)   (i)   sum(x, 1) = successor(x)

        (ii)   sum(x, successor(y)) = successor(sum(x, y))

What this says is, first in (i), that if we add *1* to a number—in this case, *x*—then the result is simply the next number in the natural ordering, in other words, the successor of *x*; and furthermore in (ii), that if we add any number other than *1* to a number—again, here called *x*—then we should first add the number that the number we add is the successor of, that is, its predecessor in the natural ordering—in this case, *y*—and then take the successor of that result. A person or a computer will always know which of (18)(i) or (ii) is needed in any specific instance, because *1* is not the successor of any number and so will never match the *successor(y)* term in (18)(ii). We say that the definition is *recursive* because the operation *sum* appears on both sides of (18)(ii), so that *sum* "calls itself" and thus recurs in the course of a calculation. However, despite the fact that it incorporates a self-reference, the definition is not circular because, whereas *sum* appears on the left with *y + 1*, it appears on the right with *y*, a lower number in the ordering that has already been passed in "climbing up the ladder" to *y + 1*.

For example, suppose we want to add *2* and *3* by using this definition; to add *2* and *3* is to evaluate (19).

(19)   sum(2, 3)

Since *3* is not *1*, (19) does not match the left-hand side of (18)(i), but it does match the left-hand side of (18)(ii), because *3* is the successor of *2*, as (20) shows.

(20)   sum(2, 3) = sum (2, successor(2))

---

[2] *Suggested excursion:* Express the distributive laws (6) and (9) in prefix notation and the recursive definition (18) in infix notation. Which notation do you prefer? Why? (*Hint:* Use words, such as *sum* and *successor*, for operation names in prefix notation and symbols, such as "+" and "*", for operation names in infix notation. Why does this make things clearer? Does it make any other difference? Which notation is better for overloading?)

The result is then given by the right-hand side of (18)(ii), as (21) shows.

(21)   sum(2, 3) = successor(sum(2, 2))

This tells us that to evaluate (19) we must first evaluate (22), which appears on the right-hand side of (21).

(22)   sum(2, 2)

Since *2* is not *1*, (22) does not match the left-hand side of (18)(i), but it does match the left-hand side of (18)(ii) because *2* is the successor of *1*, as (23) shows.

(23)   sum(2, 2) = sum(2, successor(1))

The result is again then given by the right-hand side of (18)(ii), as (24) shows.

(24)   sum(2, 2) = successor(sum(2, 1))

This tells us that to evaluate (22), which we need to do in order to evaluate (19), we need first to evaluate (25), which appears on the right-hand side of (24).

(25)   sum(2, 1)

However, this time the expression to be evaluated does match the right-hand side of (18)(i), because the number to be added is *1*. Since the right-hand side of (18)(i) contains only the operation *successor*, the repeated recursive self-calls of *sum* can finally come to an end, as (26) shows.

(26)   sum(2, 1) = successor(2)

The entire recursive calculation of (19) through (26), plus the completion of the calculation that is accomplished by successively stepping up the lattice in Figure 4 at the point in the calculation where only successor operations remain to be performed, is given in (27).

(27)   sum(2, 3)   =   sum(2, successor(2))

                          [because 3 is the successor of 2]

                     =   successor(sum(2, 2))

                          [by (18)(ii)]

                     =   successor(sum (2, successor(1)))

                          [because 2 is the successor of 1]

                     =   successor(successor(sum(2, 1)))

[by (18)(ii)]

=   successor(successor(successor(2)))

[by (18)(i)]

=   successor(successor(3))

[because the successor of 2 is 3]

=   successor(4)

[because the successor of 3 is 4]

=   5

[because the successor of 4 is 5]

The point here is that we never really need to build into a computer the capacity to do addition, as long as we build the computer in such a way that it knows how to count. As long as a computer or a person knows how to start at *1* and successively get to next larger numbers, they will also be able to do addition by using the definition (18). That definition can be provided to a person in the form of equations, as it appears here, or to a computer as a program in a suitable programming language. In reality, computers typically do have an addition facility built in, in order to save calculation time and achieve other sorts of efficiencies; however, the more general point remains, namely, that more complicated operations that might be difficult to build in can still be accomplished through this sort of definition, using whatever simpler operations the computer already has been given the capacity to perform.

For example, a computer that can count and do addition will be able to do multiplication as well, if we give it the recursive definition (28).

(28)   (i)   product(x, 1) = x

(ii)   product(x, successor(y)) = sum(product(x, y), x)

These equations define multiplication in terms of repeated addition, just as it is defined for third-graders. In other words, (i) to multiply a number—in this case, *x*—by *1*, simply leave it alone; (ii) to multiply *x* by a number other than *1*—in this case, the successor of some number *y*—add that first number—in other words, *x*—to the product of itself and the other number's predecessor, namely, *y*. Given this definition, even a person or computer who only knows how to count and do addition can now multiply any two numbers, say, *2* and *3*, through a calculation of the same sort as we saw in (27), as (29) shows.

(29) product(2, 3) = product(2, successor(2))

[because 3 is the successor of 2]

= sum(product(2, 2), 2)

[by (28)(ii)]

= sum(product(2, successor(1)), 2)

[because 2 is the successor of 1]

= sum(sum(product(2, 1), 2), 2)

[by (28)(ii)]

= sum(sum(2, 2), 2)

[by (28)(i)]

= sum(sum(2, successor(1)), 2)

[because 2 is the successor of 1]

= sum(successor(sum(2, 1)), 2)

[by (18)(ii)]

= sum(successor(successor(2)), 2)

[by (18)(i)]

= sum(successor(successor(2)), successor(1))

[because 2 is the successor of 1]

= successor(sum(successor(successor(2)), 1)

[by (18)(ii)]

= successor(successor(successor(successor(2))))

[by (18)(i)]

= successor(successor(successor(3)))

[because the successor of 2 is 3]

= successor(successor(4))

[because the successor of 3 is 4]

= successor(5)

[because the successor of 4 is 5]

= 6

[because the successor of 5 is 6]

The first five steps of (29) make use of (28) to eliminate all occurrences of the operation *product*, leaving only the operation *sum* still to be performed. The next six steps of (29) make use of (18) to eliminate all occurrences of *sum*, leaving only *successor* still to be performed. The last four steps of (29) eliminate all occurrences of *successor* by counting up to the resulting answer in accordance with the natural ordering in Figure 4.

We can get a better understanding of how these definitions work by examining their *control structures*, that is, the ways in which component operations combine to bring about an operation's overall result. Figure 6 contains a *tree graph* for the control structure of the addition operation, as defined in (18), and Figure 7 contains a tree graph for the control structure of the multiplication operation, as defined in (28).

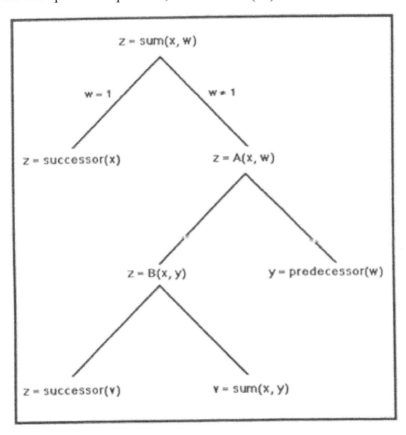

Fig. 6: Control Structure of Addition as Defined in (18)

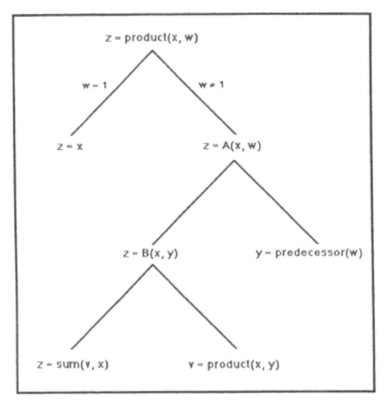

Fig. 7: Control Structure of Multiplication as Defined in (28)

In both cases, some number z, called an *output parameter*, is computed by having some operation—namely, addition or multiplication—applied to two numbers x and w, called *input parameters* or *arguments*. Also, in both cases, the respective operation consists of two alternatives, one for the case in which the second argument is *1* and one for the case in which it is some number other than *1*, in which case it is the successor of some number. When the second argument is *1*, addition is just the successor operation (Figure 6) and multiplication has no effect at all (Figure 7). When the second argument is a number other than *1*, each of the operations has further structure, comprising a component operation that we call *A* for convenience because it has no standard name. In both cases, computing the result of the operation *A* requires the computation, from the input parameter w, of an *internal parameter* y, the predecessor of w. This internal parameter appears only implicitly in (18) and (28), but it must be made explicit in the control structure, where all relevant parameters are revealed; y then serves as an argument for a component operation B, which determines the output parameter z from x and y.[3]

For addition, we get the value of z by computing the successor of the number—another internal parameter here called v—that is obtained as the sum of x and y (Figure 6). For multiplication, we get the value of z by first finding the product of x and y to get v and then adding x to that (Figure 7). In all cases, we get the value of *sum* by applying *successor*, either to the first argument itself or to the result of a sequence of previous applications of *successor*, as we saw in (27); we get the product either by doing nothing at all, when the second argument is *1*, or by applying *sum* to the result of a previous sequence of applications of *sum*, as we saw in (29). The recursive nature of these operations is revealed by the fact that, in each case, the operation that appears at the top-most node of the tree also appears somewhere else within the tree, indicating that that top-most operation is "calling itself", albeit it with a different choice of arguments. We avoid circularity because the internal call is with an argument y that is the predecessor of the higher-level argument w, so the numbers get smaller with each call, until we eventually reach the ending value of *1*, and the recursion comes to a halt, as we saw in (27) and (29).

The tree graphs in Figures 6 and 7 reveal both the similarities and the differences in the control structures of addition and multiplication, as these are defined in (18) and (28). Both operations involve three levels of decomposition, that is, of breaking up an operation into component operations that achieve its overall effect; the first of these levels involves a pair of alternatives based on whether a parameter has the value *1* or not, and the other two involve an internal parameter (namely, y) whose value is generated as the predecessor of the second input parameter (namely, w). Both also involve recursive calls to the overall operation that use that internal parameter (that is, y) to generate the value of another internal parameter (namely, v) that is used to obtain the final result. In fact, the structures are identical, except for

---

[3] *Suggested excursion:* Figure out why the figures show x and w as the input parameters, even though (18) and (28) contain x and y as the input parameters, and figure out why the figures show the need to compute *predecessor*, which does not appear at all in (18) or (28). (*Hint:* Control structures make things explicit that are only implicit in the equational definitions. The equations do include the expression $y + 1$ in a way that makes it look like a parameter.)

the operation names and the fact that z depends ultimately only on the internal parameter v in Figure 6, but on both v and the input parameter x in Figure 7. This is shown schematically in the *data dependency diagrams* in Figure 8, in which "$:$" is used to indicate that one parameter depends on—that is, requires for its computation—some other parameter, and in which the one dependency in which the two diagrams differ is highlighted in each case by being enclosed in a rectangle.

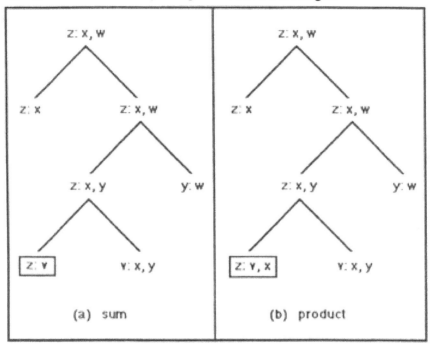

Fig. 8: Data Dependencies of Addition and Multiplication as Defined in (18) and (28)

Novices sometimes ask why control structures such as those in Figures 6 and 7 are written from right to left, rather than from left to right. The proper answer is that they are not. The view that control structures are written from right to left results from misinterpreting them as representing *data flow*, that is, the flow of parameter values through the steps of an algorithm, but this is not what they are intended to represent. Control structures are not representations of data flow—though we can derive that from them—but are *functional hierarchies* that show how the effect of what mathematicians call a function can be achieved through the joint action of other functions that comprise it. A *function* is a correspondence between two sets—that is, collections—

of objects in which each object in one collection is associated with exactly one object in the other. In Figures 6 and 7 such correspondences are established between the set of pairs of numbers and the set of numbers themselves, in the former instance by associating each pair of numbers with its sum, and in the latter by associating each pair of numbers with its product.

For addition, this correspondence can be established by either taking the successor of the first number of the pair (namely, x in Figure 6), if the second number (namely, w in the figure) is 1, or by taking whatever number the function A associates with that pair (namely, (x, w)), if w is not 1. We can get that number by determining what number the function B associates with the pair that consists of the first number with the second number's predecessor (namely, (x, y)). Finally, we can get that last number by determining what number the successor function associates with the number (namely, v) that the sum function associates with the pair (namely, (x, y)) that consists of the original first number and the predecessor of the original second number.

For multiplication, the correspondence is established by either taking the first number of the pair (namely, x in Figure 7) itself, if the second number (namely, w) is 1, or by taking whatever number the different function A associates with that pair (namely, (x, w)), if w is not 1. We can get that number, in turn, by determining what number the function again called B—though it works differently from the function called B in Figure 6—associates with the pair that consists of the first number with the second number's predecessor (namely, (x, y)). Finally, we can get that last number by determining what number the sum function associates with the pair (v, x) that consists of the number that the product function associates with the pair (x, y) and the original first number x.

In other words, rather than a right-to-left description of data flow, a control structure is more properly read as a left-to-right "recipe" that describes the functional steps we need to take, abstractly, to achieve a result, where the description of each step includes within itself a statement of its own requirements for what we must already have done in order for that step to be ready for doing. To compute *sum* for the pair *(2, 3)* (Figure 6), we need to apply *successor* to the sum of *(2, 2)*—since 2 is the predecessor of *3*—so we must take steps to ensure that that result has been made available by the time the relevant application of *successor* is reached. To compute *product* for the pair *(2, 3)* (Figure 7), we need to apply *sum* to 2 and the product of *(2, 2)*—since 2 is the predecessor of *3*—so we must take steps to ensure that

that result has been made available by the time the relevant application of *sum* is reached. Note that the symbols "*A*" and "*B*" in these figures are overloaded as *dummy names* that are strictly local to each figure. They serve mainly to keep track of data dependencies, as lower-level functions act jointly to bring about higher-level functional effects.

On the other hand, data flow does provide another useful vantage point from which to understand an algorithm, as the *data flow diagrams* for addition and multiplication shown, respectively, in Figures 9 and 10, illustrate.

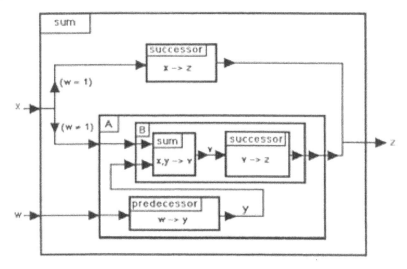

Fig. 9: Data Flow of Addition as Defined in (18)

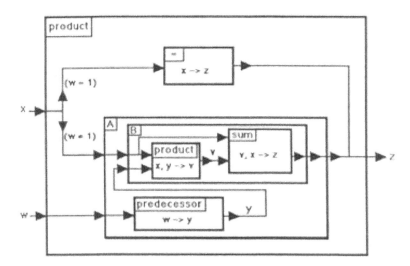

Fig. 10: Data Flow of Multiplication as Defined in (28)

We can derive each of these diagrams directly from the respective control structures in Figures 6 and 7 by examining the relations among the various parameters and the functions with which they occur. Each of the boxes in Figures 9 and 10 corresponds to one of the functions in the respective Figures 6 and 7. Boxes that correspond to lower-level functions in the control structures appear inside the boxes that represent functions that are above them in the functional hierarchies. The data dependencies are represented in the data flow diagrams by arrows. The extra arrow in the *B* box of multiplication (Figure 10) shows that *x* "flows into" *sum*, as well as into the recursive call of *product*, in contrast to the *B* box of addition (Figure 9), in which *x* is required only for the recursive call of *sum* and not for the final call of *successor*.

Figures 1 through 5 provide different vantage points on the structures of sets—collections of numbers, in the present instance—that are related to each other in various ways. Figures 6 through 10 provide different vantage points on the structures of algorithms—ways of doing things with numbers that, as we saw earlier, always bring about a definite result in a finite number of steps. Diagrams of these sorts can be implemented in programming languages either "by hand" by a human programmer or automatically (in principle) by computer by being formalized as the basis of a *specification language*, or what is sometimes called a *4GL* or *5GL* *(fourth- or fifth-generation language)*.

Programming languages differ widely in how they express particular algorithms, but the algorithms whose structures are shown in Figures 6 through 10 might be implemented in a typical *procedural programming language*, such as BASIC, FORTRAN, Pascal, or C, more or less as shown, respectively, in (30) and (31), in which *successor* and *predecessor* functions are assumed to have been defined already somewhere else in a program within which these function subprograms might occur.

(30) Function: Sum(input: x, w; output: z);

If w = 1 then z = Successor(x);

Else

y = Predecessor(w);

v = Sum(x, y);

z = Successor(v);

End Sum;

(31)   Function: Product(input: x, w; output: z);

   If w = 1 then z = x;

   Else

      y = Predecessor(w);

      v = Product (x, y);

      z = Sum (v, x);

   End Sum;

Actually, these algorithms would likely be implemented in abbreviated forms such as (32) and (33), in which the same words *Sum, Product,* and *Predecessor* are used as the names of both functions and internal parameters, as contrasted with the explicit distinction between the function names and the internal parameters *y* and *v* in the figures and in (30) and (31).

(32) Function: Sum(input: x, w);

   If w = 1 then Sum = Successor(x);

   Else   Sum = Successor(Sum(x, Predecessor(w)));

   End Sum;

(33) Function: Product(input: x, w);

   If w = 1 then Product = x;

   Else   Product = Sum(Product(x, Predecessor(w)), x);

   End Product;

This is yet another version of overloading, which we saw earlier for operation symbols and function names. It is common in programming practice, because it simplifies the programming process, as long as the algorithm's control structure, data dependencies, and data flow are well understood to begin with.

   Reversing the process of implementation, that is, extracting the control structure of a program that has already been written, can often reveal subtle errors that we might not notice readily otherwise. For example, it is very easy for a programmer working in a language like the one in (30)-(33) to arrange for the calculation of some internal parameter and then forget to include that parameter in the argument list of some internal function—also called a *subfunction*—that needs it, or to fail to arrange for the computation of some internal parameter that some subfunction requires as an argument. It is equally easy just to fail to notice that some subfunction needs to be included, when the control structure, data dependencies, and data flow have not been worked out in advance.

Note, in this connection, that we actually left Figures 6 through 10—which we derived from the program-like algorithm definitions in (18) and (28)—a bit oversimplified, in order not to make things even more complicated than they already were. These figures ignore the fact that the condition $w = 1$, which reflects the choice between (i) and (ii) in (18) and (28), itself defines a function, namely, a correspondence between the possible values of the numerical parameter w and the *truth values*, *true* (*t*) and *false* (*f*). These truth values—often referred to as *booleans* in honor of George Boole, the mathematician who first worked out the logic of truth values in the mid-1800's—are abstract objects every bit as much as numbers are, so they can serve, just as numbers do, as the values of the parameters of algorithms. We must include this function in the control structures of addition and multiplication for those functional hierarchies to be complete, because it is the internal parameter—call it, say, b, for *boolean*—that is generated by this function that determines the choice between the two cases of each of these operations. This choice is effected, for each operation, by a subfunction—call it C, since we have already chosen to call other functions A and B—that takes x, w, and b as arguments. Taking these facts into account yields Figures 11 through 13, respectively, as control structure, data dependency, and data flow diagrams for addition that are more complete than those in Figures 6, 8(a), and 9.

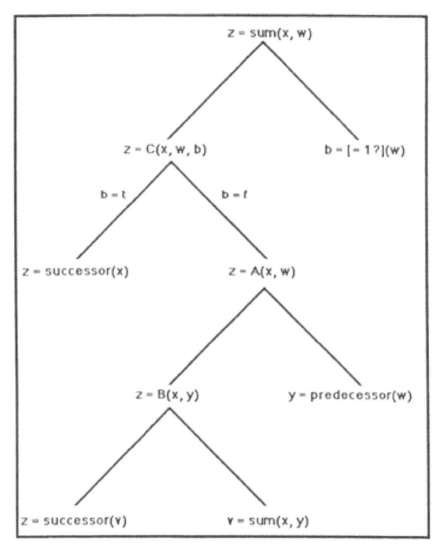

Fig. 11: Full Control Structure of Addition as Defined in (18)

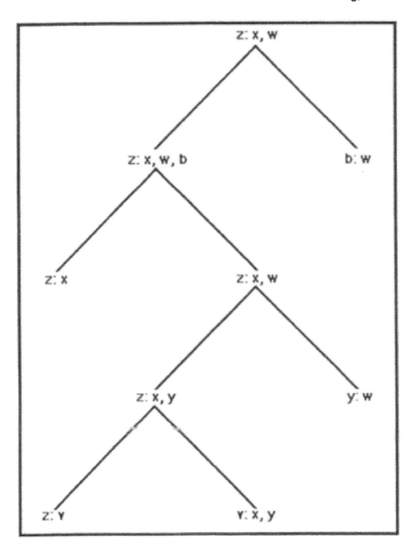

Fig. 12: Full Data Dependency of Addition as Defined in (18)

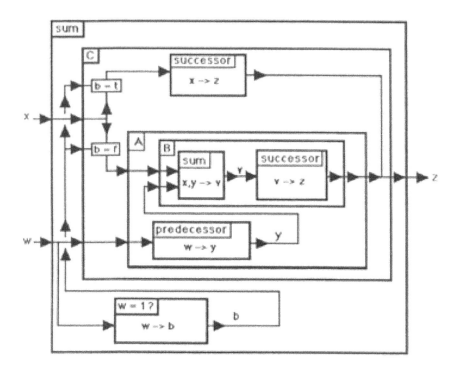

Fig. 13: Full Data Flow of Addition as Defined in (18)

Identical changes are needed in Figures 7, 8(b), and 10 for multiplication.[4]

Also observe that *b* in Figure 13 does not "flow" into any internal function box within the box for function *C*; rather, it serves as a sort of "gate-keeper" within *C*, determining whether *x* should flow into the box for *successor* or into the box for *A*. This contrasts with the numerical parameters, which are "transformed" into other such parameters as indicated by the " ⟶ " statements within the innermost boxes. As we saw for the internal edges in Figure 3, we can imagine *b*'s line-of-flow in Figure 13 as "jumping over" those of *x* and *w*, but this property of two-dimensional drawings has nothing to do with how the function itself works. The next expedition will examine how we can define non-numerical objects such as booleans in precise enough terms to be able to include them computationally in a formal algorithm.

---

[4] *Suggested excursion:* Draw these new diagrams for multiplication. (*Hint:* Take the new addition diagrams, change the function names, and then make just one change in each case. What change is that?)

2. Remembering: Types and Structures

Two student volunteers are solicited to investigate limitations on human memories. One student is given a random-number table and asked to read out random-length sequences of digits for the other student to repeat, and careful track is kept of the lists that are read back in response and, in particular, of the kinds of errors that are made. For example, upon being given the sequence (1)(a) by the first student, the second student might produce the sequence (1)(b), which is correct through the eighth digit, but then begins to fall apart.

(1)　(a)　849187562957241660
　　　(b)　849187563967421066

The ninth digit is remembered here as *3* rather than *2* and the eleventh digit is remembered as *6* rather than *5*, while the thirteenth and fourteenth digits are reversed, as are the last three digits of the sequence. After many such trials, the roles are reversed and the exercise is repeated, so that both students get to experience both roles and the results can be compared.

　　This exercise illustrates what psychologists commonly refer to as "the magic-number *7±2*," that is, the fact—first noted by psychologist George Miller in the mid-1950's—that humans typically have an upper limit on the number of items they can remember. Depending on the individual person, this limit ranges from *5* to *9*. It always turns out that a student can correctly remember sequences of numbers that have a length that is less than or equal to some upper limit, and this upper limit is always somewhere between *5* and *9*. However, despite this fact, as Miller also observed, there are strategies that people use, when they can, to overcome that limit without actually violating it, by grouping items together in various ways, through methods such as what psychologists refer to as chunking and linguistic recoding.

　　Chunking consists of grouping items together into "chunks" and then remembering the chunks as if they were individual items. For example, the ten-digit telephone number in (2)(a) is typically remembered as the three-chunk sequence in (2)(b), which consists of two three-digit chunks followed by a four-digit chunk, so the *7±2* limit is preserved for each chunk.

(2)   (a)   6175551212

(b)   617-555-1212

Linguistic recoding takes chunking one step further by replacing the chunks, when possible, with words or phrases that are more easily remembered than the chunks themselves. For example, the sixteen-digit sequence (3)(a) might be remembered as the six-word sequence (3)(b), which actually consists, in turn, of three phrases: one that consists of two words, one that consists of three words, and one that consists of one word, so the *7±2* limit is again preserved.

(3)   (a)   1861186519141918

(b)   Civil War/World War One/Dates

Such strategies are also used in computer science and, in fact, are the basis of one of its most fundamental concepts, namely, the use of data structures to organize numbers and other sorts of abstract objects in complex arrangements that are easier for both humans and computers to remember than long sequences of numbers or objects themselves are. The list data structure, for example, is a direct abstraction of chunking, as illustrated by the lists of numbers in (4), in which chunks are grouped by parentheses.

(4)   (a)   (1, 2, 3, 4, 6, 9, 12, 18, 36)

(b)   ((1, 2, 3), (4, 6, 9), (12, 18, 36))

List (4)(a) contains our old friends from Figure 1 and list (4)(b) organizes the same numbers in a very different way through a different use of parentheses. List (4)(a) contains nine members, the individual numbers themselves, which can be viewed as occupying nine different slots or positions in the list. However, list (4)(b) contains only three members, each of which is itself a list that contains three members, which are numbers. In effect, (4)(b) "chunks" the members of (4)(a) and therefore constitutes a different list.

The essential features of a list are that it has a length and that it has a slot or position for every number that is less than or equal to that length. In the technical terminology introduced on Expedition 1, that means that there are two functions associated with lists. One function—call it *length*—associates with each list some number that is its length. The other function—call it *item*—associates with each pair of a list and a number the list or number that occupies that numbered position in that list. Some instances of how these functions would apply to the lists in (4) are shown in (5).

(5) (a) length((4)(a)) = 9   length((4)(b)) = 3

 (b) item((4)(a), 1) = 1   item((4)(b), 1) = (1, 2, 3)

 item((4)(a), 2) = 2   item((4)(b), 2) = (4, 6, 9)

 item((4)(a), 3) = 3   item((4)(b), 3) = (12, 18, 36)

In other words, the length of (4)(a) is *9* and the length of (4)(b) is *3*, since (4)(a) has nine members, which are all numbers, and (4)(b) has three members, which are all lists. Furthermore, the first item in (4)(a) is *1*, but the first item in (4)(b) is *(1, 2, 3)*; the second item in (4)(a) is *2*, but the second item in (4)(b) is *(4, 6, 9)*; and the third item in (4)(a) is *3*, but the third item in (4)(b) is *(12, 18, 36)*.

Symbolically, this is written as in (6), where *LIST* and *NUMBER* are the set of all lists and the set of all numbers, respectively.

(6) (a) length: LIST → NUMBER

 (b) item: LIST X NUMBER → LIST ∪ NUMBER

LIST X NUMBER—read, "list cross number"—is the set of all pairs that consist of a list and a number. That set is called the *Cartesian product* of *LIST* and *NUMBER*, in honor of Rene Descartes, the mathematician who first studied pairs of numbers as representing geometric points in the 1600's. *LIST ∪ NUMBER*—read, "list union number"—is the set of everything that is either a list or a number. That set is called the *union* of *LIST* and *NUMBER*. In other words, *length* is a function that maps each object in *LIST* to an object in *NUMBER* and *item* is a function that maps each pair of an object in *LIST* and an object in *NUMBER* to an object in either *LIST* or *NUMBER*.

However, (6)(b) is not quite correct. What (6)(b) says is that every pair of a list and a number is mapped by the function *item* to some list or number, that is, that there is a list or number at every numbered position of every list. Actually, however, there is a list or number only at those positions in a list that are numbered less than or equal to the length of the list. There is a fifth item in (4)(a), whose length is *9*, but there is no fifth item in (4)(b), whose length is 3. In other words, there is a *constraint* on the function *item* that makes its result dependent on the function *length*, a constraint that must be incorporated into the symbolization in order for it to reflect correctly the actual situation that we intend it to describe.

To see how this incorporation is accomplished, begin by observing (7).

(7)   num $\leq$ length(lst)

This is an example of an *open statement*, that is, a statement that can be either true or false depending on the values of some symbols, called *parameters*, that can be given different values. In this case, the parameters *num* and *lst* are being used to represent specific numbers and lists, respectively, because they are more perspicuous than *x* and *y*. The open sentence (7) defines a function that maps to booleans, the truth values *t* and *f* that we encountered on Expedition 1. For some pairs (*lst*, *num*), the function that (7) defines will map to *t* and for others it will map to *f*, depending on whether the open statement (7) is itself true or false for the respective pair. For example, (7) is true, when *num* is *5* and *lst* is (4)(a), because the length of (4)(a) is *9*; however, (7) is false, when *num* is *5* and *lst* is (4)(b), because the length of (4)(b) is *3*, so the function that (7) defines maps to *t* for the pair ((4)(a), *5*), but to *f* for the pair ((4)(b), *5*).

To say that (7) is a constraint on *item* is to say that the result of *item* depends on the boolean (truth value) that is generated by the function that (7) defines, just as it does on the list and number that serve as *item*'s arguments. Specifically, to say that *item* succeeds in mapping a pair (*lst*, *num*) to some list or number is to say that (7) is true or, equivalently, that (8) is false.

(8)   num > length(lst)

Turning this around, to say that *item* fails to map a pair *(lst, num)* to a list or number is to say that (7) is false or, equivalently, that (8) is true. We can express such failure very simply by augmenting the set on the right-hand side of the arrow in (6)(b) to include a *reject* or *error* element that is not a list or number but that can still serve formally as the value of an output parameter. This is shown in (9), where *{error}* is the set, called the *singleton* of *error*, that has *error* as its only element.

(9)   item: LIST X NUMBER $\rightarrow$ LIST $\cup$ NUMBER $\cup$ {error}

In other words, *item* is not a function that maps a list and a number to a list or a number, but a function that maps a list and a number to a member of the set *LIST* or of the set *NUMBER* or of the set *{error}*, that is, to a list, a number, or the error element. For example, the instances in (5)(b) could be continued as in (10) for positions past the third, since list (4)(a) has items in those slots, but list (4)(b) does not.

(10)   item((4)(a), 1) = 1   item((4)(b), 1) = (1, 2, 3)

item((4)(a), 2) = 2   item((4)(b), 2) = (4, 6, 9)

item((4)(a), 3) = 3   item((4)(b), 3) = (12, 18, 36)

item((4)(a), 4) = 4   item((4)(b), 4) = error

item((4)(a), 5) = 6   item((4)(b), 5) = error

item((4)(a), 6) = 9   item((4)(b), 6) = error

We can now state the needed constraint very simply as the requirement that the boolean-valued function defined by the open statement (11) always produces the same result as the boolean-valued function defined by the open statement (8), that is, that the open statements (8) and (11) always have the same boolean as truth value, as (12) states.

(11)   item(lst, num) = error

(12)   (item(lst, num) = error) = (num > length(lst))

The left-hand side of (12) is (11) and the right-hand side is (8); each of these defines a function that generates a boolean, and these booleans must always be the same. A human programmer—or a type of program called a *code-generator*—must ensure that this result holds for an implementation of the function *item*, in order for that implementation to be correct. *Item* maps a list-with-number pair to *error*, if (8) is true, and to a list or a number, otherwise. In other words, to characterize the function *length* we need only the function specification (6)(a), but to characterize the function *item* we need both the function specification (9) and the constraint (12), showing the dependence of *item* on *length*. These are repeated here together as (13).

(13)   item: LIST X NUMBER → LIST ∪ NUMBER ∪ {error}

(item(lst, num) = error) = (num > length(lst))

Two further functions that are of interest in connection with lists are a function, which we will call *first*, that associates a list with its first element, and a function, which we will call *rest*, that associates a list with the result of removing its first element. For example, these functions apply to the lists in (4)(a) and (b) as (14) shows.

(14)   (a)   first((4)(a)) = 1

rest((4)(a)) = (2, 3, 4, 6, 9, 12, 18, 36)

(b)   first((4)(b)) = (1, 2, 3)

rest((4)(b)) = ((4, 6, 9), (12, 18, 36))

The first element of (4)(a) is the number *1* and the rest of it is the list *(2, 3, 4, 6, 9, 12, 18, 36)*, while the first element of (4)(b) is the list *(1, 2, 3)* and the rest of it is the list *((4, 6, 9), (12, 18, 36))*. As these examples illustrate, *first* can return either a number or a list, depending on what is in the list it is applied to, while *rest* can return only a list, because it returns what is left of a list after something has been removed from that list. If we require that these functions must apply to all lists that there are, then their respective function specifications are as (15) shows.

(15)   (a)   first: LIST → LIST ∪ NUMBER ∪{error}

(b)   rest: LIST → LIST

We include the error element in (15)(a) as an allowable result of *first* because of the possibility of applying *first* to the empty list *( )*, which contains no elements at all and thus has no first element for the function *first* to return. In contrast to (9), however, in which we really need to include *error* as an allowable result, in order to be able to state the necessary constraint (12), we can simplify (15)(a) by removing the empty list from the set of allowable inputs. This removes the need to allow *error* in the set of allowable outputs, as shown in (16), where *{( )}* is the singleton of *( )*, the set whose only element is the empty list, and where *LIST — {( )}*, called the *difference* of *LIST* and *{( )}*, is the set *LIST* with *{( )}*'s single element removed, that is, the set of all non-empty lists.

(16)   first: LIST — {( )} → LIST ∪ NUMBER

This simplification works because the empty list is the only list that would cause *first* to result in *error*, so it can simply be removed from the set of allowable argument values. This contrasts with what is the case with *item*, which depends crucially on *length* to distinguish between the cases that do and do not generate *error*.[5]

Many students express dismay at the fact that the empty list is considered to be a member of *LIST*, the set of all lists, because they correctly perceive the empty list to be a very peculiar concept. A list is supposed to be an arrangement of objects, and it is difficult to come to terms with the notion of an arrangement of objects that contains no objects. However, they eventually realize that the empty list is really no stranger than the number *0*, whose recognition as a legitimate concept was itself a fairly late development in human history; for example, the Roman numeral system had no symbol for zero. A number is supposed to be an abstraction of magnitude, that is, size or amount, and there is something peculiar about the notion that there can be a magnitude with no magnitude. Imagine trying to explain to a police officer who has cited you for not stopping at a stop sign, that *0* is an ordinary number just like any other number, so there is no essential difference between having *0* velocity at a stop sign and having any other velocity there. Clearly, there *is* a substantive difference between moving and not moving, even though we mask that reality mathematically by treating *0* as an ordinary number. However, *0* is by now an old friend that has been around for about a millennium, so we have all had time to get used to it and to see how useful it can be—though we have had no use for it yet here. In contrast, the empty list has been around for only a few decades, and its cousin, the empty set—the collection of objects that contains no objects—has been around for little more than a century, so these peculiar objects are less familiar and have had less time to demonstrate their usefulness for human concerns than *0*. However, we will see the empty list in action shortly and will then have a basis for judging its utility.

The functions *first* and *rest* are of special interest because, in contrast to *length*, which is unconstrained other than by its function specification, and to *item*, which is constrained only by its relation to *length*, the functions *first* and *rest* turn out to be *mutually* constrained, that

---

[5] *Suggested excursion:* Try to simplify (9) by removing *error* from the right-hand side of the arrow. What would you have to do to the left-hand side to make this work? (*Hint:* How would you have to restrict *LIST* to be sure that *item* does not generate *error*? Can you express this restriction without (12), that is, without already assuming that *error* is available?)

is, they are constrained in terms of each other. This is a more complex and intimate relationship than that of *item* and *length*, so it provides more difficulties to an implementer, whether a human or a machine. In particular, any list at all consists precisely of its own first element together with the rest of itself, as shown for (4)(a) and (b) in (17).

(17)   (a)   (4)(a) = (1, 2, 3, 4, 6, 9, 12, 18, 36)

so

first((4)(a)) = 1

rest((4)(a)) = (2, 3, 4, 6, 9, 12, 18, 36)

(b)   (4)(b) = ((1, 2, 3), (4, 6, 9), (12, 18, 36))

so

first((4)(a)) = (1, 2, 3)

rest((4)(a)) = ((4, 6, 9), (12, 18, 36))

However, to state the required constraints, we need to recognize a further function, which we will call *insert*. This function associates a pair of an object and a list with the list that has that object as its first element and that has that list as the rest of itself, as illustrated— making use of the results of (17)—in (18).

(18)   (a)   (4)(a) = (1, 2, 3, 4, 6, 9, 12, 18, 36)

so

(4)(a) = insert(1, (2, 3, 4, 6, 9, 12, 18, 36))

so

(4)(a) = insert(first((4)(a)), rest((4)(a)))

(b)   (4)(b) = ((1, 2, 3), (4, 6, 9), (12, 18, 36))

so

(4)(b) = insert((1, 2, 3), ((4, 6, 9), (12, 18, 36)))

so

(4)(b) = insert(first((4)(b)), rest((4)(b)))

In other words, (4)(a) is the result of inserting the number *1*, which is the first of (4)(a), into the list *(2, 3, 4, 6, 9, 12, 18, 36)*, which is the rest of (4)(a); similarly, (4)(b) is the result of inserting the list *(1, 2, 3)*, which is the first of (4)(b), into the list *((4, 6, 9), (12, 18, 36))*, which is the rest of (4)(b). In each case, the first of the list that results from *insert* is the list or number that has just been inserted, and the rest of the list that results from insert is the list that the inserted list was inserted into.[6]

The functions *first*, *rest*, and *insert* are given various and sundry names in actual programming languages, depending on the language designers' preferences. The most exotic choice of names is, perhaps, those of classic LISP, which—for obscure historical reasons that are of no interest here—uses the bizarre names *car*, *cdr*, and *cons*, respectively, for *first*, *rest*, and *insert*. Throughout this book, we avoid the terminological particularities of actual languages in order to focus on the underlying concepts, which are really what you need to understand. You can readily learn the details of each language from its respective handbook or user's guide, once you have mastered the basic generic concepts we cover here.

Since the first of a list can be either a list or a number, and since the rest of a list is always a list, we get (19) as the function specification of *insert*.

(19)   insert: (LIST $\cup$ NUMBER) X LIST $\rightarrow$ LIST

In other words, *insert* takes either a list or a number, together with a list, and generates a list. How it does this is constrained by the general requirements in (20).

(20)   (a)   first(insert(lon, lst)) = lon
           (b)   rest(insert(lon, lst)) = lst
           (c)   insert(first(lst), rest(lst)) = lst

Using *lon* as a parameter for an arbitrary list or number, these requirements state the mutual dependence—that is, the dependence on each other—of the three functions *insert*, *first*, and *rest*.

---

[6] *Suggested excursion:* Figure out what would be wrong with writing simply (i) and (ii).

(i)   (4)(a) = (first((4)(a)), rest((4)(a)))
(ii)   (4)(b) = (first((4)(b)), rest((4)(b)))

After all, these seem to show each list as its first together with its rest. What is wrong with this idea? In other words, why do we really need the function *insert* to state the relationship between first and rest? (*Hint:* Plug the lists themselves into (i) and (ii) and see if you actually get what you expected.)

In other words, inserting a list or number into a list yields a new list in which the inserted list or number is the new first, and the list that was inserted into is the new rest; inserting the first of a list into the rest of a list yields the list itself as the result. The function *insert* thus acts as a sort of inverse function to the joint action of the functions *first* and *rest* working together. Combining the constraints in (20) with the function specifications (15)(b), (16), and (19) yields (21) as a complete specification of *first*, *rest*, and *insert*.

(21)   first: LIST — {( )} → LIST ∪ NUMBER

rest: LIST → LIST

insert: (LIST ∪ NUMBER) X LIST → LIST

first(insert(lon, lst)) = lon

rest(insert(lon, lst)) = lst

insert(first(lst), rest(lst)) = lst

This is all that a programmer would need to know about these three functions to be sure of what needs to be done to implement them correctly.

We can summarize what we have seen so far on this expedition by saying that the function specifications and constraints in (22)—which combines (6)(a), (13), and (21)—constitute a *definition* of the *LIST data structure* (or, more precisely, of the *LIST OF NUMBERS* data structure).

(22)   length: LIST → NUMBER

item: LIST X NUMBER → LIST ∪ NUMBER ∪ {error}

first: LIST — {( )} → LIST ∪ NUMBER

rest: LIST → LIST

insert: (LIST ∪ NUMBER) X LIST → LIST

(item(lst, num) = error) = (num > length(lst))

first(insert(lon, lst)) = lon

rest(insert(lon, lst)) = lst

insert(first(lst), rest(lst)) = lst

Any arrangements of numbers that can be operated on by functions that behave in accordance with (22) qualify as lists, no matter what other characteristics a programmer might choose to give them and—more significantly—no matter how they might be represented physically or electronically in a computer. In a sense, then, (22) is all there is to say about lists, since it says what we can do with them and, equivalently, how they have to behave. However, there is more to be said about how the functions interact among themselves, as can be seen by asking how they might actually be computed.

It might appear from (22) that there are two independent groupings of functions on lists, namely, *length* and *item*, on the one hand, and then *first*, *rest*, and *insert*, on the other, because there is a constraint that relates the functions within each grouping but there is no constraint that relates any function in either grouping to any function in the other. However, it turns out that both *length* and *item* can be defined recursively in terms of *first*, *rest*, and *insert*, just as we saw on Expedition 1 that *sum* and *product* can be defined recursively in terms of *successor*. Moreover, we can use this fact to extract further constraints on the behavior and implementation of these functions. The function *length* can be defined in terms of the other three functions—in fact, in terms of *insert* alone, though *insert* is itself defined in relation to *first* and *rest* via (22), as shown in (23).

(23) (i) $length(( )) = 0$

(ii) $length(insert(lon, lst)) = successor(length(lst))$

What (23) says is that the empty list has length 0, and that any non-empty list—that is, any list that can be viewed as the result of some list or number having been inserted into some list—has as its length the successor of the length of the list that the list or number would have been inserted into to get the actual list whose length we desire. Compare this to (18) and (28) of Expedition 1, in which we distinguished between applying a function to *1*, the starting point, and applying a function to any other number. In the latter case, the number is necessarily the successor of some number and so appeared in that form in the equations.

For example, the length of the list (4)(b) can be computed by applying (23) as shown in (24), which gives the correct result that we observed in (5)(a).

(24) $length((4)(b))$ = $length((((1, 2, 3), (4, 6, 9), (12, 18, 36)))$

[because this is what (4)(b) is]

= length(insert((1, 2, 3), ((4, 6, 9), (12, 18, 36))))

[because (4)(b) can be considered the result of inserting (1, 2, 3) into ((4, 6, 9), (12, 18, 36))]

= successor(length(((4, 6, 9), (12, 18, 36))))

[by (23)(ii)]

= successor(length(insert((4, 6, 9),((12, 18, 36)))))

[because ((4, 6, 9), (12, 18, 36)) can be considered the result of inserting (4, 6, 9) into ((12, 18, 36))]

= successor(successor(length(((12, 18, 36)))))

[by (23)(ii)]

= successor(successor(length(insert((12, 18, 36), ( )))))

[because ((12, 18, 36)) can be considered the result of inserting (12, 18, 36) into the empty list ( )]

= successor(successor(successor(length(( )))))

[by (23)(ii)]

= successor(successor(successor(0)))

[by (23)(i)]

= successor(successor(1))

[because the successor of 0 is 1]

= successor(2)

[because the successor of 1 is 2]

= 3

[because the successor of 2 is 3]

Notice that admitting the empty list into the set of lists has forced us not only to admit a new number, namely, *0*, into our numerical menagerie, in order to be able to provide that list with a suitable length, but also to recognize that new number as a possible starting point of recursions, with the old starting point 1 as its successor. We can easily incorporate *0* into recursion, because recursion is based on the lattice in Figure 4, so we need only to move every number up one step and to relabel the bottom node as 0.[7] In contrast, there is no natural way to incorporate 0 into the lattice of Figure 5 for subtle reasons of divisibility that we will examine on Expedition 5.

The function *item* can be defined in terms of the other three functions—in fact, in terms of *insert* and *rest* alone, though—as (25) shows—these are themselves defined in terms of their relation to *first* via (22).

(25) (i)   item(( ), num) = error

    (ii)   item(lst, 0) = error

    (iii)   item(insert(lon, lst), 1) = lon

    (iv)   item(insert(lon, lst), successor(num))

         = item(rest(insert(lon, lst)), num)

What (25) says is (i) that the empty list has no items at any numbered position; (ii) that 0 is not the number of a position of any list; (iii) that the first item of a non-empty list—that is, a list that can be viewed as having been formed by inserting a list or number into some list—is that very inserted list or number; and (iv) that the item at some numbered position of a non-empty list is the same as the item at the previously numbered position of the list that is the rest of that non-empty list. The fourth clause of (25) works because the rest of a list ignores the list's first element, so the numbered positions of the other elements are all decreased in the rest by one.

For example, the third item of the list (4)(b) can be obtained by applying (25) as shown in (26), which gives the correct result that we observed in (5)(b).

(26)   item((4)(b), 3)   =   item(((1, 2, 3), (4, 6, 9), (12, 18, 36)), 3)

                                  [because this list is what (4)(b) is and we want the item in position 3]

                           =   item(insert((1, 2, 3), ((4, 6, 9), (12, 18, 36))), successor(2))

---

[7] *Suggested excursion:* Reformulate (18) and (28) of Expedition 1 to allow their recursions to start with 0 instead of 1. (*Hint:* The sum of any number with 0 is the number itself, and the product of any number with 0 is 0. Do you have to change (ii) in either case?)

[because (4)(b) can be considered the result of inserting (1, 2, 3) into ((4, 6, 9), (12, 18, 36)) and 3 is the successor of 2]

= item(rest(insert((1, 2, 3), ((4, 6, 9), (12, 18, 36)))), 2))

[by (25)(iv)]

= item(((4, 6, 9), (12, 18, 36)), 2)

[by (20)(b)]

= item(insert((4, 6, 9), ((12, 18, 36))), successor(1))

[because ((4, 6, 9), (12, 18, 36)) can be considered the result of inserting (4, 6, 9) into ((12, 18, 36)) and 2 is the successor of 1]

= item(rest(insert((4, 6, 9), ((12, 18, 36)))), 1)

[by (25)(iv)]

= item(((12, 18, 36)), 1)

[by (20)(b)]

= item(insert((12, 18, 36), ( )), 1)

[because ((12, 18, 36)) can be considered the result of inserting (12, 18, 36) into the empty list]

= (12, 18, 36)

[by (25)(iii)]

The occurrence of *( )* in the next-to-last line of (26) is an argument to the function *insert*, not to *item* itself, so we never reach a point in this calculation that requires (25)(i). The recursion ends when we reach a *num* value of *1*, because that is the least number that we need to consider as numbering a position in a list, so we never reach (25)(ii) either. Those are the two cases that can generate *error*, so that result does not occur in this calculation.

We need to include (25)(ii) in the definition of *item*, because we had to recognize *0* as a number, in order to get a full definition of *length* for every list, including the empty one; the latter is needed to start recursions, even though *item* itself has no use for *0*. We could eliminate the need for (25)(ii) by changing *item*'s function specification to exclude *0* from its possible arguments by replacing *NUMBER* on the left-hand side of the item arrow in (22) with *NUMBER — {0}* in the same sort of way that *( )* was removed from the possible arguments of *first*. However, we already need to include *error* anyway as a possible output of *item* because of positions numbered greater than a list's length—(25)(i) is itself really just a special case of this, so we might just as well keep (25)(ii) to specify a further case in which the error value occurs. In fact, from the algorithm definitions in (23) and (25) it is possible to prove the constraint in (12), because, as a comparison of (24) and (26) reveals, the number of successor steps from (25)(iv) that it takes to get to the *1* of (25)(iii) in finding the highest-numbered item of a list is always one less, for any given list, than the number of successor steps from (23)(ii) that it takes to get to the *0* of (23)(i) in finding the list's length. Any further such steps in a calculation from (25) will get to (25)(i) by depleting all the elements in the list and leaving it empty, thereby ending the recursion, but with the error element as the result.[8]

Tree graphs for the control structures of *length* and *item* are shown, respectively, in Figures 14 and 15. As Figure 14 shows, a number is computed as the length of a list in a manner that depends on the value of a boolean that distinguishes between the case that ends a sequence of recursions and the case of the recursion itself. In the former case, in which the list is empty, the number for the length is simply *0*; in the latter case, in which the list is not empty, the number for the length is determined by taking the successor of the number that is computed as the length of the list that is the original list without its first element. Perhaps surprisingly, the control structure for *length* thus turns out to be identical to that for *sum*, except for the specific functions that appear at each node and the number of input parameters involved:, two such parameters are required for *sum* but only one for *length*, as a comparison of Figure 14 with Figure 11 reveals. The internal subfunction names, *A*, *B*, and *C*, have also been given a more natural alphabetical ordering in Figure 14, but these are dummy names

---

[8] *Suggested excursion:* Figure out exactly what it is about (25) that enables it to give the correct results, namely, *error*, when an item is asked for at a position that is numbered greater than a list's length. Which of (i) or (ii) is producing the *error* element in such a case? (*Hint:* Clause (25)(iv) recurs on both the *lst* parameter (via *rest*) and the *num* parameter (via *successor*), but the numerical recursion stops at clause (iii). Try to compute the fourth item of (4)(b) and see what happens.)

anyway, serving mainly to keep track of data dependencies, as we observed on Expedition 1. However, the virtual identity of the control structures of these two functions should really not be surprising, because computing the length of a list is really nothing more than counting off the elements of the list one by one, while addition is nothing more than counting off upward steps one by one in the lattice of Figure 4.[9]

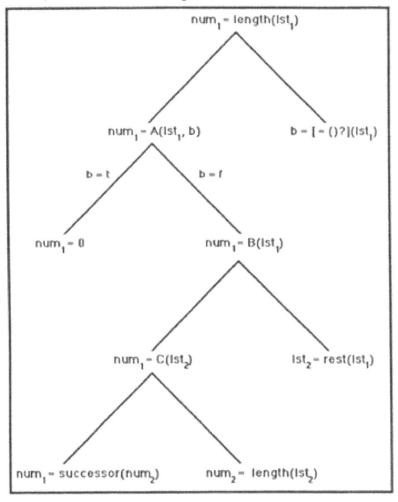

Fig. 14: Control Structure of length as Defined in (23)

---

[9] *Suggested excursion:* Draw the data dependency and data flow diagrams of *length*. (*Hint:* Carefully trace the relations among the input, output, and internal parameters in Figure 14. Remember that each function in the control structure becomes a box in the data flow diagram.)

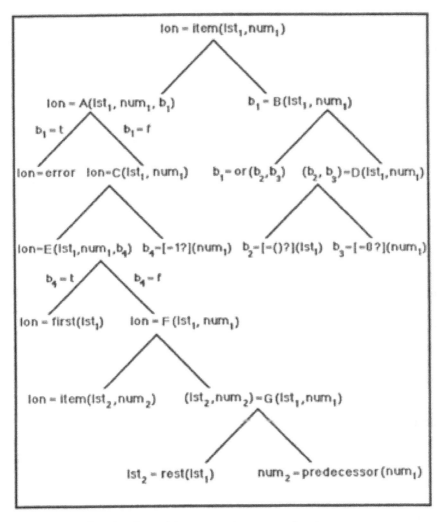

Fig. 15: Control Structure of item as Defined in (25)

However, as Figure 15 reveals, the control structure of *item* is a different matter altogether. A list or number is computed as the item of a list at some numbered position based on a boolean test that itself consists of two such tests, one to see if the list is empty and the other to see if the numbered position is the zero[th] one. The function *or*—which logicians refer to as *inclusive or* or *inclusive disjunction*—takes two booleans as arguments and generates *t* (*true*), if either or both of those arguments are *t*, and generates *f* (*false*), otherwise, that is, if both of the arguments are *f*. There exists another function, *xor*—which logicians call *exclusive or* or *exclusive disjunction*—that is the same as inclusive *or* except that it produces *f*, if both arguments are *t*, thus clearly distinguishing between two incompatible alternatives. However, the inclusive function is the one that is required in Figure 15, because of the possibility that both *lst* = *( )* and *num* = *0* are true, that is, the possibility of trying to compute the zero[th] position of the empty list, which will result in *error* by either of the relevant tests, both of which generate *t*. Furthermore, as the control structure reveals, these two tests are independent, since one depends only on the list and the other depends only on the position number, so they could be implemented in parallel, if a parallel computer—that is, one that contains multiple independently functioning processing units—is available. On a more conventional sequential computer, which can compute only one function at a time, a programmer would have to sequence these tests in some order and would have to do so arbitrarily, since there is nothing about them that requires that either test must be done before the other. The latter would be the case, for example, if an internal parameter were to be generated by one function that the other might then need as an argument, as is the case in the other control structures that we have seen here so far.

As long as the result of the *or* test is *f*, the list or number *lon* that is the num_1[th] item of lst_1 is computed only from lst_1 and num_1 by the function that is called C in the figure just to provide it with a convenient name, but that works in accordance with the further structure that is indicated in the tree. As that structure specifies, that function also depends on the result of a boolean test, which, as in the other examples we have seen, distinguishes the case that ends a sequence of recursions from the case of the recursion itself. However, in this instance, unlike the others, the recursive call to the overall function, that is, the lower occurrence of *item*, itself generates the final output parameter from a pair of internal parameters. This contrasts with *sum*, *product*, and *length*, which, as we saw in Figures 6, 7, 11, and 14, each generates an internal parameter that is then "finished off" by a further function—*successor*, in the case of *sum* and *length*, and *sum*, in the case of *product*. That is the reason for the long sequences of *successor* that occur in the final steps of (24) (and of *successor* and of *sum* and *successor* in (27) and (29) of Expedition 1, respectively), but not in (26), in which *item* just seems to be waiting around to finish the job, after other functions have done theirs. Like the two booleans that are computed in the initial test that gets *item* started to begin with, the two internal parameters that the recursive call to *item* takes as arguments are independent, one of which, the rest of the list, depends only on the list and the other of which, the new lower position number, depends only on the position number. These, too, can therefore be computed in parallel, if the computer they are implemented on has a facility for parallel computation.[10]

Three further data structures that are very widely used in computer programming and that we will make use of later in this book are stacks, arrays, and trees. A *stack* is an arrangement of objects—for the time being, of numbers, though we will also make use of stacks of letters on Expedition 3—that can be accessed only through the object that has most recently been "pushed" onto it. That object is considered to be its "top" element and is the only one we can remove; we do this by what is known as "popping" the stack. For example, if we push the number *36* onto the stack in (27)(a), we get the stack in (27)(b), which contains all of the numbers in Figure 1 as its elements, with *36* as its top element.

(27)

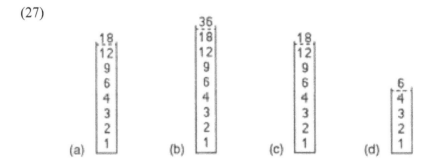

Any other number in the stack is hidden from the user's view and can be accessed only by successively popping stacks, until it becomes the top element. Popping the stack in (27)(b) yields (27)(c), which is

---

[10] *Suggested excursion:* Draw the data dependency and data flow diagrams of *item*. (*Hint:* Carefully trace the relations among the input, output, and internal parameters in Figure 15. Remember that each function in the control structure becomes a box in the data flow diagram. Because of the greater complexity in this case, also observe that input parameters and internal parameters, when they are used as arguments, can be viewed as "flowing downward" in the control structure, whereas output parameters and internal parameters, when they are generated, can be viewed as "flowing upward" in the control structure.)

identical to (27)(a) and thus has 18 as its top element; popping stacks successively three more times yields the stack in (27)(d), which has 6 as its top element. Stacks in programming are often referred to as *push-down stacks*, reflecting their resemblance to stacks of dishes in a cafeteria. They are useful for keeping track of how many instances of a particular number (or letter) have been processed so far, as we will see on Expedition 3.

To define the *STACK* data structure formally, we need to provide functions that satisfy constraints that express the sort of behavior that we just described. There must be (i) a function *push* that takes a number and a stack and returns a stack, reflecting the fact that a number can be pushed onto a stack to get another stack; (ii) a function *pop* that takes a stack and returns a stack, reflecting the fact that exactly one number, namely, the "visible" one, can be removed from a stack; and (iii) a function *top* that takes a stack and returns a number, namely, the number that was "visible" at the top of the stack. This yields the function specifications in (28).

(28)   push: NUMBER X STACK → STACK

pop: STACK → STACK ∪ {error}

top: STACK → NUMBER ∪ {error}

We need to include *error* as a possible output value of *pop* and *top* because, as we saw in the case of numbers and lists, there needs to be a "starting point." In this case, the starting point is an *empty stack*, ▱, the stack of numbers with nothing in it, an object that by now should seem perfectly natural. Applying *top* to ▱ cannot return a number, because there is no number there to return, and applying *pop* to ▱ cannot return a stack, because there is no number there to remove to obtain a remaining stack from. Figure 16 illustrates both of these facts.

Fig. 16: The Constraints on the Empty Stack

We therefore need to provide constraints on these two functions that require them to return *error*, when they are applied to ☐. These constraints are given in (29).

(29)   pop(☐) = error

top(☐) = error

When *top* is applied to a non-empty stack, it returns the number that is at the top of the stack. Another way of saying this is that it returns the number that would have been pushed onto the remainder of the stack. In other words, taking the top of a stack that is the result of pushing a number onto a stack yields that very number, as illustrated in Figures 17(a) and (b) and as stated in the constraint (30), in which *stk* is a parameter for an arbitrary stack.

(30)   top(push(num, stk)) = num

Fig. 17: The Constraints (30) on top and push (a)(b)
and (31) on pop and push (c)(d)

Similarly, when *pop* is applied to a non-empty stack, it returns the stack with the top number removed. Another way of saying this is that it returns the stack that that number would have been pushed onto. In other words, popping a stack that is the result of pushing a number onto a stack yields the stack that that number was pushed onto, as illustrated in Figures 17(c) and (d) and as stated in the constraint (31).

(31)   pop(push(num,stk)) = stk

Combining the function specifications in (28) with the constraints in (29) through (31) yields (32) as the full definition of the data structure *STACK* (of numbers).

(32)   push: NUMBER X STACK $\rightarrow$ STACK

pop: STACK $\rightarrow$ STACK $\cup$ {error}

top: STACK $\rightarrow$ NUMBER $\cup$ {error}

pop($\square$) = error

pop(push(num,stk)) = stk

top($\square$) = error

top(push(num,stk)) = num

Any arrangements of numbers that can be operated on by functions that behave in accordance with (32) qualify as stacks, no matter what other characteristics a programmer might choose to give them and, more significantly, no matter how they might be represented physically or electronically in a computer. As we saw in the case of (22) for lists, (32) is, in essence, all there is to say about stacks, since it says what we can do with them and, equivalently, how they have to behave.[11]

It is instructive to compare stacks to queues, a related data structure that is also widely used in programming, for example, to model situations in which people stand in lines, such as those at ticket counters or teller's windows. Queues differ from stacks in being what are called *first-in/first-out* structures, rather than *last-in/first-out* structures. In other words, a number can enter or exit only at the top of a stack, the last one that entered being the first one that can exit; however, a number enters only at the end of a queue and exits only at the front, the first one that entered being the first one that can exit. For example, if the number *36* enters the queue in (33)(a), which has *1* as its front element and *18* as its rear-most element, it must enter from the rear, thereby producing the queue in (33)(b), which contains all of the

---

[11] *Suggested excursion:* Think of some further functions that might be of interest in connection with stacks, and give recursive definitions of those functions in terms of *push*, *pop*, and *top*. Draw the control structure, data dependency, and data flow diagrams for the functions you define. (*Hint:* How about the *height* or *depth* of a stack? How does that compare to the *length* of a list?)

numbers in Figure 1 as its elements, with *36* as its new rear-most element and *1* still as its front element.

(33)

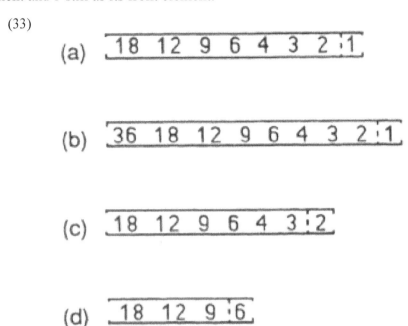

(a) 18 12 9 6 4 3 2 1

(b) 36 18 12 9 6 4 3 2 1

(c) 18 12 9 6 4 3 2

(d) 18 12 9 6

Any number other than the front element, namely the *1* in (33)(a) and (b), is hidden from view and can be accessed only by having front numbers successively exit queues, until the number itself becomes the front number of one of the queues that results. The front number exiting the queue in (33)(b) yields (33)(c), which—in contrast to what we saw in (27) is the case for stacks—is not identical to (33)(a), but has *2*, rather than *1*, as its front element, *1* being the only number in the queue that had a right to exit in (33)(b). Front numbers successively exiting queues three more times yield the queue in (33)(d), which, like the stack in (27)(d), now has *6* as its front—that is, its accessible—element. However, *6* has become accessible in the queue (33)(d) by successively removing *1*, *2*, and *3* from the front, in contrast to the stack (27)(d), in which *6* became accessible by successively removing *18*, *12*, and *9* from the top. Numbers in stacks never know how long they will have to stay there, because all of the activity takes place at the top, so the length of a stay depends on how many other numbers decide to visit; in contrast, numbers in queues know that they will each get their turn and eventually get to leave by patiently passing through.

Formally, we need three functions, together with constraints, that express the sort of behavior that was just described. We need (i) a function *enter* that takes a number and a queue and returns a queue, reflecting the fact that a number can enter a queue to yield another queue; (ii) a function *exit* that takes a queue and returns a queue, reflecting the fact that exactly one number, namely, the "visible" one, can be removed from a queue; and (iii) a function *front* that takes a queue and returns a number, namely, the number that was "visible" at the front of the queue. These functions thus have the function specifications in (34).

(34)   enter: NUMBER X QUEUE $\rightarrow$ QUEUE

exit: QUEUE $\rightarrow$ QUEUE $\cup$ {error}

front: QUEUE $\rightarrow$ NUMBER $\cup$ {error}

Again, we must include *error* as a possible output value of *enter* and *exit* because—as we saw was the case with stacks—there has to be an *empty queue*, ⬛, the queue of numbers with nothing in it. Applying *front* to ⬛ cannot return a number, because there is no number there to return, and applying *exit* to ⬛ cannot return a queue, because there is no number there to remove. Figure 18 illustrates both of these facts.

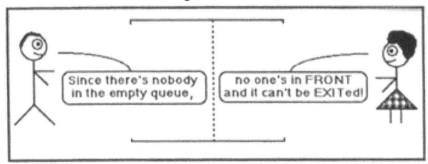

Fig. 18: The Constraints (35) on the Empty Queue

We must therefore provide constraints on these two functions that require them to return *error*, when they are applied to ⬛. These constraints are given in (35).

(35)   exit(⬛) = error

front(⬛) = error

However, the behavior of *enter* is a bit more complicated than that of its cousin, *push*. Since all of the activity in stacks takes place at the top, there is never any need to worry about the remainder of a stack and, in particular, about its bottom; in contrast, numbers pass through queues, so care must be taken to maintain the proper relation between the queues' two ends, not only the front, which numbers leave from, but also the rear, which numbers enter. If a number enters the empty queue, it becomes the new front element of the queue that results, but if a number enters a non-empty queue, the front element of the resulting queue remains the same as it was in the queue that was entered. It is thus necessary to have two constraints to express the relation between *enter* and *front*, as shown in (36), in which *qu* is a parameter for an arbitrary queue; this contrasts with the one constraint that was needed in (30) to express the relation between *push* and *top*.

(36) $front(enter(num, \blacksquare)) = num$

$front(enter(num_2, enter(num_1, qu))) = front(enter(num_1, qu))$

The point here is that *enter(num_1, qu)* is always a non-empty queue, because even if the queue *qu* itself is empty, the queue that results from the number *num_1* entering it is not. Furthermore, every non-empty queue can be considered to be of that form, that is, to have been obtained as the *enter(num_1, qu)* of some queue *qu*, because any non-empty queue can be obtained by having some number enter some queue, which may or may not itself be empty. In other words, the constraints in (36) separate all non-empty queues into two cases, distinguishing those which contain exactly one number—which can be viewed as having been obtained by having a number enter $\square$—from those which contain two or more numbers— which can be viewed as having been obtained by having a number enter some other non-empty queue. As Figures 19(a) and (b) illustrate, the first constraint says that a queue that contains exactly one number has that number as its front number.

*Fig. 19: The Constraints (36) on front and enter (a)–(b)
and (37) on exit and enter (c)–(d) for the empty queue*

As Figures 20(a) and (b) illustrate, the second constraint says that a queue that contains two or more numbers has the same front number as the queue that it would have been obtained from, because a number entering that queue would have had to do so from the rear, with no consequent effect on fronts.

*Fig. 20: The Constraints (36) on front and enter (a)–(b)
and (37) on exit and enter (c)–(h) for a non-empty queue*

Fig. 20 (cont.): The Constraints (36) on front and enter (a)–(b)
and (37) on exit and enter (c)–(h) for a non-empty queue

Similarly, if a number enters the empty queue and the resulting queue is then exited, the result is the empty queue again, because the number that entered the empty queue from the rear is the only element there and is therefore the new front element, the one that exiting removes. That is illustrated in Figures 19(c) and (d). However, if a number enters a non-empty queue and the resulting queue is then exited, the result is the same queue that would have resulted if the original queue had been exited first and that number had then entered that resulting queue. That is illustrated in Figures 20(c) and (d). We therefore need to have two constraints to express the relation between *enter* and *exit*, as (37) shows, in contrast to the one constraint that we needed in (31) to express the relation between *push* and *pop*.

(37) $\text{exit}(\text{enter}(\text{num}, \blacksquare)) = \blacksquare$

   $\text{exit}(\text{enter}(\text{num}_2, \text{enter}(\text{num}_1, \text{qu})))$

   $= \text{enter}(\text{num}_2, \text{exit}(\text{enter}(\text{num}_1, \text{qu})))$

Again, *enter(num₁, qu)* is just a convenient functional way of referring to an arbitrary non-empty queue, in order to distinguish that case from the case of the empty queue.

Observe that we cannot express the necessary second constraints in (36) and (37) simply as (38)(a) and (b), respectively.

(38)　　(a)　　front(enter(num, qu)) = front(qu)

　　　　(b)　　exit(enter(num, qu)) = enter(num, exit(qu))

According to the function specifications of *front* and *exit* in (34), the parameter *qu* can take any queue as its value, whether that queue is empty or not; however, neither (38)(a) nor (b) is true when *qu* is replaced with ▱ because of (35), which stipulates that applying *front* or *exit* to ▱ results in *error*. According to (34), *error* is not a possible argument for *enter*, no matter what *num* value is chosen as the other argument, so the right-hand sides of (38) have no meaning in that case, a fact that requires that the constraints be restricted to non-empty queues, that is, queues of the form *enter(num, qu)*, as (36) and (37) state.

Combining the function specifications in (34) with the constraints in (35) through (37) yields (39) as the full definition of the data structure *QUEUE* (of numbers).

(39)　　enter: NUMBER X QUEUE → QUEUE

　　　　exit: QUEUE → QUEUE ∪ {error}

　　　　front: QUEUE → NUMBER ∪ {error}

　　　　exit(▣) = error

　　　　exit(enter(num, ▣)) = ▣

　　　　exit(enter(num₂, enter(num₁, qu)))

　　　　　　　　　　　= enter(num₂, exit(enter(num₁, qu)))

　　　　front(▣) = error

　　　　front(enter(num, ▣)) = num

　　　　front(enter(num₂, enter(num₁, qu))) = front(enter(num₁, qu))

Again, any arrangements of numbers that we can operate on using functions that behave in accordance with (39) qualify as queues, no matter what other characteristics a programmer might choose to give them and, more significantly, no matter how they might be represented physically or electronically in a computer. As we saw for the respective definitions of lists and stacks, (39) is essentially all there is to queues, since it says what we can do with them and, equivalently, how they behave.[12]

As we saw on Expedition 1, we can facilitate comparison of different sets of functions by overloading, that is, by using the same symbols for corresponding functions in each set. It is instructive to compare the data structures *QUEUE* and *STACK* by overloading the symbols *STRUCTURE*, *f*, *g*, and *h* for their respective sets of instances and functions, and the symbol *empty* for their respective empty instances, as (40) indicates.

(40)		stacks	queues
	STRUCTURE:	STACK	QUEUE
	f:	push	enter
	g:	pop	exit
	h:	top	front
	empty:	□	▣

Given (40), both (28) and (34) become (41), so the function specifications of stacks and queues turn out to be identical, other than for the names that we have chosen to give their respective instances and functions.

(41)   f: NUMBER X STRUCTURE → STRUCTURE

g: STRUCTURE → STRUCTURE ∪ {error}

h: STRUCTURE → NUMBER ∪ {error}

However, their constraints differ in some very subtle ways. Given (40) and using *str* as a *STRUCTURE* parameter, the stack constraints in (32) become (42), and the queue constraints in (39) become (43).

(42)   g(empty) = error

g(f(num, str)) = str

---

[12] *Suggested excursion:* Think of some further functions that might be of interest in connection with queues and give recursive definitions of those functions in terms of *enter*, *exit*, and *front*. Draw the control structure, data dependency, and data flow diagrams for the functions you define. (*Hint:* How about the *length* of a queue? How does that compare to the *length* of a list?)

$$h(empty) = error$$
$$h(f(num, str)) = num$$

(43) $g(empty) = error$
$$g(f(num, empty)) = empty$$
$$g(f(num_2, f(num_1, str))) = f(num_2, g(f(num_1, str)))$$
$$h(empty) = error$$
$$h(f(num, empty)) = num$$
$$h(f(num_2, f(num_1, str))) = h(f(num_1, str))$$

The constraints for the empty case in (42) and (43) are identical, namely, those repeated in (44).

(44) $g(empty) = error$
$$h(empty) = error$$

In effect, these can be understood as being a definition of what it is for a stack or queue to be empty.

The remaining constraints for stacks and queues, those for the non-empty case, are repeated in (45) and (46), respectively.

(45)   (a) $g(f(num, str)) = str$
(b) $h(f(num, str)) = num$

(46)   (a)   (i) $g(f(num, empty)) = empty$
(ii) $g(f(num_2, f(num_1, str))) = f(num_2, g(f(num_1, str)))$
(b)   (i) $h(f(num, empty)) = num$
(ii) $h(f(num_2, f(num_1, str))) = h(f(num_1, str))$

Remember, from (40), that *f(num, empty)* is the stack or queue that results from putting a number into the empty stack or queue and is therefore itself non-empty, even though the name *empty* appears in its description. The constraint (46)(a)(i) is the same as (45)(a) for the single case in which the parameter *str* has the value *empty*. We can thus reformulate (46)(a)(i) as (47), which says exactly that.

(47) $(g(f(num, str)) = str) = (str = empty)$

In other words, (47) says that the open statement (48)(a) always has the same boolean truth value as the open statement (48)(b), so the equivalent statement (46)(a)(i), which applies to queues, is just a restricted version of (45)(a), which applies to stacks, the same statement but restricted in its applicability to only one case.

(48)   (a) $g(f(num, str)) = str$

        (b) $str = empty$

Since (46)(a)(ii) applies specifically to the non-empty queue $f(num_1, str)$, that expression for the queue $f(num_1, str)$ can be replaced in (46)(a)(ii) with the single parameter str, as long as the requirement that str itself is non-empty is stated in some other way. We can thus reformulate (46)(a)(ii) as in (49), which says that the overloading version of (38)(b), which we saw to be a false statement when taken by itself, is true exactly when (48)(b) is false.

(49) $(g(f(num, str)) = f(num, g(str))) = (str \neq empty)$

The functions f and g on queues are thus seen to have what is called the *commutative property*, that is, they produce the same result when applied in either order, first f then g or first g then f, but only as long as they are restricted to non-empty queues. In contrast, the functions f and g on stacks exhibit this behavior only when the number that is being put on the stack is the same as the one that was just removed. According to (45)(a), applying g to the result of applying f to a number and a stack returns exactly that stack. If g is applied first to the stack, then its top element is lost and only what is left of the stack is retained. We can restore the original stack only by keeping track of the fact that the number that was removed was the former top element; in other words, it is necessary to invoke h to state the conditions under which g and f behave in a commutative way. In contrast to the queue constraint (49), then, the much more restricted condition (50) states the circumstances in which the commutative property is operative for f and g on stacks.

(50) $(g(f(num, str)) = f(num, g(str))) = (num = h(str))$

The relation between (46)(b)(i) and (45)(b) is essentially the same as what we have seen for (46)(a)(i) and (45)(a), namely, that (46)(b)(i) is the same as (45)(b) for the single case in which str is empty, so (46)(b)(i) can be reformulated as the equivalent statement (51).

(51) $(h(f(num, str)) = num) = (str = empty)$

Again, the queue constraint turns out to be a stack constraint restricted to a particular parameter value. However, the relation between (46)(b)(ii) and (45)(b) is very different from the relation between (46)(a)(ii) and (45)(a). Since $f(num_1, str)$ in (46)(b)(ii) is any non-empty queue, (46)(b)(ii) can be reformulated as (52), which has *str* instead of $f(num_1, str)$ plus the requirement that *str* is not empty. What (52) says is that the front element of a queue that has had a number put into it is the same as the front element of the queue that the number was put into, as long as the queue that the number was put into was not empty to begin with.

$$(52)\quad (h(f(num, str)) = h(str)) = (str \neq empty)$$

The issue here, then, is not the commutative property, as it was in connection with (49) and (50), but the *vacuous* effect of f on h, that is, the fact that the behavior of h on queues is unaffected by the prior application of f, as long as the queues are non-empty. In stark contrast to this situation—as (45)(b) states—the result of h on stacks, far from being unaffected by the prior behavior of f, is entirely determined by that behavior, because the result of h will be whatever number f has just placed on the stack. This is perhaps the most striking and fundamental difference between queues and stacks.[13]

Despite such differences, stacks and queues, as well as lists, have one key feature in common: they are all one-dimensional. Whether we consider their elements as being arranged horizontally, as lists and queues are usually portrayed, or vertically, as stacks are usually visualized, those elements are most naturally thought of as being arranged in a straight line, as we have represented them here. In contrast to such *linear* data structures, the *SQUARE ARRAY* data structure, which we will use on Expedition 4 to represent puzzles and games, arranges numbers (or letters, as on Expedition 4) in a *two-*dimensional way. This is illustrated in (53), which shows the numbers in Figure 1 arranged in a square array.

---

[13] *Suggested excursion:* Use overloading to compare *stacks* and *queues* with *lists*. (*Hint: Insert* combines *first* with *rest* to produce a list. Observe that lists can have lists as elements. What about (44)?)

(53)

$$\begin{bmatrix} 1 & 2 & 3 \\ 4 & 6 & 9 \\ 12 & 18 & 36 \end{bmatrix}$$

The square array in (53) is said to be a *3 X 3*—read "three by three"—array, because it has its elements arranged in three rows and three columns. There can also be *rectangular arrays*, such as *3 X 4, 3 X 5, 5 X 6*, and so on, in which the numbers of rows and columns differ; however, square arrays will suffice for our purposes here.[14] Like stacks and queues, but unlike lists, a square array of numbers (or letters) can contain as elements only numbers (or letters), rather than further instances of the same data structure, such as lists containing lists as elements, as well as containing numbers as elements.

In contrast to the three linear data structures we have examined, square arrays are *static*, that is, they do not grow or shrink as they are used, but have a fixed size that is specified once and for all when they are first *declared* (that is, introduced) in a program. This tells the computer to reserve a specific number of storage locations in its memory for storing the elements of the arrays. We therefore need to recognize not an "empty array," from which other arrays are "grown," in a way that is analogous to what we saw in connection with lists, stacks, and queues, but an *empty element* or *blank*, $\square$, instead. This fills the slots in a square array that we have not yet placed numbers into, and we can use them to erase such numbers when necessary without destroying the slots that contained them.[15] For example, we

---

[14] *Suggested excursion:* As you read the account of square arrays being developed here, think about how you would modify that account to accommodate rectangular arrays. How would the function specifications and constraints differ? How do *1 X n* and *n X 1* arrays, for some number *n*, differ from lists, stacks, and queues? (*Hint:* You need two numbers, not just one, to specify the size of a rectangular array. The size does not change, once it is fixed.)

[15] *Suggested excursion:* What if you wanted a programming language to have a facility for defining *dynamic arrays*, which can grow and shrink like lists. As you read the account of square arrays being developed here, think about how you would

might have created the square array in (53) by starting with (54)(a)—which is not empty, that is, lacking even in slots, but contains the element $\square$ in every slot—and then successively placing the numbers one by one, as (54)(b) through (d) illustrate for the first row of (53).

(54)

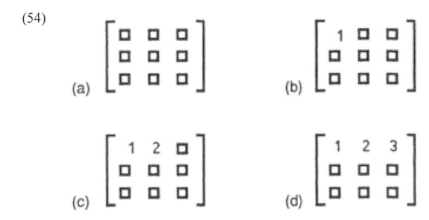

(a)   (b)   (c)   (d)

When square arrays are used mainly for storing data, rather than for manipulating data to count things or to model situations, we only need two functions to use with them: (i) a function, *write*, that puts a number into a slot and (ii) a function, *read*, that says what number, if any, is already in some slot. Any number or $\square$ can be put into any slot. When a number or $\square$ is put into a slot, it replaces the number or $\square$ that is already there. Any slot can be filled with any number or $\square$; however, there is a fixed number of slots depending on the size for which the arrays have been declared, so there is also a need for a further function, *size*, to state the constraint on size.

Formally, these functions have the function specifications and constraints contained in (55), in which *SQUARRAY* is the set of all square arrays of numbers, *sqry* is a parameter for an arbitrary member of that set, and *nob* is a parameter for an arbitrary number or $\square$.

(55)   size: SQUARRAY $\rightarrow$ NUMBER

      read: SQUARRAY X NUMBER X NUMBER

           $\rightarrow$ NUMBER $\cup$ {$\square$} $\cup$ {error}

      write: SQUARRAY X NUMBER X NUMBER

---

modify that account to accommodate such arrays. (*Hint:* Think in terms of the rectangular arrays described on the previous excursion.)

$$X \; (\text{NUMBER} \cup \{\square\}) \rightarrow \text{SQUARRAY} \cup \{\text{error}\}$$

(read(sqry, num_1, num_2) = error)

$\qquad$ = or((num_1> size(sqry)), (num_2> size(sqry)))

(write(sqry, num_1, num_2, nob) = error)

$\qquad$ = or((num_1> size(sqry)), (num_2> size(sqry)))

read(write(sqry, num_1, num_2, nob), num_1, num_2) = nob

The function *size* associates a square array with the number of rows and columns that it has. The size of each of the square arrays in (53) and (54) is *3*, because each of those arrays has three rows and three columns, as (56) states for (53).

(56)   size((53)) = 3

The function *read* takes a square array, a row number, and a column number and says what object—a number or $\square$—occupies the slot that is in that numbered row and that numbered column in the indicated square array. For example, the square array in (53) contains a *9* in the second row/third column slot and contains an *18* in the third row/second column slot, whereas the square array in (54)(b) contains $\square$ in both of those slots. Therefore, *read* will give the results that (57) indicates for those slots in those arrays.

(57)   read((53), 2, 3) = 9   read((53), 3, 2) = 18

$\qquad$ read((54)(b), 2, 3) = $\square$ read((54)(b), 3, 2) = $\square$

The function *write* places a number or blank in a numbered row/column slot in a square array, thereby replacing whatever is already there. For example, we can obtain (54)(d) from (54)(a) by three applications of *write*, as (58) shows.

(58)   write((54)(a), 1, 1, 1) = (54)(b)

$\qquad$ write((54)(b), 1, 2, 2) = (54)(c)

$\qquad$ write((54)(c), 1, 3, 3) = (54)(d)

First, a *1* is placed in the first row/first column slot of (54)(a) to produce (54)(b); then, a *2* is placed in the first row/second column slot of (54)(b) to produce (54)(c); and, finally, a *3* is placed in the first row/third column slot of (54)(c) to produce (54)(d).

The first constraint in (55) says that if an attempt is made to read a slot that a square array does not have, the result will be *error*, rather than a number or $\square$. That happens for a row or column number that is greater than the size of the array, such as the non-existent second row/fifth column slot for (53), as (59) states.

(59)   read((53), 2, 5) = error

Similarly, the second constraint in (55) says that if an attempt is made to write a number or $\square$ in a slot that a square array does not have, the result will be *error*, rather than a square array. An example would be trying to place a *12* in the non-existent second row/fifth column slot of (53), as (60) states.

(60)   write((53), 2, 5, 12) = error

The third constraint in (55) requires that *read* must behave as an inverse of *write*, just as *insert* acts as an inverse to the joint effect of *first* and *rest* for lists. Reading what is in a numbered row/column slot of a square array that has had something written in that slot will yield whatever number or $\square$ has most recently been written there. If we write a *9* in the second row/third column slot of (54)(d), then reading what is in that slot will yield *9* as the result, as (61) illustrates.

(61)   write((54)(d), 2, 3, 9)

$$= \text{write}\left(\begin{bmatrix} 1 & 2 & 3 \\ \square & \square & \square \\ \square & \square & \square \end{bmatrix}, 2, 3, 9\right)$$

$$= \begin{bmatrix} 1 & 2 & 3 \\ \square & \square & 9 \\ \square & \square & \square \end{bmatrix}$$

so

read(write((54)(d), 2, 3, 9), 2, 3)

$$= \text{read}\left(\begin{bmatrix} 1 & 2 & 3 \\ \square & \square & 9 \\ \square & \square & \square \end{bmatrix}, 2, 3\right)$$

$$= 9$$

Observe that there is no fourth constraint requiring *write* to behave as an inverse to *read*. Any number at all or $\square$ can be written in a slot of a square array, no matter what might be there already. The only requirement is that when something is written in a slot, reading that slot must have as its result the very thing that was written. This is what the third constraint in (55) says.

As was the case with the previous data structures, the function specifications and constraints in (55) contain all of the information that a programmer would need to know about square arrays to be able to implement them so that they will behave in the ways that we would want them to. We can use the functions in (55) to define a further function on square arrays that we will need on Expedition 4, where we will use them to represent puzzles and games. In that connection we will need a function that interchanges or switches two elements of a square array, as the function *switch* defined in (62) does.

(62)   switch(sqry, num_1, num_2, num_3, num_4)

=   write(write(sqry, num_3, num_4, read(sqry, num_1, num_2)),

num_1, num_2, read(sqry, num_3, num_4))

What (62) says is that we switch the number or $\square$ that is in the *num₁* row/*num₂* column slot of a square array with the number or $\square$ that is in the *num₃* row/*num₄* column slot of that array by writing into the *num₃* row/*num₄* column slot of that array what we read in the *num₁* row/*num₂* column slot of that array, and then writing into the *num₁* row/*num₂* column slot of the resulting array what we read in the *num₃* row/*num₄* column slot of the *original* array. Since placing the new *num₃* row/*num₄* column value into the array erases the value that was already there, steps must be taken, when implementing this function, to ensure that that former value has been previously read and stored somewhere in the computer's memory in order for it to be still available for its new role as the *num₁* row/*num₂* column value in the square array that we finally get. The equation in (62) serves as a general *constraint* on the allowable implementations of the function *switch*, but it says nothing at all about such details of any *particular* implementation.

We can switch the second row/first column value in (53) with its third row/second column value, for example, as shown in (63).

(63)   switch((53), 2, 1, 3, 2)

$$= \quad \text{switch}\left(\begin{bmatrix} 1 & 2 & 3 \\ 4 & 6 & 9 \\ 12 & 18 & 36 \end{bmatrix}, 2, 1, 3, 2\right)$$

$$= \quad \text{write}\left(\text{write}\left(\begin{bmatrix} 1 & 2 & 3 \\ 4 & 6 & 9 \\ 12 & 18 & 36 \end{bmatrix}, 3, 2,\right.\right.$$

$$\left.\text{read}\left(\begin{bmatrix} 1 & 2 & 3 \\ 4 & 6 & 9 \\ 12 & 18 & 36 \end{bmatrix}, 2, 1\right)\right), 2, 1,$$

$$\left.\text{read}\left(\begin{bmatrix} 1 & 2 & 3 \\ 4 & 6 & 9 \\ 12 & 18 & 36 \end{bmatrix}, 3, 2\right)\right)$$

$$= \quad \text{write}\left(\text{write}\left(\begin{bmatrix} 1 & 2 & 3 \\ 4 & 6 & 9 \\ 12 & 18 & 36 \end{bmatrix}, 3, 2,\right.\right.$$

$$\left.\text{read}\left(\begin{bmatrix} 1 & 2 & 3 \\ 4 & 6 & 9 \\ 12 & 18 & 36 \end{bmatrix}, 2, 1\right)\right), 2, 1, 18)$$

$$= \quad \text{write}\left(\text{write}\left(\begin{bmatrix} 1 & 2 & 3 \\ 4 & 6 & 9 \\ 12 & 18 & 36 \end{bmatrix}, 3, 2, 4\right), 2, 1, 18\right)$$

$$= \quad \text{write}\left(\begin{bmatrix} 1 & 2 & 3 \\ 4 & 6 & 9 \\ 12 & 4 & 36 \end{bmatrix}, 2, 1, 18\right)$$

$$= \quad \begin{bmatrix} 1 & 2 & 3 \\ 18 & 6 & 9 \\ 12 & 4 & 36 \end{bmatrix}$$

We read two values independently from the original array and then write them consecutively into a first and then a second resulting array. The control structure for *switch*, given in Figure 21, shows the general way in which this happens.

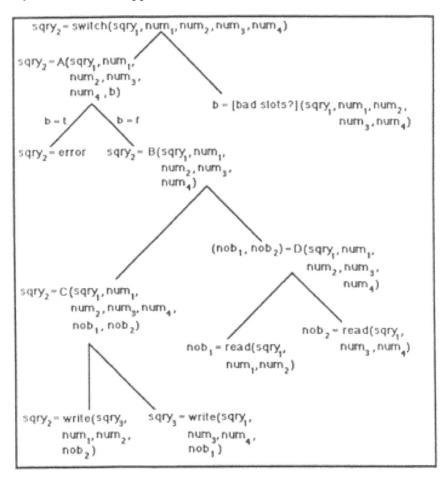

Fig. 21: Control Structure of switch as Defined in (62)

As the control structure shows, we find two numbers or $\square$ by reading twice from *sqry₁*, once from its *num₁*, *num₂* slot and once from its *num₃*, *num₄* slot. These readings are independent and can be implemented in parallel, if a facility for such implementation is available. Otherwise, the programmer must sequence them arbitrarily. Once these read values are available, they become further arguments for determining the final array *sqry₂*. We do this by writing the value that was in the *num₃*, *num₄* slot of the original array *sqry₁* into the

num_1, num_2 slot of the array $sqry_3$ that results from having read the value that was in the num_1, num_2 slot of $sqry_1$ into $sqry_1$'s own num_3, num_4 slot. Like the other functions whose control structures we have seen, *switch* depends on the result of a boolean test—still to be filled in, in Figure 21[16]—this time to see if the numbers that determine the slots exceed the size of the square array whose elements are to be switched. However, unlike other control structures we have seen, there are no internal calls to the overall function in Figure 21, that is, *switch* does not call itself within its own control structure. The reason for this is that *switch* is not recursive, but simply does its thing once and then is finished. We can see this also from (62), in which *switch* appears only on the left-hand side of the single equation that defines it.[17]

Trees are another non-linear data structure that we will find useful on Expedition 4; in effect, we have already seen them. As we saw on Expedition 1, control structures can be viewed as trees of functions that are very tightly constrained by the requirements of data flow. On Expedition 4 we will need trees of square arrays, when we examine methods that we can use to get computers to solve puzzles and play games. However, to simplify the discussion of trees themselves, and to facilitate their comparison with the other data structures that we have seen, we will restrict attention for now to trees of numbers, such as those in (64), which contain the numbers in Figure 1 in two different arrangements.

---

[16] *Suggested excursion:* Complete Figure 21 by defining the boolean function *[bad slots?]*. Draw the control structure, data dependency, and data flow diagrams for that function. (Hint: Compare this test function to the one in Figure 15. You need two numbers to define a slot and you are examining two slots.)

[17] *Suggested excursion:* Draw the data dependency and data flow diagrams of *switch*. (Hint: Assume that the corresponding diagrams for *[bad slots?]* have already been drawn. Remember that *switch* is not recursive.)

(64)   (a)   (b)

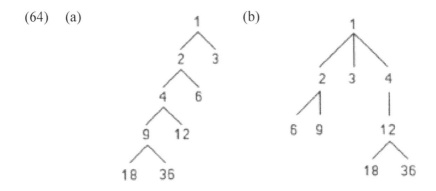

Unlike square arrays, but like the linear data structures, trees have no predetermined size; they can grow and shrink as needed.

As in square arrays, the numbers in trees can be accessed through their numbered locations—called *nodes* for trees—in the data structure; however, a tree's nodes are numbered not by pairs of numbers, but by sequences of numbers of varying length called *node indexes* or *indices*. Each number in a tree is at some position from the left at some level of the tree, so a node is uniquely identifiable by the index that consists of the sequence of numbers that identify those positions at successive levels. For example, in both (64)(a) and (b), *1* is at the *root* of the tree, the zero level, which is indexed by the empty sequence, *[ ]*, the sequence that contains no numbers at all. Also, in both (64)(a) and (b), *2* is at node *[1]*, because it is the first item from the left below the root, and *3* is at node *[2]*, because it is the second item from the left below the root. However, *4* is at different nodes in the two trees; it is at node *[1, 1]* in (64)(a), because it is the first number from the left under the number at node *[1]*, but it is in node *[3]* in (64)(b), because it is the third number from the left below the root. Similarly, *9* is at node *[1, 1, 1]* in (64)(a), because it is the first number from the left under the number that is at node *[1, 1]*, but it is at node *[1, 2]* in (64)(b), because it is the second number from the left under the number that is at node *[1]*. Finally, *36* is at node *[1, 1, 1, 2]* in (64)(a), because it is the second number from the left under the number that is at node *[1, 1, 1]*, but is in node *[3, 1, 2]* in (64)(b), because it is the second number from the left under the number that is the first number from the left under the number that is at node *3*. The full set of node indices for each of the respective trees in (64) is shown in (65).

(65) (a) 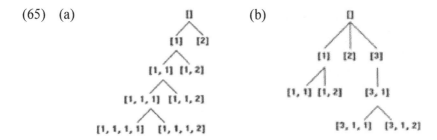   (b)

It is convenient to stipulate that a tree of numbers contains the blank element ⊡ at every node below its lowest nodes, called *terminal nodes*, *leaf nodes*, or *leaves*—for example, below nodes *[2]*, *[1, 2]*, *[1, 1, 2]*, *[1, 1, 1, 1]*, and *[1, 1, 1, 2]* in a tree like (64)(a), and below nodes *[2]*, *[1, 1]*, *[1, 2]*, *[3, 1, 1]*, and *[3, 1, 2]* in a tree like (64)(b)—so we can assume that any sequence of non-zero numbers will identify either a number or ⊡ for any tree. For example, the sequence *[1, 1, 1, 2]* identifies *36* in (64)(a), but ⊡ in (64)(b), while the sequence *[3, 1, 2]* identifies *36* in (64)(b), but ⊡ in (64)(a). We can attach a new number to a tree only at a node for which there already is a number, rather than ⊡, at the node immediately above or to the left of it. For example, *18* can be attached to (66)(a) at node *[1, 1, 1, 1]* to get (66)(b), because (66)(a) already has a number, not ⊡, at node *[1, 1, 1]* immediately above, and 36 can be attached to (66)(b) at node *[1, 1, 1, 2]* to get (64)(a), because (66)(b) already has a number, not ⊡, at *[1, 1, 1, 1]* immediately to the left.

(66) (a) 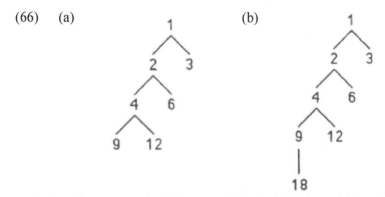   (b)

In contrast, no number can be attached to (64)(b) at node *[1, 1, 1, 1]*, because (64)(b) has no number at node *[1, 1, 1]* immediately above *[1, 1, 1, 1]*, and no number can be attached to (64)(b) at node *[1, 1, 1, 2]*, because (64)(b) has no number at node *[1, 1, 1, 1]* immediately to the left of [1, 1, 1, 2].

To formalize all this, we first need to characterize *sequences* as a data structure, in order to clarify what functions are available to us to apply to them, before we can use them to identify tree nodes. Sequences of numbers are essentially the same as lists of numbers, except that they can contain as elements only numbers, rather than further lists, and we typically attach new elements at the end of a sequence, rather than at the beginning. We can therefore obtain a definition of sequences by modifying the function specifications and constraints for lists in (22) in accordance with these differences, as (67) shows.

(67)   last: SEQUENCE — {[ ]} → NUMBER

initial: SEQUENCE → SEQUENCE

attach: NUMBER X SEQUENCE → SEQUENCE

last(attach(num, seq)) = num

initial(attach(num, seq)) = seq

attach(last(seq), initial(seq)) = seq

SEQUENCE in (67) is the set of all sequences of numbers, and *seq* is a parameter for an arbitrary member of that set. The function *last* finds the number that is at the end of a sequence, and the function *initial* returns the same sequence with that final element removed. *Attach* acts as a sort of inverse to the joint action of *last* and *initial*, just as *insert* does for the list functions *first* and *rest*.[18] We do not need to include analogs for *length* or *item* as functions in (67), because we can define these for sequences in terms of *last, initial*, and *attach* in much the same way that *length* and *item* themselves were defined for lists in terms of *first, rest*, and *insert* in (23) and (25), respectively.[19] In fact, the functions *length* and *item* no longer need to be included in the definition of lists, as (22) states it, since those functions have now been otherwise defined in terms of the rest of that definition.

───────────────

[18] *Suggested excursion:* Use overloading to compare *sequences* with *lists*. Does the contrast between (67) and (22) really distinguish adequately between *first* and *last*? What further constraint might be helpful? (*Hint:* Define functions that compare sequences and lists by examining their elements one by one. Try this excursion again after studying the discussion of (72).)

[19] *Suggested excursion:* Define functions for sequences that are analogous to the list functions *length* and *item*. (*Hint:* Use (23) and (25) as guides.)

Now that sequences are available, along with the functions that we can use to manipulate them, we can use them to define trees as the data structure that has the function specifications and constraints given in (68), in which *TREE* is the set of all trees of numbers, *tree* is a parameter for an arbitrary member of that set, and ◢ is the empty

tree, ⟨tree symbol⟩ , which contains $\square$ at every node, that is, for every member of *SEQUENCE*.[20]

(68)　grow: TREE X SEQUENCE X NUMBER → TREE ∪ {error}

graft: TREE X SEQUENCE X NUMBER → TREE ∪ {error}

chop: TREE X SEQUENCE → TREE ∪ {error}

fruit: TREE X SEQUENCE → NUMBER ∪ {$\square$} ∪ {error}

leaf: TREE X SEQUENCE → BOOLEAN

leaf(tree, seq) = and((fruit(tree, attach(num, seq)) = $\square$),

not(fruit(tree, seq) = $\square$))

(grow(tree, seq, num) = error) = not(leaf(tree, seq))

(graft(tree, seq, num) = error)

= or(leaf(tree, seq), (fruit(tree, seq) = $\square$))

chop (◢, seq) = error

chop(grow(tree, seq, num), seq) = tree

―――――――――――――――――――

[20] *Suggested excursion:* Figure out why ⟨tree symbol⟩ is described here as the empty tree,

even though $\begin{bmatrix} \square & \square & \square \\ \square & \square & \square \\ \square & \square & \square \end{bmatrix}$ was said to be *not* empty in connection with (54).

(*Hint:* The square array $\begin{bmatrix} \square & \square & \square \\ \square & \square & \square \\ \square & \square & \square \end{bmatrix}$ has three rows and three columns. How

many levels does the tree ⟨tree symbol⟩ have? Ask yourself what the empty square array *would* look like.)

chop(graft(tree, seq, num), seq) = tree

fruit(■, seq) = □

fruit(grow (tree, seq, num), seq) = num

fruit(graft(tree, seq, num), seq) = num

This time there are two construction functions: *grow,* which attaches a number to a leaf node, and *graft,* which attaches a number to a node that already has a number "hanging" from it. The reason for this is that these two ways of putting a number into a tree have different effects on the resulting node indices. As (65) illustrates, a number that is grown onto a tree has a node index that can be obtained by attaching a *1* at the end of the index of the node it is grown from, while a number that is grafted onto a tree has a node index that can be obtained by adding *1* to the last element of the node index of another number that is already "hanging" from the same node. As before, there are two access functions: *chop,* which returns what is left of a tree when a number is removed from some node, and *fruit,* which tells us what number is at some node in a tree. The boolean-valued function, *leaf,* is an auxiliary function that identifies leaf nodes, as defined explicitly in the first constraint. It serves mainly as an abbreviation to simplify the formulation of the constraints and, like all abbreviations, could be dispensed with entirely by replacing (69)(a) with (69)(b) wherever it appears in the other constraints.

(69)   (a)   leaf(tree, seq)

(b)   fruit(tree, attach(num, seq)) = □.

The next two constraints provide the error conditions on the construction functions, and the rest describe the effects of each access function on the empty and non-empty cases. The first error condition prohibits growing a number onto a tree at a node that is not a leaf node on that tree; *not* is the *negation* function, which reverses truth values, changing *t* to *f* and *f* to *t,* wherever it finds them. The constraint says that (70)(a) and (b) always have the same truth-value, that is, that *grow* will produce *error* whenever *leaf* produces *f.*

(70)   (a)   grow(tree, seq, num) = error

(b)   not(leaf(tree, seq))

The second error condition prohibits grafting a number onto a tree at a leaf node and also at any node whose fruit is □, that is, any node that is not otherwise connected to the tree; the latter condition is already included for the first constraint through (70)(b), since an unconnected node is inherently not a leaf node.

The first *chop* constraint says that the empty tree cannot be chopped, just as the empty stack cannot be popped and the empty queue cannot be exited. The next two say that chopping a tree at a node at which it has just had a number grown or grafted onto it yields the original tree back. The first *fruit* constraint says that the empty tree has $\square$ at every node. The next two say that the fruit at a node of a tree at which a number has just been grown or grafted is the number that has just been grown or grafted there. Together these constraints ensure that the access functions and the construction functions for trees behave as mutual inverses, in the ways that we seen for the previously examined data structures.[21, 22, 23, 24]

---

[21] *Suggested excursion:* Think of some further functions that might be of interest in connection with trees and give definitions of those functions in terms of the functions in (68). Draw the control structure, data dependency, and data flow diagrams for the functions you define. (*Hint:* How about the *number of elements* in a tree? How does that compare to the *length* of a list? How about a function that *searches* a tree to find the node at which a particular number resides? How many different search functions can you think up?)

[22] *Suggested excursion:* Use overloading to compare *trees* with *square arrays*. Do you discover anything interesting? (*Hint: Square array* elements are accessed via a pair of numbers, but *tree* elements are accessed via a sequence of numbers of arbitrary length.)

[23] *Suggested excursion:* Use overloading to compare *trees* with *lists*. Do you discover anything interesting? (*Hint:* Compare *chop(*■*)* with *rest(( ))* and *fruit(*■*)* with *first(( ))*.)

[24] *Suggested excursion:* A tree is equivalent to a special kind of list, called a *labeled bracketing*, in which numbers at leaf nodes of a tree are elements of the corresponding list at some internal level of *nested* parentheses and numbers at non-leaf nodes of a tree serve as *labels* on the parentheses. For example, the trees (64)(a) and (b) are equivalent, respectively, to the labeled bracketings (i) and (ii).

(i) $(_1 (_2 (_4 (_9 18 \quad 36)_9 \quad 12)_4 6)_2 \quad 3)_1$

(ii) $(_1 (_2 6 \quad 9)_2 \quad 3 \quad (_4 (_{12} 18 \quad 36)_{12})_4)_1$

What, if anything, might be gained by writing trees as labeled bracketings? What, if anything, might be lost? Define labeled bracketings formally as a data structure and then use overloading to compare them to trees and to lists. (*Hint:* Lists are linear; trees are not. Trees are equivalent to labeled bracketings; lists are equivalent to trees with unlabeled non-leaf nodes.)

The functions *and*, *not*, and *or*, which appear in the first three conditions of (68), are among the functions that we can use to characterize booleans, just as we can use suitably constrained functions, as we have seen, to define various data structures. Unlike the data structures, booleans are not arrangements of abstract objects, but are abstract objects themselves. They therefore constitute a *data type*, rather than a data structure.

Function specifications and constraints defining the *BOOLEAN* data type are given in (71).

(71)   BOOLEAN = {t, f}

not: BOOLEAN → BOOLEAN

or: BOOLEAN X BOOLEAN → BOOLEAN

and: BOOLEAN X BOOLEAN → BOOLEAN

not(t) = f	or(t, t) = t	and(t, t) = t
not(f) = t	or(t, f) = t	and (t, f) = f
t = (1 = 1)	or(f, t) = t	and (f, t) = f
	or(f, f) = f	and (f, f) = f

Since (71) defines a *kind* of object, rather than an *arrangement* of objects that are assumed to exist already—such as numbers—we need to specify those objects in some way, as well as what functions we can use with them; in this case, the objects are identified as *t* and *f*. Since this data type contains only two objects, the constraints primarily take the form of specifying what value is returned by each function for each choice of parameter values. The *not* in (71) is the negation function that we just saw in (68), and the *or* is the inclusive disjunction function that we first saw in connection with Figure 15, and that also appears in (68). The *and* in (71) is the *conjunction* function, which generates *t*, when both of its arguments are *t*, and generates *f*, otherwise. In other words, *and* tells us when both of the boolean conditions it applies to are true, just as *or* tells us when one or the other or both are true. These functions mirror more or less accurately one of the ways the words *not*, *or*, and *and* are used in everyday English, but we will have more to say about the actual subtleties of those words on Expedition 5.[25]

The remaining constraint in (71), repeated in (72), is needed to break the symmetry of the rest of (71).

(72) $t = (1 = 1)$

The functions *or* and *and* are *duals*, in the sense that each of them becomes the other when the symbols *t* and *f* are interchanged. There is nothing else in (71) that distinguishes these two symbols to ensure that they are implemented in accordance with their intended meanings as abstract representations of the respective intuitive notions of truth and falsity, rather than the other way around. The *names* of the functions *or* and *and*, as well as those of the symbols *t* and *f*, have meaning to a person who reads them, but they have no meaning in themselves to a computer that we implement them on. Their computational significance resides entirely in the relationships that we explicitly state for them in the function specifications and constraints, regardless of the names that we assign to them. Including (72) or some equivalent in (71) informs the human or machine programmer of the requirement that the abstract symbol *t* must be implemented to represent truth, rather than falsity, since it is identified in (72) as the value of a true statement.

As a further example, we can define *times* as abstract objects that are different from numbers and that comprise a separate data type, by specifying functions that we can use with times, but not with numbers. One advantage of doing this in programming is that it prevents a programmer from applying to times any number functions that are really not appropriate to times, such as greatest common divisor or least common multiple. One way of characterizing times as a data type, using the twelve-hour system that is standard in the U.S., is shown in (73),

---

[25] *Suggested excursion:* The definition of booleans can be simplified by reformulating it in terms of only one function *nor*, which generates *t*, when both of its arguments are *f*, and generates *f*, otherwise, because each of the three functions *not*, *or*, and *and* can be defined entirely in terms of *nor*. Figure out how to do this. (*Hint:* The result of applying *not* to some argument is the same as the result of applying *nor* to that argument and itself.)

where *TIME* is the set of all times and *time* is a parameter for an arbitrary member of that set.[26]

(73) TIME =   {1 AM, 2 AM, 3 AM, 4 AM, 5 AM, 6 AM,

7 AM, 8 AM, 9 AM, 10 AM, 11 AM, 12 noon,

1 PM, 2 PM, 3 PM, 4 PM, 5 PM, 6 PM,

7 PM, 8 PM, 9 PM, 10 PM, 11 PM, 12 mdnt}

o'clock: NUMBER $\rightarrow$ TIME

measure: TIME $\rightarrow$ NUMBER

later: TIME X NUMBER $\rightarrow$ TIME

measure(1 AM) = 1	measure(9 AM) = 9	measure(5 PM) = 17
measure(2 AM) = 2	measure(10 AM) = 10	measure(6 PM) = 18
measure(3 AM) = 3	measure(11 AM) = 11	measure(7 PM) = 19
measure(4 AM) = 4	measure(12 noon) = 12	measure(8 PM) = 20
measure(5 AM) = 5	measure(1 PM) = 13	measure(9 PM) = 21
measure(6 AM) = 6	measure(2 PM) = 14	measure(10 PM) = 22
measure(7 AM) = 7	measure(3 PM) = 15	measure(11 PM) = 23
measure(8 AM) = 8	measure(4 PM) = 16	measure(12 mdnt) = 0

measure (o'clock(num)) = num

o'clock(measure(time)) = time

o'clock(num) = o'clock(remainder(num, 24))

later(time, num) = o'clock(sum(measure(time), num))

Again, as with booleans, the members of the set can be explicitly listed, because, in contrast to numbers, there are only finitely many of

---

[26] *Suggested excursion:* Define *time* as a data type using the twenty-four hour system that is common in much of the world outside the U.S. Can you extend this to a definition that includes minutes, as well as hours? (*Hint:* A time and its measure will look the same. Will your extended version of *time* be a data type or a data structure?)

them. The first twenty-four constraints provide each time with a numerical measure, and the next two constraints specify that the functions *measure* and *o'clock* act as inverses. The second *o'clock* constraint provides a time for any number at all, even those that are not explicitly provided as measures for times in the measure constraints. The function *remainder*, which appears in the second *o'clock* constraint, returns the remainder when one number is divided by another number, in this case, 24; it is assumed to be already available for numbers by the time we get around to defining times as a data type.[27] The last constraint says how to compute the time that is some number of hours later than some given time.[28]

For example, determining what time is *10* hours after *3 PM* requires computing the value of (74).

(74)   later(3 PM, 10)

According to the *later* constraint in (73), (74) is equivalent to (75).

(75)   o'clock(sum(measure((3 PM), 10))

The measure constraints in (73) say that (75) is equivalent to (76), because the measure of *3 PM* is *15*, and, therefore, that (76) is equivalent to (77), because of the way we defined *sum* on Expedition 1, that is, because we can compute the sum of *15* and *10*, by that definition, to be *25*.

(76)   o'clock(sum(15, 10))

(77)   o'clock(25)

---

[27] *Suggested excursion:* Define the function *remainder* that returns the remainder when we divide one number by another. (*Hint:* You can define *remainder* without reference to division, if you use a recursive definition. The value of *remainder(num$_1$, num$_2$)* can be obtained, without division, by starting at the node at which *num$_1$* appears in the lattice in Figure 4 and counting down by steps of size *num$_2$* as many times as possible, until you arrive at a node whose number is smaller than *num$_2$*. The number you end up at is the number you want.)

[28] *Suggested excursion:* The *later* constraint in (73) is really an explicit definition of the function *later* in terms of the other time functions *measure* and *o'clock*. Draw the control structure, data dependency, and data flow diagrams of *later*. (*Hint:* This definition is not recursive.)

The second *o'clock* constraint tells us that (77) is equivalent to (78) and thus to (79), because dividing *25* by *24* leaves a remainder of *1*.

(78)   o'clock(remainder(25, 24))

(79)   o'clock(1)

According to the first *o'clock* constraint, the o'clock of a number that is the measure of a time is the time that that number is the measure of, so (79) turns out to be equivalent to (80), because *1 AM* is identified in (73) as the time whose measure is *1*.

(80)   1 AM

In other words, we have computed from (73) the correct result that *10* hours after *3 PM* is *1 AM* by applying to times only functions that are defined for times and applying functions that are defined for numbers only to numbers themselves. Inside the computer, all of this computation does get done in terms of numbers, but defining times as a data type enables a programmer who needs to write a program about times to think explicitly in terms of times, as humans more naturally do, leaving all the distracting numerical work entirely up to the machine.[29]

The data types of a program are the kinds of objects that it can deal with, its data structures are the ways in which it organizes those objects in order to deal with them most effectively, and its algorithms are what it does with them. Making extensive use of abstract objects that are formally defined as data types—a style of computer utilization known as *object-oriented programming*, exemplified by such languages as C++ and Java—contrasts with an older style of programming in which, in effect, a programmer has to model everything explicitly in terms of numbers. The newer style has the advantage of enabling the programmer to think in terms of the sorts of objects the program is really supposed to be about, such as times in a program that is dealing with scheduling, so that extraneous characteristics of numbers no longer get in the way of figuring out what to do with those objects. For example,

---

[29] *Suggested excursion:* Define data types *month* and *day* and then use them to define a data type *date* whose elements each have a month and a day. (*Hint:* Different months have different numbers of days.)

representing truth and falsity by t and f, respectively, as defined in (71), rather than by, say, 1 and 0, as programmers used to have to and often still have to do, enables a programmer to avoid the temptation of applying functions to truth values that make no sense for them, simply because they work for numbers. According to (71), a programmer can use on t and f the functions *not*, *or*, *and*, and any other functions that we have defined explicitly in terms of those three functions, but cannot use on t and f such functions as *subtraction* or *successor*, which are meaningless for t and f. If those numbers were to be used instead of t and f to represent truth and falsity, a programmer might inadvertently err by applying such numerical functions meaninglessly to 1 and 0, with potentially misleading consequences.[30, 31, 32, 33]

---

[30] *Suggested excursion:* Define *fractions* as a data type. (*Hint:* The numerator and the denominator of a fraction are both numbers. Some fractions are equal, even though they have different numerators and denominators. That gives you one of your constraints. How should you define addition and multiplication for fractions?)

[31] *Suggested excursion:* Define *signed numbers*, that is, positive and negative whole numbers together with zero, as a data type. (*Hint:* The numbers $+2$ and -2 have the same *absolute value*, but different *signs*.)

[32] *Suggested excursion (difficult):* Having now seen several examples of data structure definitions, define *lattices* as a data structure. *(Hint:* The basic functions have to behave like *maximum* and *minimum* for Figure 4 and like *least common multiple* and *greatest common divisor* for Figure 5. What constraints on those functions would express such behavior? Do you need any further functions to formulate such constraints? What is the maximum of the maximum of two numbers and the minimum of those same numbers? What other such combinations of *maximum* and *minimum* can you come up with and what must their results be?)

[33] *Suggested excursion (very difficult):* Having now seen several examples of data type definitions, take a crack at defining *numbers* as a data type. *(Hint:* Look back at what we said about the principle of mathematical induction in connection with Figure 4. How might we express that principle formally? More on this on Expedition 5.)

3. Recognizing: States and Machines

I ask six student volunteers to leave the room, after telling them that those who remain will make up a story for them to guess, when they return, by asking only questions that can be answered *yes* or *no*. After the guessing group leaves, I tell the remaining students that there will really be no story. If the guessers ask a question that ends in one of the vowels in (1), the answer will be *yes*, and if they ask a question that ends in any other letter, the answer will be *no*.

(1)   a, e, i, o, u, y

For example, if the guessers ask (2)(a), the answer will be *yes*, but if they ask (2)(b), the answer will be *no*.

(2)   (a)   Is the story about people?

        (b)   Is the story about a person?

If the guessers ask (3)(a), the answer will be *no*, but if they ask (3)(b), the answer will be *yes*.

(3)   (a)   Is the story about animals?

        (b)   Are there animals in the story?

It matters that *y* be considered a vowel in this exercise, because someone among the guessers inevitably asks the question (4).

(4)   Is there really a story?

Considering *y* to be a consonant would immediately end the exercise by necessitating the answer *no*.

    This exercise illustrates the concept of *creativity*, which lies at the core of the distinction between humans and machines. The guessers always end up constructing a story of their own, based on their own interests and backgrounds, in response to what are, in effect, random answers that have nothing to do with the content of their questions. Furthermore, they construct these stories without even realizing that they are doing it. One time, for example, after being told that the story was not about a person, an animal, a plant, a continent, a rock formation, an ocean, a planet, and so on, one guesser, who had apparently been studying physics, asked if it was about plasma. The story quickly turned into a science fiction fantasy about a plasma creature that was trying to conquer the universe. A philosophically minded guesser once asked, after a long sequence of *no* answers, if the story was about an idea. After the required *yes* answer, the story became a historical fantasy about a debate between Plato and Aristotle. More often, guessers ask if the story is about someone at the college, someone taking the course, or someone sitting right here. After that, the questioning turns into a fishing expedition for gossip about friends, professors, or advisors, and the story takes shape accordingly.

It is a simple matter to program a computer to play the role of responder in this exercise, because it is easy to distinguish vowels from consonants—assuming that written language is used and communication is done by keyboard—and to respond *yes* or *no* accordingly. Questions can be represented as sequences of words, and words can be represented as sequences of letters, so to distinguish, for example, between (2)(a) and (b), the computer needs only to evaluate the expressions (5)(a) and (b), where *last* is overloaded for the two different kinds of sequences.[34]

(5)   (a)   last(last([[Is] [the] [story] [about] [people]]))

(b)   last(last([[Is] [the] [story] [about] [a] [person]]))

For (5)(a), the computer would perform the calculation in (6)(a), in which it first finds the last element of the sequence of the words in (2)(a) (without the question mark) and then finds the last element of the sequence of letters that comprises that word, and for (5)(b), it would perform the corresponding calculation in (6)(b) in exactly the same way, but with a different result.

(6)   (a)   last(last([[Is] [the] [story] [about] [people]]))

$$= last([people]) = e$$

(b)   last(last([[Is] [the] [story] [about] [a] [person]]))

$$= last([person]) = n$$

---

[34] *Suggested excursion:* Define the data structures *sequence of words* and *sequence of letters,* where a word is a sequence of letters. *(Hint:* Replace the set *NUMBERS* in the definition of *sequence of numbers* with some other appropriate set. Remember that there are only twenty-six letters, and that these have to be identified.)

In a typical programming language, the computer would be given an instruction something like (7), in which *member* is a function that tests to see if some object is in some sequence.[35]

(7)   If member(last(last(seq)), [a, e, i, o, u, y])

then Response = yes;

Else

Response = no;

Print Response;

If *member* returns the value *t*, the parameter *Response* gets the value *yes*; if *member* returns the value *f*, then *Response* gets the value *no*.[36]

It is not as easy to program a computer to play the role of guesser in this exercise, and whether it is even possible to do so realistically is still an open question. Guessers have to draw on their knowledge and life experience in ways that are not yet fully understood; it is easy to give a computer an extensive knowledge base, simply by filling it with factual statements written in some suitable programming language, but how to give it a full human life experience is not clear at all. Psychologists distinguish between

---

[35] *Suggested excursion:* Define the function *member*. *(Hint:* This function maps a pair of an object and a sequence to a boolean. If the object is in the sequence, the result is *t;* otherwise, it is *f.)*

[36] *Suggested excursion:* More sophisticated programs might treat a sentence as a *list* of words and a word as a *string* of letters. Strings are defined primarily by a function *concatenate,* which forms a new string from two existing strings by placing one after the other, as in (i).

(i)   concatenate(light, house) = lighthouse

concatenate(house, keeper) = housekeeper

Using lists makes it possible to express phrasal differences in what would otherwise be the same sequence of words, such as the three-word phrase (ii), which can be internally phrased as either of the two two-word phrases (iii) or (iv), which have very different meanings.

(ii)   light house keeper

(iii)   ((lighthouse) keeper)

(iv)   (light (housekeeper))

Define *lists of words* and *strings of letters* as data structures. *(Hint:* Compare strings to lists and sequences. What functions act as inverses to *concatenate?)*

semantic memory, which consists of the facts that a person learns from books, lessons, lectures, and so on, and *episodic memory*, which consists of rememberings of one's own personal experience. The two sorts of memory seem to be stored and accessed differently in human brains, and it is far from clear how that distinction could be implemented meaningfully in a computer, or what it would even mean to say that a computer has had some experience. Guessers must use what they draw from their knowledge and experience to formulate meaningful questions that are relevant and responsive to the whole pattern of *yes/no* answers that they have been presented with, and they must do all this with the aim of figuring out a story that has supposedly, but not really, already been constructed. Progress has been made in getting computers to do such things, through what are called goal-directed programs, as we will see on Expedition 4 in connection with puzzles and games, and in more sophisticated natural-language understanding systems, but no program has yet been constructed that behaves anything at all like a real person.

Moreover, it is far from easy to program a computer even to play the role of responder, if we require that the responses, just as much as the questions, must be relevant and meaningful, as we would expect them to be in real life, rather than mechanical and virtually random, as they are in the exercise. In fact, the ability to give meaningful and relevant answers to questions has been proposed as a key distinguishing feature of human intelligence. According to the *Turing Test*—named for the mathematician, Alan Turing, who introduced it in the 1950's—we can consider a machine to have human intelligence if a human cannot distinguish its responses to questions from those that another human would give. Given a machine that is claimed to have human intelligence, the machine and a human are both subjected to a long sequence of questions by another human, who is not told which is which, as Figure 22 illustrates. If, regardless of what questions are asked, the questioner cannot tell which answers are coming from the human and which are coming from the machine, then we must conclude that the machine—at least, according to this test—has human intelligence.

Fig. 22: The Turing Test: "Answer these questions."

A "Robotman" cartoon by Jim Meddick nicely illustrates a curious paradox in the Turing Test. In the dialog (8), Robotman initiates the Turing Test with his human mentor and gives some very human answers, but he then fails the test, when he is confronted with the obviously definitive question.

(8)   Human: Why are you standing behind a large piece of cardboard?

      Robotman: I want to take the artificial intelligence test. It's a test that was designed by the British mathematician Alan Turing. A person holds a conversation with an unseen respondent. If the person can't tell whether the respondent is

	human or computer, then artificial intelligence has been achieved.
Human:	Uh. Ok. Crazy weather we've been having, huh?
Robotman:	I hate rain.
Human:	And what about the deficit?
Robotman:	It's outta control!
Human:	Are you a computer?
Robotman:	Yeah.
Human:	Aha!
Robotman:	Nuts.

Except for the last one, the questions in (8) are not *yes/no*, like the questions in the exercise, but they could easily be reformulated that way. More interesting is the fact that the Turing Test, as it is usually formulated, does not require responders to give true answers. Humans regularly err or lie, and a computer programmed to have human intelligence would presumably exhibit those behaviors as well. Robotman would not have failed the test so easily, if he had lied in response to the final question in (8), rather than telling the truth.

What is paradoxical about this is that a human would not have to lie in response to that question in order to be judged to be exhibiting human intelligence, but could answer it truthfully—as Robotman does—but with the opposite result. In other words, a computer can demonstrate human intelligence only by not practicing human ethics, at least in some instances. To pass the Turing Test and be judged to have human intelligence, a computer—whatever else it might be asked—must answer *yes* to (9)(a) and *no* to (9)(b), even though both of these answers are lies.

(9) (a)   Are you a human?

(b)   Are you a computer?

A human—that which the computer is trying to emulate—can give exactly the same answers, but truthfully, with no ethical violation. The very interesting questions that this raises about the relation between ethical behavior and intelligence are, unfortunately, beyond the scope of this book.

A more sophisticated and more difficult test for human intelligence—proposed by computer scientist Lotfi Zadeh in the 1980's—makes creativity, rather than answering questions, the defining feature of the human/machine distinction. Rather than a succession of questions, the tester would present the computer and the human with an extensive set of statements to "summarize in your own words," as Figure 23 illustrates.

Fig. 23: The Zadeh Test: "Summarize in your own words."

On the one hand, humans differ among themselves so widely in how they would perform that task that a sufficiently clever computer might very well be able to lose itself in all that variation. By exhibiting a level of intelligence that is indistinguishable from that of at least some real humans a computer could come out looking like just "one of the guys." In fact, the colorful creativity of some of Robotman's answers in (8) (as well as the fact that it was he who initiated the test in this instance!) suggests that he might be able to pass this test if only he could get over his non-human commitment to truthfulness. On the other hand, this test requires a much deeper level of understanding on the part of the test subjects of what is being said to them than is required in the Turing test, as well as the ability to formulate coherent relevant answers. The tester would thus have that much more information to make use of in the attempt to distinguish the human from the machine, and the conclusion that the machine has human intelligence would have that much more credibility if the tester could still not tell them apart.

We can clarify the difference between humans and machines still further by defining machines as a data type, along the lines we discussed for other sorts of objects at the end of Expedition 2. This also has the further benefit of enabling us to write computer programs that can manipulate machines as objects. We can identify a *machine* abstractly with the set of *states* it can be in and the kinds of *transitions* it can make from one state to another in response to environmental influences. For example, an automobile can be idling, accelerating, moving steadily, decelerating, or turned off. Stepping on the gas pedal makes the automobile accelerate, when it is idling, moving steadily, or decelerating, but leaves it in the state it is in, when it is already accelerating or is turned off. Stepping on the brake pedal makes the automobile decelerate, when it is moving steadily or accelerating, but leaves it in the state it is in, when it is already decelerating or is idling or turned off. Turning the ignition makes an automobile idle, if it is turned off, and turns it off, if it is idling, but has no effect otherwise. We can thus conceptualize an automobile as consisting of five possible states among which it shifts back and forth in response to three possible inputs, as summarized in the *state transition diagram* for an automobile shown in Figure 24. The figure represents each of the five states by a node and each of the possible transitions between states by an arc that is labeled with the input that triggers the respective transition.

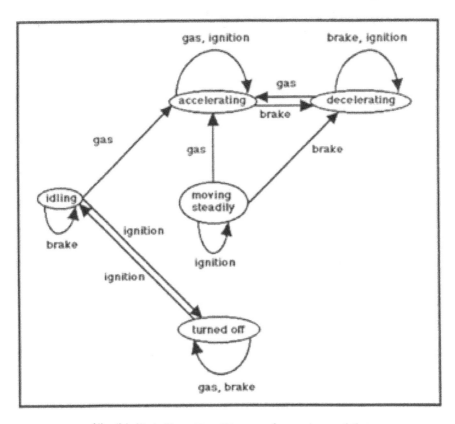

Fig. 24: State Transition Diagram for an Automobile

In effect, the diagram defines a function, which can be expressed by the *state transition function table* (10), that associates each pair of a state and an input with a state, the *next state* for that state and input, thereby providing a full description of how the machine operates.[37]

---

[37] *Suggested excursion:* Actually, the description is a bit oversimplified. What further states or inputs must we include to get a more fully realistic account of an automobile? Draw the state transition diagram and define the state transition function of your more complete description. *(Hint:* What happens when you remove your foot from the gas or brake pedal? How do you get from decelerating to idling? What really happens when you turn the ignition in the accelerating, decelerating, and steady states?)

(10)

input / state	gas	brake	ignition
	automobile		
idling	accel	idling	off
accel	accel	decel	accel
decel	accel	decel	decel
steady	accel	decel	steady
off	off	off	idling

For the purpose of formal definition, we can assume that there is an infinite set, *MACHINE*, of possible machines and an infinite set, *STATE*, of possible machine states, where each machine in *MACHINE* can be in any of some number of states in *STATE*. For the machines that we will be examining here, we can assume also that inputs can be numbers or letters. It is convenient to assume, further, that the elements of *STATE* are ordered beginning with state s_1—so there is a function *statenum* that associates each state with its number in that ordering—and that each machine has associated with it some finite number of states beginning with s_1.[38] There must also be a function *numstates* that associates each machine with the number of states in *STATE* that it can actually be in, beginning with s_1, and a

---

[38] *Suggested excursion:* This works as long as we are looking only at individual machines, as we are doing here, but not when we want to combine simpler machines to build more complicated machines, as is often done in more sophisticated settings. Figure out how to modify the definition of data type *machine* in (11) to be able to account for combining different machines. *(Hint:* Say that two machines are *isomorphic* if their state transition diagrams are identical except for the state names that label their nodes. Replace a machine with an isomorphic machine with completely different node labels, when it is to be combined with a machine that has some of the same node labels it has. Modify (11) to reflect this new capacity by permitting a machine's states to start with a state other than s_1.)

further function *trans*—the *machine transition function*—that associates each triple of a machine, a state, and an input with the state that that machine, in that given state, presented with that input, will enter as its next state. The function *trans* will take a machine into some state for some input only from a state that is one of the states of that machine—that is, only from a state that is ordered in *STATE* with a number that is not greater than the number of states the machine has—so this fact must be incorporated as a constraint into the definition of the machine data type. The full definition is given in (11), where *mach* and *state* are parameters for arbitrary members of *MACHINE* and *STATE*, respectively, and *nol* is a parameter for an arbitrary number or letter.[39]

(11)   LETTER =   {a, b, c, d, e, f, g, h, i, j, k, l, m, n, o, p,

q, r, s, t, u, v, w, x, y, z}

STATE =   { s_1, s_2, s_3, s_4, s_5, s_6, s_7, s_8, ... }

statenum: STATE $\rightarrow$ NUMBER

numstates: MACHINE $\rightarrow$ NUMBER

trans: MACHINE X STATE X (NUMBER $\cup$ LETTER)

$\rightarrow$ STATE $\cup$ {error}

(trans(mach, state, nol) = error)

= (statenum(state) > numstates(mach))

Some of the most useful machines in computer science are those that recognize when some sequence of symbols is or is not a word or sentence of some language. Programs written in a programming language that is intelligible to a human must first be translated into a form that can actually be processed by a computer, and the first step of translation is to make sure that the sequence of symbols to be translated is really a well-formed sentence of the programming language; otherwise, programmers must be sent an error message telling them to clean up their act. Such translations are performed by

---

[39] *Suggested excursion:* Is the function *statenum* really defined adequately in (11)? What else might be needed to constrain it sufficiently? *(Hint:* First define the data type *state* separately from machines, and then use it to define data type *machine.)*

computer programs called *compilers* that are already entered into the machine by the time a specific program is to be run. Those programs function as *abstract machines* that turn the actual machine, the computer, into a translating machine, when we run one of them on it. We stipulate that such a *recognition machine* is in its *initial state*, when it reads the first symbol of a candidate sentence, and that it will be in one or more of its *accepting states*, after reading the last symbol of an input sequence that really does represent a sentence of the language that we have designed the machine to recognize. We indicate the initial state of a machine by an arrow in the machine's state transition diagram, and the accepting states by a doubly bordered node in that diagram and by a circle in the machine's state transition function table.

For example, the machine M_1 in Figure 25(a) has the *state transition function table* (12)(a) and recognizes the language L_1 whose "sentences" consist of zero or more occurrences of either a or b or both in any arrangement, while the machine M_2 in Figure 25(b) has the state transition function table (12)(b) and recognizes the language L_2 whose "sentences" consist of one or more occurrences of a followed by one or more occurrences of b.

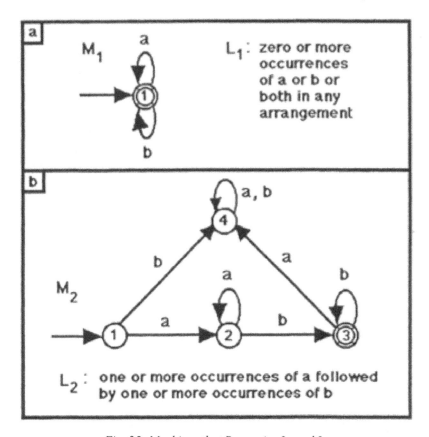

Fig. 25: Machines that Recognize L_1 and L_2

(12)   (a) M_1 (b) M_2

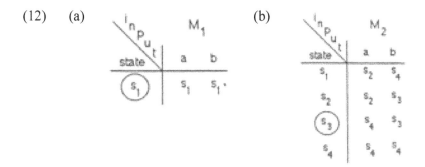

The machine M_3 in Figure 26(a) has the state transition function table (13)(a) and recognizes the language L_3 whose sentences consist of one or more occurrences of *ab* or one or more occurrences of *ba*, but not both, while the machine M_4 in Figure 26(b) has the state transition function table (13)(b) and recognizes the language L_4 whose sentences consist of one or more occurrences of *ab* followed by one or more occurrences of *ba*.

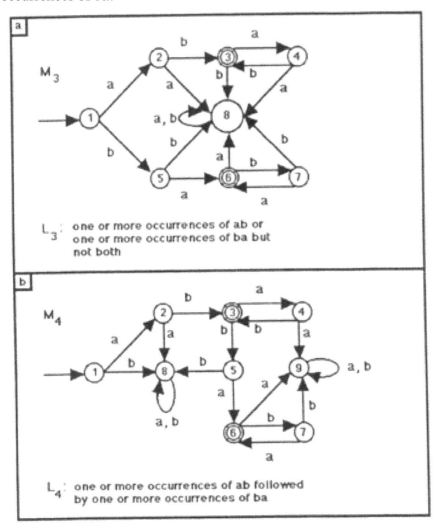

Fig. 26: Machines that Recognize L3 and L4

(13)   (a)

M_3

state	a	b
s_1	s_2	s_5
s_2	s_8	s_3
(s_3)	s_4	s_8
s_4	s_8	s_3
s_5	s_6	s_8
(s_6)	s_8	s_7
s_7	s_6	s_8
s_8	s_8	s_8

(b)

M_4

state	a	b
s_1	s_2	s_8
s_2	s_8	s_3
(s_3)	s_4	s_5
s_4	s_9	s_3
s_5	s_6	s_8
(s_6)	s_9	s_7
s_7	s_6	s_9
s_8	s_8	s_8
s_9	s_9	s_9

For example, the sentence ab is in all four languages and the corresponding sequence *[a, b]* is accepted by all four machines. For M_1, the machine reads a while in the initial state s_1 and so re-enters state s_1; it then reads b while in the state s_1 and so re-enters s_1 again, thereby ending in an accepting state. For each of M_2, M_3, and M_4, the machine enters state s_2, after reading a in state s_1, and then ends up in the accepting state s_3, after reading b in state s_2. In contrast, the sentence *abba* is in L_1 and L_4, but is not in L_2 or L_3 and, accordingly, the sequence *[a, b, b, a]* is accepted by M_1 and M_4, but not by M_2 or M_3. When M_1 reads [a, b, b, a], it keeps recycling back to s_1, its only state and an accepting one. When M_4 reads [a, b, b, a], it makes the transitions to states s_2, s_3, s_5, and s_6, thereby ending in an accepting state. However, when M_2 tries to read *[a, b, b, a]*, it enters s_2 by reading a in s_1 and then enters s_3 by reading b in s_2; then it re-enters s_3 by reading b in s_3 and ends up in the non-accepting state s_4 by reading a in s_3. Similarly, when M_3 tries to read *[a, b, b, a]*, reading a in s_1 puts it into s_2 and then reading b in s_2 puts it into s_3; reading b in s_3 then puts it into the non-accepting state s_8 and reading a again in s_8 keeps it there. For both M_2 and M_3, the machine does enter an accepting state along the way, so what has been read up to that point does represent what would be an acceptable sentence of the respective machine's language, but the machine does not end up in an accepting state after reading the entire sequence, so the sentence that that sequence represents is not a sentence of the machine's language.[40, 41]

Each of the states s_4 in machine M_2 and s_8 in machine M_3 is a *sink* or *dead state*, from which no escape is possible. Such states are reminiscent of "black holes" in physics, with the transitions into them providing a metaphor for gravitation. Machine M_4 is designed with two dead states, s_8 and s_9, only to make it visually clearer.[42] A machine enters a dead state as soon as it reads an input symbol that would prevent the sequence it is reading from representing a sentence of the machine's language. no matter what further symbol it might read from then on. In an implemented machine, entering a dead state could be used as a signal that no further reading of the sequence need be done.

A *translation machine* is like a recognition machine except that it has the further ability to generate output sequences in some language, as well as the ability to read input sequences in the same or a different language. Formally, this means replacing the function specification for the machine transition function *trans* in (11) with (14), which says that a machine in a state presented with an input symbol will not only enter a new state but will also generate an output symbol.

(14)   trans: MACHINE X STATE X (NUMBER $\cup$ LETTER)

→   (STATE X (NUMBER $\cup$ LETTER)) $\cup$ {error}

---

[40] *Suggested excursion:* Yes, there is such a thing as "the empty sentence" and machine M_1 does accept it. Figure out a general rule for how to ensure that a machine that you design will not accept the empty sentence. *(Hint:* Compare M_1 to M_2)

[41] *Suggested excursion:* Notice that these machines are assumed to read sequences from left to right, which mirrors the way an English-speaking person would normally read them, even though sequences were defined on Expedition 2 in terms of a function that identifies their right-most element, which mirrors the way such a person would likely write them. Define a function that successively extracts the elements of a sequence from left to right. *(Hint:* The function has to be recursive and defined in terms of functions that are already available for sequences. Compare it to *item* on lists.)

[42] *Suggested excursion:* Redesign machine M_4 to contain only one dead state. Give both the state transition diagram and the state transition function table for your new machine. *(Hint:* Let all transitions that go to s_9 go to s_8 instead or vice versa.)

In fact, a recognition machine is equivalent to a translation machine that generates, say, *y* for *yes*, when it enters an accepting state and *n* for *no* when it enters a non-accepting state. A sequence can be considered to have been accepted by such a machine if it gets translated by that machine into a sequence that ends in *y* and not to have been accepted otherwise, so there is no longer any need to identify accepting states in the diagrams or function tables of such machines.

For example, the recognition machines M_1 and M_2 in Figure 25 are equivalent, respectively, to the translation machines M_1' and M_2' in Figure 27.

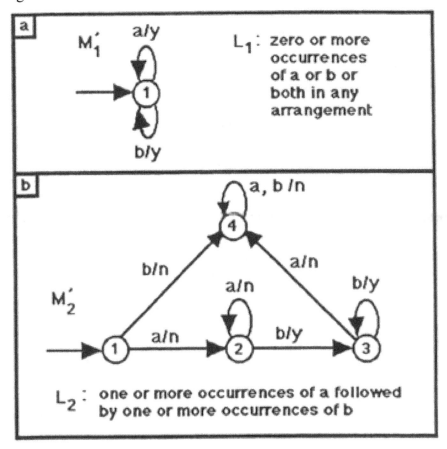

Fig. 27: Translation Machines Equivalent to M_1 and M_2

The state transition function tables of M_1' and M_2' contain generated outputs but no distinction between accepting and non-accepting states, as (15) shows.[43]

(15)   (a)

state	a	b	a	b
s_1	s_1	s_1	y	y

(b)

state	a	b	a	b
s_1	s_2	s_4	n	n
s_2	s_2	s_3	n	y
s_3	s_4	s_3	n	y
s_4	s_4	s_4	n	n

When M_1' reads the sequence *[a, b]*, it not only re-enters state s_1 twice, as machine M_1 does, but also generates the sequence *[y, y]*, thereby signaling that *ab* is accepted as a sentence of L_1 because that output sequence ends in *y*. When M_2' reads the sequence *[a, b]*, it not only enters state s_2 and then state s_3, as M_2 does, but also generates the sequence *[n, y]*, which signals that *ab* is in the language L_2 for the same reason. When M_1' reads the sequence *[a, b, b, a]*, it not only re-enters s_1 four times, as M_1 does, but also generates the sequence *[y, y, y, y]*, again signaling acceptance of the corresponding sentence, this time *abba*, for the language L_1, because this output sequence also ends in *y*. However, when M_2' reads *[a, b, b, a]*, it not only enters the states s_2, s_3, s_3 again, and then s_4, as M_2 does, but generates the sequence *[n, y, y, n]*, thereby signaling that *abba* is not accepted as a sentence of its language L_2, because the output sequence ends in *n*, rather than *y*.

Translation machines can serve not only as language recognizers and as straightforward translators from one language to another, but also as machines that compute functions. The machine M_5 in Figure 28, for example, translates sequences of decimal digits that represent numbers into sequences of decimal digits that represent their doubles, that is, it multiplies numbers by two.

---

[43] *Suggested excursion:* Design translation machines that are equivalent to M_3 and M_4. Give both their state transition diagrams and their state transition function tables. *(Hint:* Just put the appropriate outputs on the arcs, *n* when going to a non-accepting state and *y* when going to an accepting state.)

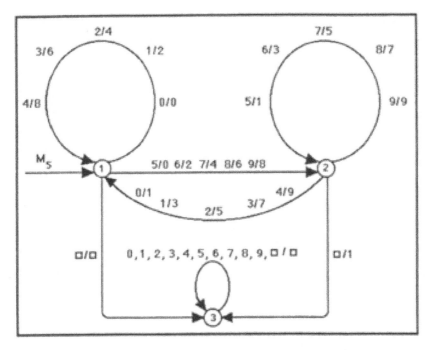

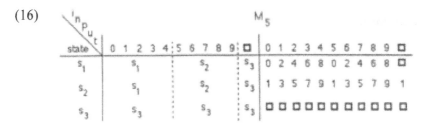

Fig. 28: A Machine that Doubles Numbers

Its state transition function table is given in (16).

(16)

state	0	1	2	3	4 : 5	6	7	8	9 : □	0	1	2	3	4	5	6	7	8	9	□
s_1	s_1					s_2				s_3	0	2	4	6	8	0	2	4	6	8	□
s_2	s_1					s_2				s_3	1	3	5	7	9	1	3	5	7	9	1
s_3	s_3					s_3				s_3	□	□	□	□	□	□	□	□	□	□	□

Since the machine is translating from the language L_5 of numbers to L_5 itself—or, more precisely, from the language of numbers to the language of even numbers—in a way that achieves the computation of an arithmetic function, it makes sense to stipulate that it will both read input sequences and also generate output sequences from right to left. This is the way a person would normally compute such a function.[44]

---

[44] *Suggested excursion:* Design a recognition machine and an equivalent translation machine that each recognizes L_5. Give both the state transition diagram and the state transition function table for each machine. *(Hint:* The "sentences" of L_5 are all

We also need to assume that (14) has been modified to allow special symbols other than numbers or letters—such as $\square$—to be used as input or output symbols. For example, the machine needs to know when it has just read the left-most digit, so it will know to generate *1* as an explicit carry digit, rather than adding *1* to a next-left output digit.[45]

In effect, s_1 in M_5 is the state of not having just now read a digit whose double requires a carry, and s_2 is the state of having just now read such a digit. When the machine is in s_1, either it generates the double of a digit that does not require a carry and stays in s_1, or it generates the right-most digit of the double of a digit that does require a carry and goes to s_2. When the machine is in s_2, either it generates the successor—in the sense of Figure 4 discussed on Expedition 1—of the double of a digit that does not require a carry and goes to s_1, or it generates the successor of the right-most digit of the double of a digit that does require a carry and stays in s_2. State s_3 is a dead state that the machine enters when it reads a $\square$, which is placed as the left-most element of the sequence that represents the number to be doubled as a signal to the machine that the reading of the number has been completed. If the $\square$ is read when the machine is in s_1, the machine generates a $\square$, because it is in that state at that point precisely because the preceding digit did not require a carry. If the $\square$ is read when the machine is in s_2, the machine generates a *1*, because it is in that state at that point precisely because the preceding digit did require a carry.

For example, to double the number *92754*, the machine is presented with the sequence *[$\square$, 9, 2, 7, 5, 4]* while it is in its initial state s_1. The machine reads *4* in s_1 and therefore generates *8* and returns to s_1, because doubling *4* does not require a carry. It then reads *5* in s_1 and so generates *0* and enters s_2, because doubling *5* does require a carry. Then it reads *7* in s_2 and so generates *5* and re-enters s_2, because doubling *7* requires a carry, after which it reads *2* in s_2 and so generates *5* and enters s_1, because doubling *2* does not require a carry. Finally, the machine reads *9* in s_1 and so generates *8* and enters s_2, because doubling *9* requires a carry, after which it reads $\square$ in s_2 and

---

numbers written in standard decimal notation and the "words" are the digits *0* through *9*.)

[45] *Suggested excursion:* Figure out the modified version of (14). *(Hint:* Define a set *SYMBOLS* that contains the desired further symbols and include it on both sides of the arrow. Where exactly does it go?)

so generates the final carry digit 1, ending the computation by entering s_3. The entire computation is summarized in (17).[46]

(17)

in state	read input	generate output	enter state
s_1	4	8	s_1
s_1	5	0	s_2
s_2	7	5	s_2
s_2	2	5	s_1
s_1	9	8	s_2
s_2	□	1	s_3

Machines that are characterized as in (11) and (14) can recognize and translate lots of languages and compute many useful functions, but there are languages and functions that are of practical significance that are beyond their power to handle. For example, consider what it would take to have a recognition machine for the language L_6 whose sentences consist of one or more occurrences of a followed by *exactly the same number* of occurrences of b. This language models, for example, the way parentheses are used in algebraic notation, which requires a correct algebraic expression to have exactly the same number of right-hand parentheses—")"—as it has left-hand parentheses—"(". In sentences of L_6 the number of b's depends on the number of a's, in contrast to sentences of L_2, in which the number of b's is entirely arbitrary. All of the sentences in (18), for example, are in L_2, but only (a), (d), (e), and (h) are in L_6, because only those sentences have equal numbers of a's and b's.

(18) (a) ab   (b) aab   (c) abb   (d) aabb

(e) aaabbb   (f) aaabb   (g) aabbb   (h) aaaabbbb

M_2 or M_2' will not distinguish between the sentences in (18) that are in L_6 and those that are not, because the self-loops on the nodes for states s_2 and s_3 in Figures 25(b) and 27(b) work independently, with no way for the b loop to know how many a's were generated before the b's got

---

[46] *Suggested excursion:* Design a machine that triples decimal numbers, that is, that multiplies numbers by three. Give both its state transition diagram and its state transition function table. *(Hint:* Replace each double in the doubling machine with the corresponding triple. Be careful to note the cases for which a carry is necessary, since they may not be the same for the two machines.)

started. This is always the case with self-loops, which are the only way to get such a machine to accept infinitely many sentences.

The simple machine in Figure 29(a) recognizes the trivial language that consists of the single sentence (18)(a), while the only slightly less simple machine in Figure 29(b) recognizes the slightly less trivial language that contains only the sentences (18)(a) and (d).

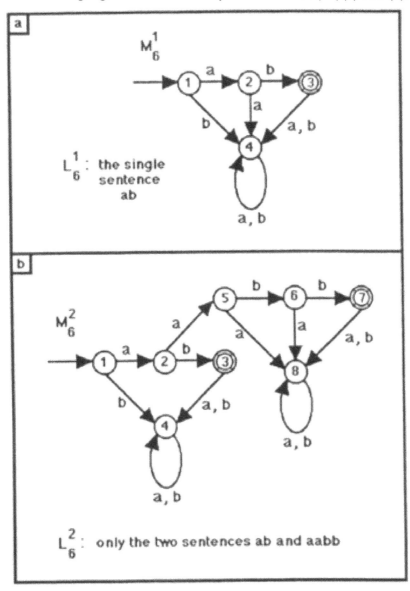

Fig. 29: Machines that Recognize Pieces of L_6

The machine in Figure 29(c) recognizes the language that contains exactly the sentences (18)(a), (d), and (e).[47]

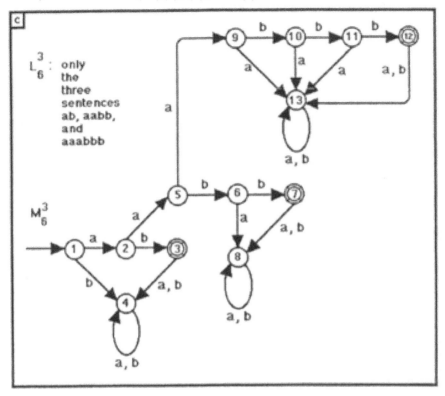

Fig. 29 (cont.): Machines that Recognize Pieces of L_6

Following this pattern—which is the only way to get all of the sentences of L_6 with this kind of machine, since self-loops will not do the job—would result in the machine in Figure 30, which does recognize L_6 but only by violating (11), by having infinitely many states and thus no function *numstates* to constrain *trans*, as (11) requires.[48]

---

[47] *Suggested excursion:* Design a machine that recognizes the language that consists entirely of the four sentences (18)(a), (d), (e), and (h). Give both its state transition diagram and its state transition function table. *(Hint:* Just build another layer with four *b* accepting states on top of the machine in Figure 29(c). Be careful that no node has more than one arrow leaving it for any one input symbol.)

[48] *Suggested excursion:* Redesign the machines in Figures 29(b), 29(c), and 30 and, if necessary, in excursion 47 so that each contains just one dead state. Can you design

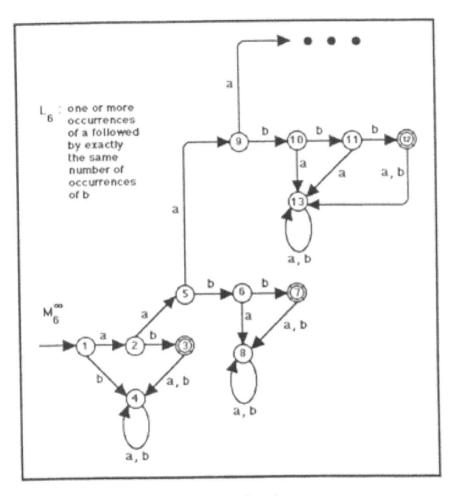

Fig. 30: An Infinite State Machine that Recognizes L6

Machines such as the one in Figure 30—called *infinite state automata* or *infinite state machines*—are of interest to mathematicians, logicians, and computer theoreticians, who enjoy thinking about abstractions for their own sake, but they are difficult to conceptualize (let alone draw fully!) and are of little use in understanding how real computers work. A more standard—and

these new machines to contain not only just one dead state, but also just one accepting state? Give both the state transition diagram and the state transition function table for each new machine. *(Hint:* Don't worry if it's a mess. Taking excursion 42 first might help.)

more useful—way of coming to grips with languages like L_6 is to stick with machines that satisfy the constraint in (11)—called *finite state automata* or *finite state machines*, since the effect of that constraint is to ensure that each machine has a definite finite number of states—but to give those machines the further ability to manipulate stacks, one of the data structures we discussed on Expedition 2. In addition to showing what new state is entered—for a recognition machine—or showing what new state is entered and what output symbol is generated—for a translation machine—a state transition diagram or state transition function table will also show whether a machine pushes some symbol onto a stack, pops a stack, or neither, for each input that is read in each state of the machine.

For recognition machines with stacks,[49] we need to replace the function specification for *trans* in (11) with (19), and to replace the constraint in (11) with (20), which still ensures that any particular machine will have only finitely many states, while taking into account the fact that stacks, as well as states, are also being affected.

(19)   trans: MACHINE X STATE X (NUMBER ∪ LETTER) X STACK

$\rightarrow$ (STATE X (STACK ∪ {error})) ∪ {error}

(20)   (trans(mach, state, nol, stk) – error)

= (statenum(state) > numstates(mach))

We also need the further constraint (21), where *stker* is a parameter for an arbitrary stack or error, to ensure that the stack that results from a state transition is related in the allowable ways to the stack that was there before the transition took place.[50]

(21)   or ((not(trans(mach, state$_1$, nol$_1$, stk) = (state$_2$, stker))) ,

(stker = stk) ,

(stker = pop(stk)) ,

---

[49] *Suggested excursion:* Determine the new *trans* for translation machines with stacks. *(Hint:* Compare (19) to (14).)

[50] *Suggested excursion:* Figure out why *error* has to appear twice in (19). *(Hint:* Strange things can happen when you pop a certain stack, even when the state is okay.)

$$(stker = push(stk, nol_2)))$$

$$= t$$

What (21) says is that at least one of the open statements in (22) is true for any choice of machine, input symbol, and before and after states and stacks.

(22)   (a) $not(trans(mach, state_1, nol_1, stk) = (state_2, stker))$

      (b) $stker = stk$

      (c) $stker = pop(stk)$

      (d) $stker = push(stk, nol_2)$

If none of (22)(b), (c), or (d) is true, that is, if the new resulting stack is not the same as the previous stack, the result of popping the previous stack, or the result of pushing a number or letter onto the previous stack, then (22)(a) has to be true and so the indicated transition is not allowed. In other words, (23) can be true for the indicated parameters only if (22)(a) is false and thus only if one of (22)(b), (c), or (d) is true.

(23) $trans(mach, state_1, nol_1, stk) = (state_2, stker)$

We will develop a simpler and more perspicuous way of saying all this on Expedition 5, where we will examine the logic of *if...then* statements in more depth. Note that we are now allowing stacks to contain letters, as well as numbers. This assumes that we have made the minor alteration that is required in the definition of stacks in (32) of Expedition 2.[51]

Machines that satisfy (19), (20), and (21) are known as *pushdown automata* or *pushdown stack machines*. We assume that such a machine starts in the initial state s_1 with the empty stack, and we consider a sentence to have been accepted if the machine ends up in one of its accepting states with the empty stack again, after reading the last input symbol of the sentence. A machine of this sort that recognizes L_6 is easy to design. We simply use the stacks to count up the number of occurrences of a, and then use them again to count off the same number of occurrences of b. The machine M_6 in Figure 31 illustrates this.

---

[51] *Suggested excursion:* Identify that alteration and reformulate (32) of Expedition 2 accordingly. *(Hint:* Do you really need a hint for this one?)

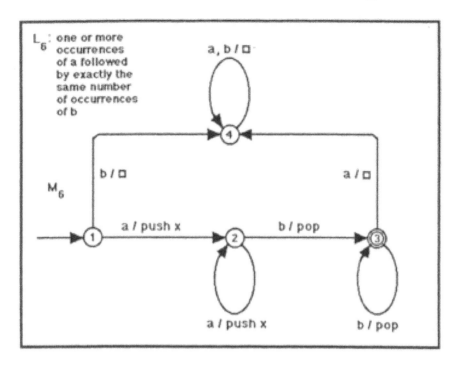

Fig. 31: A Pushdown Stack Machine that Recognizes L₆

The state transition function table of M_6 is given in (24).

(24)

state	input a	input b	M₆ a	M₆ b
s_1	s_2	s_4	push x	□
s_2	s_2	s_3	push x	pop
(s_3)	s_4	s_3	□	pop
s_4	s_4	s_4	□	□

Essentially, M_6 is just M_2 with a counting device that is designed to rule out sentences of L_2 that are not also in L_6. For example, this is illustrated in (25) for the sentence *aaabbb*.

(25)

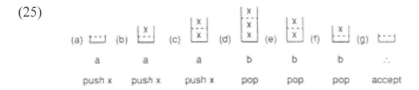

To recognize *aaabbb*, the machine reads the sequence *[a, a, a, b, b, b]* from left to right, starting—as always—in state s_1 with the empty stack (25)(a). After reading *a* in s_1, it pushes an *x* onto that stack, thereby replacing it with the stack in (25)(b), which contains one *x*, and then enters s_2. After reading *a* in s_2, it pushes an *x* onto that stack, thereby replacing it with the stack in (25)(c), which contains two *x*'s, and then re-enters s_2. After reading another *a* in s_2, it pushes an *x* onto that stack, thereby replacing it with the stack in (25)(d), which contains three *x*'s, and then again re-enters s_2. The machine then reads *b* in s_2 and so pops that stack, thereby replacing it with the stack in (25)(e), which contains two *x*'s, and enters s_3. After reading *b* in s_3, it pops that stack, thereby replacing it with the stack in (25)(f), which contains one *x*, and then re-enters s_3. Finally, it reads the last symbol of the sentence, namely, another *b*, while in s_3, so it pops that stack, thereby replacing it with the empty stack (25)(g), and then again re-enters s_3. Since the machine finds itself in an accepting state with the empty stack after having read the last symbol, the machine has accepted the sentence.[52]

In contrast, when the machine tries to recognize a sentence that is not in L_6, something very different happens. For example, when it tries to recognize *aaabb*, it reads the sequence *[a, a, a, b, b]* and thereby generates the succession of stacks in (26)(a) through (f).

(26)

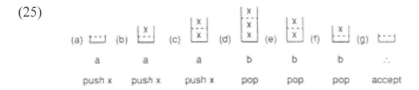

When it tries to recognize the sentence *aabbb*, it reads the sequence *[a, a, b, b, b]* and thereby generates the succession of stacks in (27)(a) through (e), but then it generates *error*, after reading the final *b*, when it tries to pop the empty stack.

(27)

In both cases, it finishes its reading in an accepting state, but with a non-empty stack in the case of (26), and with no stack at all in the case of (27). In each case, the result shows that the respective sentences *aaabb* and *aabbb* are not accepted by the respective machine.

Pushdown automata can recognize languages involving very intricate relations between the required numbers of occurrences of two different symbols. For example, Figure 32 contains a machine M_7 that recognizes the language L_7 whose sentences consist of one or more occurrences of *a* followed by exactly twice that number of occurrences of *b*, while Figure 33 contains a machine M_8 that recognizes the language L_8 that consists of any non-zero even number of occurrences of *a* followed by exactly half that number of occurrences of *b*.[53]

---

[53] *Suggested excursion:* Give the state transition function tables for M_7 and M_8. *(Hint:* Just translate the diagrams into tables.)

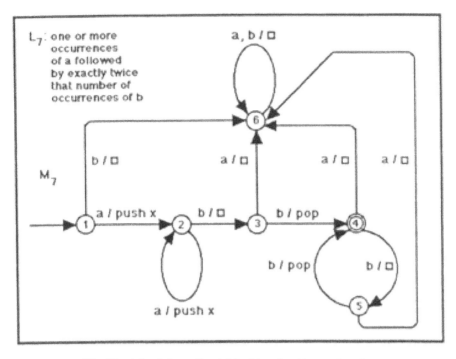

Fig. 32: A Pushdown Stack Machine that Recognizes L₇

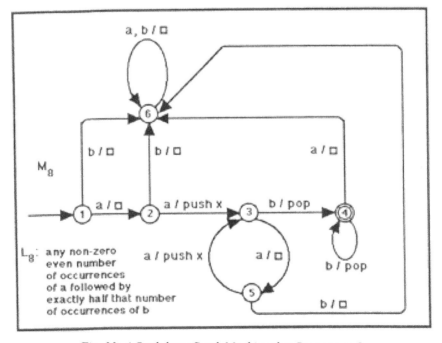

Fig. 33: A Pushdown Stack Machine that Recognizes L₈

Such machines accomplish their respective tasks by doing their counting in a staggered way, for example, by having some transitions that push x and others that leave the stack alone, but without going to a dead state, after reading a, or by having some transitions that pop a stack and others that leave the stack alone, again without going to a dead state, after reading b. In particular, M_7 counts off a pair of b's for each a that it reads, and M_8 counts off one b for each pair of a's that it reads.[54] When M_6, M_7, and M_8 each try to recognize the sentence *aabbbb*, they generate the respective successions of stacks in (28), and when they try to recognize the sentence *aaaabb*, they generate the respective successions of stacks in (29).

(28)   aabbbb:

(29)   aaaabb:

---

[54] *Suggested excursion:* Design a machine that recognizes the language whose sentences consist of one or more occurrences of a followed by *exactly three times* that number of occurrences of b, and then another machine that recognizes the language whose sentences consist of any non-zero number of occurrences of a that is a *multiple of* 3 followed by *exactly one-third* that number of occurrences of b. Give both the state transition diagram and the state transition function table for each machine. *(Hint:* Put new states and transitions into M_7 and M_8 that stagger the counting differently.)

M_6: (a) [ ] (b) [ ] (c) [ ] (d) [ ] (e) [ ] (f) [ ] (g) [ ]

a   a   a   a   b   b   ∴

push x   push x   push x   push x   pop   pop   reject

M_7: (a) [ ] (b) [ ] (c) [ ] (d) [ ] (e) [ ] (f) [ ] (g) [ ]

a   a   a   a   b   b   ∴

push x   push x   push x   push x   □   pop   reject

M_8: (a) [ ] (b) [ ] (c) [ ] (d) [ ] (e) [ ] (f) [ ] (g) [ ]

a   a   a   a   b   b   ∴

□   push x   □   push x   pop   pop   accept

These show that, of these three machines, only M_7 accepts *aabbbb*, and only M_8 accepts *aaaabb*.

Machines that can manipulate stacks can recognize more languages than machines that cannot, but they too turn out to have limited power. In other words, there are languages that even they cannot recognize and functions that they cannot compute. For example, the language L_9 whose sentences consist of one or more occurrences of *a* followed by exactly the same number of occurrences of *b* followed by exactly the same number of occurrences of *c* cannot be recognized by any machine that satisfies (19), (20), and (21), because the manipulation of the stacks cannot keep track of both the relation between the numbers of *a*'s and *b*'s and the relation between the numbers of *b*'s and *c*'s at the same time. While the machine is manipulating stacks to count off *b*'s to match the number of *a*'s that it has already read and counted off, it cannot use the same stacks to count off *b*'s for the purpose of counting off the *c*'s that it will read later.[55]

---

[55] *Suggested excursion:* Try to design a pushdown stack machine that recognizes L_9. *(Hint:* Try to get one succession of stacks to correlate *a*'s with *b*'s and *b*'s with *c*'s simultaneously. Don't try too hard. Do just enough to see why it can't be done.)

However, we *can* get a machine to recognize L_9 if we allow it access to *two* "stack-holders," rather than just the single one that (19) permits, that is, if the machine can start with two instances of the empty stack and then manipulate a succession of stacks from each of them independently.[56] Such machines are known as *two-stack automata* or *two-stack pushdown machines*. We consider such a machine to have accepted a sentence, if it ends up in an accepting state with both stack-holders containing the empty stack, when it finishes reading the last symbol of the sentence. For example, the machine M_9 in Figure 34 recognizes L_9.

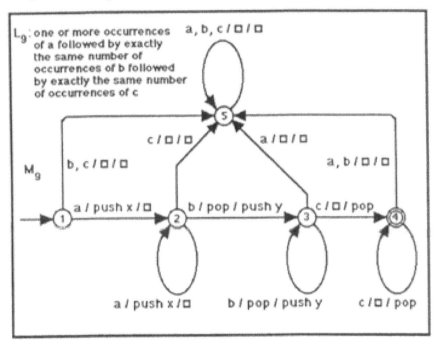

Fig. 34: A Two-Stack Pushdown Machine that Recognizes L_9

The state transition function table of M_9 is given in (30).

---

[56] *Suggested excursion:* Reformulate (19), (20), and.(21) to be adequate for defining such a machine. *(Hint:* Reformulate (19) with another *(STACK $\cup$ {error})* and (20) with another *stkr* parameter. Exactly where do they go in each case? Be sure to account for all possible combinations in putting another *stkr* parameter into your reformulated (21).)

(30)

M_9

input / state	a	b	c	a	b	c	a	b	c
s_1	s_2	s_5	s_5	push x	□	□	□	□	□
s_2	s_2	s_3	s_5	push x	pop	□	□	push y	□
s_3	s_5	s_3	s_4	□	pop	□	□	push y	pop
(s_4)	s_5	s_5	s_4	□	□	□	□	□	pop
s_5	s_5	s_5	s_5	□	□	□	□	□	□

M_9's acceptance of *aabbcc*, but not *aabbc*, *aabcc*, or *abbcc*, respectively, is illustrated in (31).

(31)   aabbcc:

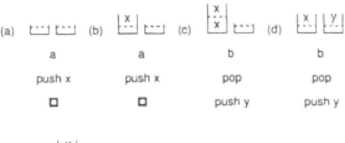

aabbc:

(a)			(b)			(c)			(d)		
	a			a			b			b	
	push x			push x			pop			pop	
	□			□			push y			push y	

(e)			(f)		
	c			∴	
	□			reject	
	pop			(not both empty[57])	

aabcc:

(a)			(b)			(c)			(d)		
	a			a			b			c	
	push x			push x			pop			□	
	□			□			push y			pop	

(e)			(f)	error
	c			∴
	□			reject
	pop			(no second stack)

---

[57] *Suggested excursion:* Find a sentence that leaves the empty stack in the second stack-holder, but *not* in the first, and another sentence that leaves non-empty stacks in both stack-holders, when each is processed by M_9. (*Hint:* You need to count more *x's* than *y's.)

abbcc:

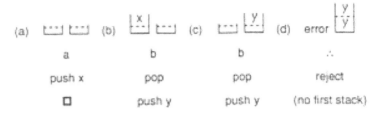

In each case, the machine starts in the initial state s_1 with the empty stack in both stack-holders. It finishes reading *[a, a, b, b, c, c]* in the accepting state s_4 with two empty stacks again, thereby indicating that it accepts the sentence *aabbcc*. It also finishes reading *[a, a, b, b, c]* in s_4, but with a non-empty stack in the second stack-holder, thereby indicating that it rejects the sentence *aabbc*. For both *[a, a, b, c, c]* and *[a, b, b, c, c]*, the machine generates *error* for one or the other of its two stack-holders by trying to pop the empty stack, thereby indicating that it rejects the respective sentences *aabcc* and *abbcc*. In the former case, this happens at the very end of the computation because the number of *c*'s exceeds the number of *b*'s, emptying the second stack-holder too soon. In the latter case, the rejection happens in the middle of the computation, when the number of *b*'s exceeds the number of *a*'s, emptying the first stack-holder too soon, so the machine does not even get to finish reading the input sequence.[58]

In a similar vein, it would be easy to design a three-stack machine to recognize a language like L_{10} whose sentences consist of one or more *a*'s followed by exactly the same number of *b*'s followed by exactly the same number of *c*'s followed by exactly the same number of *d*'s by continuing the pattern suggested by the ways in which M_6 and M_9 handle L_6 and L_9,

---

[58] *Suggested excursion:* Design a two-stack pushdown machine that recognizes the language whose sentences consist of one or more occurrences of *a* followed by exactly twice that number of occurrences of *b* followed by exactly twice as many occurrences of *c* as there are of *b*, and then another such machine that recognizes the language whose sentences consist of any non-zero even number of occurrences of *a* followed by exactly half that number of occurrences of *b* followed by exactly twice as many occurrences of *c* as there are occurrences of *a*. (*Hint:* Use one stack-holder to correlate *a*'s with *b*'s and the other to correlate *b*'s with *c*'s. Use enough states to ensure that the right number of input symbols gets counted by each stack element.)

respectively. The first stack-holder would count up a's and count off b's, the second one would count up b's and count off c's, the third one would count up c's and count off d's, and that would be that.[59] Surprisingly, however, it turns out that *two* stack-holders are really all we need to recognize L_{10}. Returning to the empty stack in either stack-holder frees it up for another counting task, which the machine can begin while the other stack-holder is still being used for something else. In other words, the third stack-holder turns out to be unnecessary, because the first stack-holder empties out before the third one needs to start counting anything, so the first one can be reused to count whatever the third one would have been used to count. The relation between the numbers of a's and b's has no bearing on the relation between the numbers of c's and d's other than through the relation between the numbers of b's and c's, so the number of a's no longer needs to be remembered by the time the number of d's becomes an issue.

The two-stack pushdown machine M_{10} shown in Figure 35 uses this device to recognize L_{10}.

---

[59] *Suggested excursion:* Design a three-stack machine that recognizes L_{10}. (*Hint:* Just put further suitable counting states into M_9.)

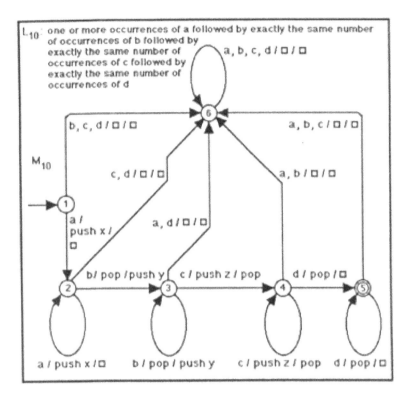

Fig. 35: A Two-Stack Pushdown Machine that Recognizes L_{10}

M_{10}'s state transition function table is given in (32).

(32)

state	a	b	c	d	a	b	c	d	a	b	c	d
s_1	s_2	s_6	s_6	s_6	push x	□	□	□	□	□	□	□
s_2	s_2	s_3	s_6	s_6	push x	pop	□	□	□	push y	□	□
s_3	s_6	s_3	s_4	s_6	□	pop	push z	□	□	push y	pop	□
s_4	s_6	s_6	s_4	s_5	□	□	push z	pop	□	□	pop	□
(s_5)	s_6	s_6	s_6	s_5	□	□	□	pop	□	□	□	□
s_6	s_6	s_6	s_6	s_6	□	□	□	□	□	□	□	□

The successions of stacks through which M_{10} accepts *aabbccdd*, but not *aabbccd*, *aabbcdd*, or *aabbccddd* are shown in (33).

(33)   aabbccdd:

(a)	(b)	(c)	(d)
a	a	b	b
push x	push x	pop	pop
□	□	push y	push y

(e)	(f)	(g)	(h)	(i)
c	c	d	d	∴
push z	push z	pop	pop	accept
pop	pop	□	□	(both empty)

aabbccd:

(a)	(b)	(c)	(d)
a	a	b	b
push x	push x	pop	pop
□	□	push y	push y

(e)	(f)	(g)	(h)
c	c	d	∴
push z	push z	pop	reject
pop	pop	□	(not both empty[60])

60

aabbcdd:

---

[60] *Suggested excursion:* Find a sentence that leaves the empty stack in the first stack-holder, but *not* in the second, and another sentence that leaves non-empty stacks in both stack-holders, when each is processed by M_{10}. *(Hint:* You need to count more *y*'s than *z*'s.)

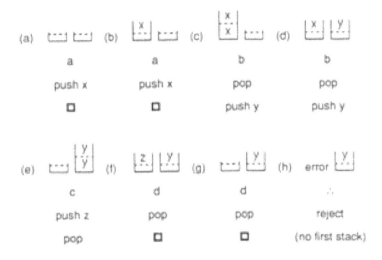

aabbccddd:

In fact, two stack-holders always suffice for *any* solvable problem. A kind of machine called a *Turing machine*—because it was invented in the 1930's by the same mathematician who first proposed the Turing Test—is generally considered by people who think about these things for a living to be the most powerful possible kind of computing device. Essentially, a Turing machine is a finite state machine together with an infinite tape from which it reads input symbols, just as we can view the machines we have examined here as doing. However, a Turing machine can also write output symbols onto its tape, moving in either direction along the tape as far and as often as it needs to. Numerous attempts of various sorts have been made for over half a century to define a most general kind of computing machine, and every sort of device that has resulted from such attempts has turned out to be provably equivalent to a Turing machine. The computer scientist Marvin Minsky proved this result in general as a theorem for two-stack pushdown machines in the 1960's. There do exist computational problems that have been proven to have no solution at all, but for any problem that cannot be proven to have no solution, there is a machine with two stack-holders that can discover its solution.[61]

---

[61] *Suggested excursion (very difficult):* Design a two-stack pushdown machine that recognizes the language whose sentences consist of any *prime* number of occurrences of *a*, and then another such machine that recognizes the language whose sentences consist of any number of occurrences of *a* that is a *power of two. (Hint:* For the first machine, figure out what it would take to check to see if a number is one of those on the first level of the lattice in Figure 5. For the second machine, figure out what it would take to check to see if a number is one of those on the left-most vertical branch path of that lattice. Taking excursion 38 first might help.)

4. Reconnoitering: Goals and Strategies

I ask for a student volunteer to help investigate the use of strategies by participating in one or more games of Mastermind. In this game one player chooses a pattern of shapes and/or colors for the other player to figure out. The second player makes guesses at what the target pattern might be and receives answers as to how many—but not which—of the shapes or colors are correct or correctly matched. For example, (1) shows one possible move in a version of the game that involves pairs of shapes, rather than shapes and colors.

(1)

Target Pattern   Guessed Pattern

Response (to Guesser)	Explanation (Not Reported to Guesser)
1. One pair is correctly matched and is in the correct position.	1. Guessed pair in Position 3 from left is correct.
2. One pair is correctly matched but is in an incorrect position.	2. Guessed pair in Position 1 from left should be in Position 2.
3. One item is correct in the correct position but is incorrectly matched.	3. Guessed item in lower Position 2 from left is correct.

In this case, the guessed pattern is completely correct in the third position from the left, because both the man and the downward-pointing arrow appear in that position in the target pattern. It is partly correct in that the cat and the rightward-pointing arrow that appear in its left-most position do appear matched in the target pattern, but in a different position, namely, the second from the left. It is also partly correct in that the cat that appears in its lower second-from-left position appears in that position in the target pattern. The guesser is told that one pair is completely correct, that one pair is correct but in the wrong position, and that one item is in the correct position but incorrectly matched, but is not told specifically which items or positionings are correct ones and which are not.

First, I ask the student to try to guess target patterns that I have chosen and to explain his or her strategy, if any; we then examine and discuss that strategy. Second, I try to guess the student's choice of target patterns, using three standard strategies: successive scanning, conservative focusing, and focus gambling.

In the strategy of *successive scanning*, we assume one pattern as an initial hypothesis and then compare it to deliberate counterexamples that serve as further hypotheses. For example, having tried the guessed pattern in (1) as an initial hypothesis, the guesser might then guess the very different pattern in (2), which violates that hypothesis by differing in every choice of shapes except the left-most two arrows.

(2)

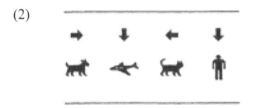

For this guess, the guesser would be told that, again, one pairing is completely correct (because of the dog and the rightward-pointing arrow in the left-most position), but that, this time, two pairs are correctly matched but in the wrong positions (because of the cat and the leftward-pointing arrow in the third position from the left and the man and the downward-pointing arrow in the right-most position). Scanning the succession of responses that such very different guessed patterns evoke helps a guesser to figure out the target pattern by narrowing down the range of possibilities that can fit all of the evoked responses.

In the strategy of *conservative focusing*, we assume one pattern as a hypothesis that serves as a reference point and then vary it one attribute at a time to get further hypotheses as guesses. For example, instead of the guessed pattern in (1), the guesser might start with the pattern in (3), taking the cat and the rightward-pointing arrow as a reference point from which to base further hypotheses.

(3)

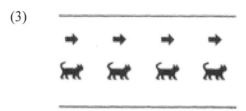

After being told that this pattern contains one pair that is completely correct (because of the items in the second position from the left) and two items that are each in the correct position but not correctly matched (because of the left-most arrow and the right-most cat), the guesser knows for sure that the target pattern contains a matched cat and rightward pointing arrow in some position and a further such arrow and a further cat that are not matched. The guesser might then try the pattern in (4), choosing arrow direction as the one attribute to be varied this time.

(4)

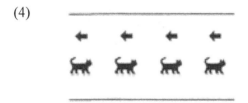

In response to this pattern the guesser would be told that there now is one pair that is completely correct (because of the items in the right-most position) and one item that is in the correct position but incorrectly matched (because of the cat in the second position from the left) and so can conclude that the known further cat is matched with a leftward pointing arrow. The guesser might then choose to vary arrow direction again in a different way or might choose a pattern like the one in (5), in which arrows stay as in (4) but the cats all change to dogs.

(5)

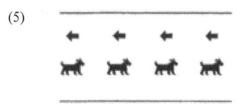

This time the guesser would be told that there are no correctly matched pairs but that two items are in the correct positions, though incorrectly matched (because of the left-most dog and the right-most arrow), so (5) is worse than (4) as a hypothesis for the target pattern.

The strategy of *focus gambling* is the same as conservative focusing except that more than one attribute is varied at a time. For example, the guesser might go directly from (3) to (5), varying both arrow direction and figure-type in one guess, thereby covering more territory in terms of feature variability, but missing out on the information that is provided by the responses to (4). This strategy can work faster than conservative focusing, when it works, but it requires more careful reasoning to sort out which of the varied features is responsible for the various changes in the responses.

Each of these strategies is an example of a *heuristic*, a "rule of thumb" that, when formalized, can provide the basis for game-playing programs and more general decision-making programs in artificial-intelligence systems. Heuristics differ from algorithms in that they do not always produce a result. For example, in the Mastermind case a guesser could play forever using any of these three strategies and still not see the solution. However, a heuristic for solving some problem will tend to make progress toward a solution more quickly than an algorithm would, even when an algorithm for that problem is already known to exist.

In fact, there is a very simple algorithm for playing Mastermind. All a guesser has to do is to generate all possible patterns of the allowed symbols and ask the responder whether each successive pattern is the correct one. This algorithm produces a definite correct result when the responder truthfully answers, "Yes." We can easily implement the patterns themselves on a computer as sequences of symbols, and we can tell the computer to generate all such sequences. However, the enormous number of such sequences makes this a frivolous scenario. For the version of Mastermind described in (1) through (5), there are four possible arrow directions for each of four possible positions, and there are four possible figures for each of four possible positions. Since the choice of what to put in each position is entirely independent of any of the others, there are $(4 * 4 * 4 * 4) * (4 * 4 * 4 * 4) = 4^8 = 2^{16} = 65,536$ possible patterns, as spelled out in (6).

(6)

In practice, this game is of interest only because it can be won after a limited number of guesses. No responder is going to be willing to sit through a questioning session in which all possible sequences are checked in succession, when the number of such sequences is 65,536. The use of heuristics opens the possibility that we will not find a solution, but it also increases the likelihood that we will find a solution in a reasonable length of time. This makes the problem tractable and the game fun.

We can best discuss how to make heuristics formal enough to be implemented on a computer by using a simpler example. Consider what it would take to have a computer program that could solve an instance of the *15-puzzle*, a one-person game illustrated in Figure 36 that every toy store sells. The game consists of fifteen numbered square tiles arranged in a square of sixteen slots, one of which is empty. We can move tiles only horizontally or vertically into the empty slot, if they are adjacent to it. The goal is to arrange the tiles in some desired target pattern by moving them one at a time from whatever positions they start in.

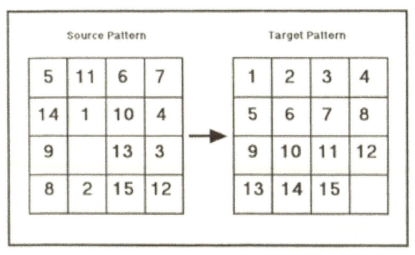

Fig. 36: A Typical Instance of the 15-Puzzle

As with Mastermind, there is a simple algorithm that is guaranteed abstractly to solve this puzzle: exhaustively generate all possible moves from the source pattern until the target pattern is arrived at. There are only finitely many possible game patterns and, using this algorithm, we will eventually reach every one of them. However, again as with Mastermind, the number of possible patterns that this algorithm generates rapidly gets way beyond anything that anyone—even Robotman—can reasonably be expected to deal with.[62] An alternative is to use a heuristic that generates only a few moves at a time and evaluates each one to determine which move results in a pattern that is closer to the desired target. This is not guaranteed to bring about a solution, because it could happen that the process enters a cycle in which successive moves result in patterns that are first closer and then further away from the target pattern. However, if we can find a suitable evaluation method, then we can expect to arrive at the target without having to generate all of the possible patterns along the way.

There are many possible ways to evaluate patterns in the 15-puzzle, but the simplest and most immediately natural—though not necessarily the most efficient—is *city-block distance*. This consists of the sum of the number of "blocks"—that is, slots in the puzzle—that separate each tile from where we want it to be in the target.[63] For example, in Figure 36 tile *5* is one block up in the source pattern from where we want it to be in the target pattern, and tile *12* is one block down in the source from where we want it to be in the target pattern. Consequently, each of these tiles has a city-block distance of *1* from where we want it to be, as Figure 37 shows.

---

[62] *Suggested excursion:* Calculate the number of possible patterns of the 15-puzzle. *(Hint:* There are sixteen slots that can each contain any one of fifteen numbered tiles or blank.)

[63] *Suggested excursion:* Think up some ways of evaluating patterns in the 15-puzzle other than city-block distance, and rework the following discussion in terms of them. *(Hint:* Should corners count more or less than middle slots?)

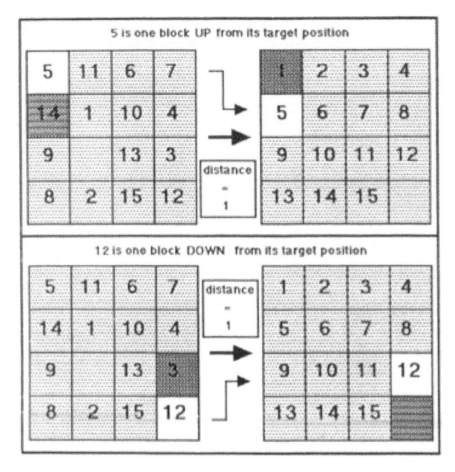

Fig. 37: City-block Distances of 5 and of 12 from Source to Target in Figure 36

Tile *1* is one block to the right and one block down in the source from where we want it to be in the target, and tile *10* is one block to the right and one block up from where we want it to be, so each of these tiles has a city-block distance of *2*, as Figure 38 shows.

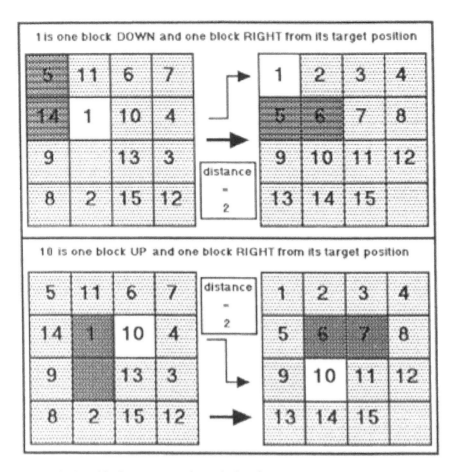

Fig. 38: City-block Distances of 1 and of 10 from Source to Target in Figure 36

Tile *13* is two blocks to the right and one block up in the source from where we want it to be, so it has a city-block distance of *3*, and tile *8* is three blocks to the left and two blocks down in the source from where we want it to be, so it has a city-block distance of *5*, as Figure 39 shows.

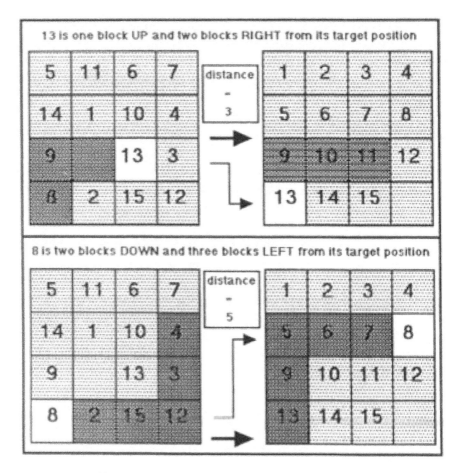

Fig. 39: City-block Distances of 13 and of 8 from Source to Target in Figure 36

Tiles *9* and *15* in the source pattern in Figure 36 are already where we want them to be, so they each have a city-block distance of *0*, as Figure 40 shows.

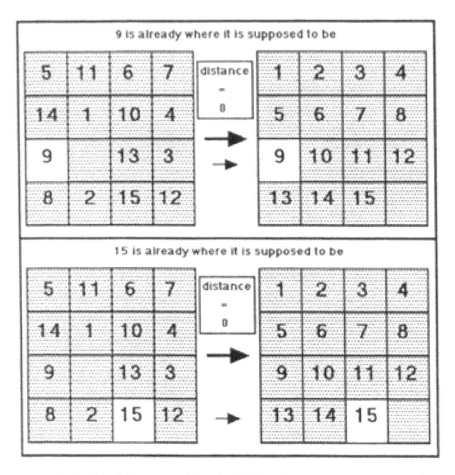

Fig. 40: City-block Distances of 9 and of 15 from Source to Target in Figure 36

The full set of individual city-block distances for the tiles in the source pattern in Figure 36 is given in Figure 41.[64]

---

[64] *Suggested excursion:* Verify the distance values in Figure 41. *(Hint:* Just count the number of "blocks" in each case.)

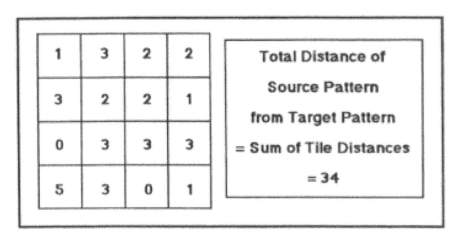

Fig. 41: City-block Distances for Each Tile from Source to Target and Total Pattern Distance in Figure 36

Since the sum of all the numbers in the pattern in Figure 41 is *34*, we can say that the source pattern itself in Figure 36 has a city-block distance of *34* from the target pattern, as (7) shows.

(7) distance of source pattern from target pattern

= sum of distances of each tile in source from its target position

= 1 + 3 + 2 + 2 + 3 + 2 + 2 + 1 + 0 + 3 + 3 + 3 + 5 + 3 + 0 + 1

= 34

In computer terms, city-block distance defines an *evaluation function* for the 15-puzzle. It associates each pair of same-size square arrays with a number, the "distance"—that is, the degree of difference—between the first square array and the second, as (8) states.[65]

(8) distance: SQUARRAY X SQUARRAY → NUMBER ∪ {error}

A pattern of the 15-puzzle can be represented as a 4 X 4 square array. We can move tiles by switching them with the blank tile, ▱, that we can consider to be occupying the empty slot, using the function *switch*

---

[65] *Suggested excursion:* Figure out why *error* has to be included as a possible result of *distance* in (8), and formulate a suitable constraint for distinguishing the cases that result in *error* from the cases that do not. *(Hint:* The set SQUARRAY contains all square arrays of all sizes. What happens when you apply the function *distance* to a pair of square arrays of different sizes?)

that we defined on Expedition 2. Solving the problem that Figure 36 poses—that is, getting from the indicated source pattern to the indicated target pattern—therefore consists in finding a suitable sequence of applications of *switch* to $\square$ and some adjacent tile that starts with the square array in (9)(a) and ends with the square array in (9)(b).

$$(9) \quad (a) \begin{bmatrix} 5 & 11 & 6 & 7 \\ 14 & 1 & 10 & 4 \\ 9 & \square & 13 & 3 \\ 8 & 2 & 15 & 12 \end{bmatrix} \quad (b) \begin{bmatrix} 1 & 2 & 3 & 4 \\ 5 & 6 & 7 & 8 \\ 9 & 10 & 11 & 12 \\ 13 & 14 & 15 & \square \end{bmatrix}$$

We can determine the first of these applications of *switch* by examining all possible ways that we can apply *switch* to the square array in (9)(a), for $\square$ and some adjacent tile, and then applying the function *distance* to determine how far each of the resulting square arrays is from the square array in (9)(b). We then take the resulting square array that we find to be the closest to the one in (9)(b)—that is, the one with the smallest distance value from (9)(b)—as a new starting point and apply *distance* to each possible result of applying *switch* to it, for $\square$ and some adjacent tile. Repeating that process successively for each square array that we determine has the best value at each step generates a tree of square arrays that we can reasonably expect to end eventually with the desired target square array at some leaf node. This happens without our having to generate the full tree of square arrays that result from all possible applications of *switch*, for $\square$ and some adjacent tile, to *all* resulting square arrays.[66]

There are exactly four ways in which we can apply *switch* appropriately for the 15-puzzle to the square array in (9)(a), because there are exactly four tiles that are horizontally or vertically adjacent to $\square$, namely, tiles *1*, *9*, *13*, and *2*. Only tiles that are situated in that way are allowed to move into the empty slot for this puzzle. Since the respective positions of these tiles in (9)(a) are those in (10), the corresponding *switch* applications are those in (11).

---

[66] *Suggested excursion:* Figure out how to modify the definition of the data structure *tree* in (68) of Expedition 2 to account for trees of square arrays. *(Hint:* That definition is for trees of numbers. How is that fact indicated in the definition?)

(10)

(a) tile 1: row 2, column 2
     tile ☐: row 3, column 2

(b) tile 9: row 3, column 1
     tile ☐: row 3, column 2

(c) tile 13: row 3, column 3
     tile ☐: row 3, column 2

(d) tile 2: row 4, column 2
     tile ☐: row 3, column 2

(11)

(a) switch$\left(\begin{bmatrix} 5 & 11 & 6 & 7 \\ 14 & 1 & 10 & 4 \\ 9 & ☐ & 13 & 3 \\ 8 & 2 & 15 & 12 \end{bmatrix}, 2, 2, 3, 2\right)$

(b) switch$\left(\begin{bmatrix} 5 & 11 & 6 & 7 \\ 14 & 1 & 10 & 4 \\ 9 & ☐ & 13 & 3 \\ 8 & 2 & 15 & 12 \end{bmatrix}, 3, 1, 3, 2\right)$

(c) switch$\left(\begin{bmatrix} 5 & 11 & 6 & 7 \\ 14 & 1 & 10 & 4 \\ 9 & ☐ & 13 & 3 \\ 8 & 2 & 15 & 12 \end{bmatrix}, 3, 3, 3, 2\right)$

(d) switch$\left(\begin{bmatrix} 5 & 11 & 6 & 7 \\ 14 & 1 & 10 & 4 \\ 9 & ☐ & 13 & 3 \\ 8 & 2 & 15 & 12 \end{bmatrix}, 4, 2, 3, 2\right)$

These *switch* applications result in the respective square arrays in (12).[67]

(12)

(a)
$$\begin{bmatrix} 5 & 11 & 6 & 7 \\ 14 & \square & 10 & 4 \\ 9 & 1 & 13 & 3 \\ 8 & 2 & 15 & 12 \end{bmatrix}$$

(b)
$$\begin{bmatrix} 5 & 11 & 6 & 7 \\ 14 & 1 & 10 & 4 \\ \square & 9 & 13 & 3 \\ 8 & 2 & 15 & 12 \end{bmatrix}$$

(c)
$$\begin{bmatrix} 5 & 11 & 6 & 7 \\ 14 & 1 & 10 & 4 \\ 9 & 13 & \square & 3 \\ 8 & 2 & 15 & 12 \end{bmatrix}$$

(d)
$$\begin{bmatrix} 5 & 11 & 6 & 7 \\ 14 & 1 & 10 & 4 \\ 9 & 2 & 13 & 3 \\ 8 & \square & 15 & 12 \end{bmatrix}$$

The individual city-block distances of each tile in each pattern in (12) from where we want each tile to be in the target pattern (9)(b) are shown in (13).

(13)

(a)
$$\begin{bmatrix} 1 & 3 & 2 & 2 \\ 3 & 4 & 2 & 1 \\ 0 & 3 & 3 & 3 \\ 5 & 3 & 0 & 1 \end{bmatrix}$$

(b)
$$\begin{bmatrix} 1 & 3 & 2 & 2 \\ 3 & 2 & 2 & 1 \\ 4 & 1 & 3 & 3 \\ 5 & 3 & 0 & 1 \end{bmatrix}$$

(c)
$$\begin{bmatrix} 1 & 3 & 2 & 2 \\ 3 & 2 & 2 & 1 \\ 0 & 2 & 2 & 3 \\ 5 & 3 & 0 & 1 \end{bmatrix}$$

(d)
$$\begin{bmatrix} 1 & 3 & 2 & 2 \\ 3 & 2 & 2 & 1 \\ 0 & 2 & 3 & 3 \\ 5 & 2 & 0 & 1 \end{bmatrix}$$

---

[67] *Suggested excursion:* Verify this claim in each case by explicitly working out the steps of each calculation. *(Hint:* See (63) of Expedition 2 as an example of how *switch* works.)

The resulting total distances of the patterns themselves from the target pattern (9)(b) are given in (14).

(14)   (a)   36   (b)   36

      (c)   32   (d)   32

The *switch* applications in (10)(a) and (b) each turn out to increase the distance from the target pattern from *34* to *36*, thereby moving the puzzle further away from where we want it to be going, while the *switch* applications in (10)(c) and (d) each turn out to decrease the distance from the target pattern from *34* to *32*, thereby moving the puzzle closer to where we want it to be going. We can conclude that, at least as far as city-block distance is concerned, either of the moves (10)(c) or (d)—that is, switching either *13* or *2* with *☐*—is preferable to either of the moves (10)(a) or (b)—that is, switching either *1* or *9* with *☐*—so the latter two moves can be ignored as we work the puzzle out further.

In practice, when we are actually writing a program to implement a heuristic that involves an evaluation function, we need to decide ahead of time on a *tie-breaking criterion*, so the computer will know what to do when two patterns turn out to have the same evaluation. Figuring out the best tie-breaking criterion for a particular game can be as difficult as figuring out the best evaluation function, but, for illustrative purposes, just for now, we can decide to use the criterion of choosing the pattern with the fewer further moves. This is a reasonable criterion to start with, because the motivation for using a heuristic rather than an algorithm in the first place was precisely to reduce the number of game patterns we would have to generate and examine. In the current instance, it tells us to choose (12)(d), rather than (12)(c), as the next starting point. Even though we have found both patterns to have distances of *32* from the target pattern, (12)(c) has the potential for four further moves, because *☐* can be switched with either *10*, *13*, *3*, or *15*, whereas (12)(d) has the potential for only three further moves, because *☐* can be switched with either *2*, *8*, or *15*. Choosing the pattern with the fewer further moves, we can repeat the entire process with (12)(d), rather than (9)(a), as the new starting point for further evaluation.

Of the three moves that are available in (12)(d), we only need to consider two, because the third—namely, switching *☐* with *2*—would return the pattern to (9)(a) and therefore be superfluous. The patterns that result from these two moves are shown in (15), the respective distances of their tiles from their target positions are shown in (16), and the total distances of the patterns themselves from the target pattern are shown in (17).[68]

(15)   (a)
$$\begin{bmatrix} 5 & 11 & 6 & 7 \\ 14 & 1 & 10 & 4 \\ 9 & 2 & 13 & 3 \\ \square & 8 & 15 & 12 \end{bmatrix}$$
(b)
$$\begin{bmatrix} 5 & 11 & 6 & 7 \\ 14 & 1 & 10 & 4 \\ 9 & 2 & 13 & 3 \\ 8 & 15 & \square & 12 \end{bmatrix}$$

(16)   (a)
$$\begin{bmatrix} 1 & 3 & 2 & 2 \\ 3 & 2 & 2 & 1 \\ 0 & 2 & 3 & 3 \\ 3 & 4 & 0 & 1 \end{bmatrix}$$
(b)
$$\begin{bmatrix} 1 & 3 & 2 & 2 \\ 3 & 2 & 2 & 1 \\ 0 & 2 & 3 & 3 \\ 5 & 1 & 1 & 1 \end{bmatrix}$$

(17)   (a)   32   (b)   32

Again, evaluation results in a tie, with both patterns having a distance value of *32* from the target pattern. There are only two further possible moves from (15)(a)—namely, switching $\square$ with tiles *9* or *8*—and there are three further possible moves from (15)(b)—namely, switching $\square$ with tiles *13*, *15*, or *12*—so the criterion of choosing the pattern with the fewer further moves yields (15)(a) as the new starting point for further evaluation. Since switching $\square$ with tile *8* in (15)(a) returns the pattern to (12)(d), we need to examine only the other of its two moves—namely, switching $\square$ with tile *9*. This results in the pattern in (18), which has the individual tile distance shown in (19), and thus the total distance from the target pattern shown in (20).

---

[68] *Suggested excursion:* Write the *switch* applications for these moves. *(Hint:* Include the square array and the row and column numbers of the tiles to be switched.)

(18)

$$\begin{bmatrix} 5 & 11 & 6 & 7 \\ 14 & 1 & 10 & 4 \\ \square & 2 & 13 & 3 \\ 9 & 8 & 15 & 12 \end{bmatrix}$$

(19)

$$\begin{bmatrix} 1 & 3 & 2 & 2 \\ 3 & 2 & 2 & 1 \\ 4 & 2 & 3 & 3 \\ 1 & 4 & 0 & 1 \end{bmatrix}$$

(20)   34

Unfortunately, this move has increased the city-block distance from *32* to *34*, so (18) is further from the target pattern than (15)(a) is; alas, the heuristic is leading the puzzle in the wrong direction. As we noted earlier, a heuristic, unlike an algorithm, is not guaranteed to produce a result. An algorithm is figured out and proven to work through entirely mathematical methods, but a heuristic is arrived at experimentally, through intuition, guesswork, and trial-and-error testing, so it might not give us a solution in every case we apply it to. On the other hand, we can always refine and improve a particular heuristic as we test it and as we learn more about the problem we want to use it to solve. In the present case, the heuristic consists of two parts, an evaluation function and a tie-breaking criterion. Either of these could be the source of the heuristic's apparent dysfunction. Any experienced 15-puzzler could point out, for example, that city-block distance is too global a measure to be able to solve this puzzle efficiently. A human solver would work more locally by focusing on getting particular tiles into the right slots, largely ignoring those that are not yet being worked on or have already been placed in their proper locations. For example, we might begin by working to get the tiles properly placed in the top row or in the upper left region of the puzzle and then ignore those tiles while we are working to get the tiles properly placed in the second row or in the lower left region, not worrying about getting $\square$ in the lower right corner until the very end. Furthermore, we occasionally need to displace one or more tiles that have already been properly positioned, in order to make room for others to get by. This could very well increase the city-block distance of the puzzle as a whole for at least one step of the solution process.[69, 70]

On the other hand, the problem with this heuristic could be not the evaluation function, but the tie-breaking criterion; perhaps city-block distance would work, if we chose to break ties differently. For example, consider what would have happened if we had decided to choose between (12)(c) and (d) by the criterion of picking the pattern with the larger number of further possible moves, rather than the smaller. One of the moves available in (12)(c)—namely, switching $\square$ with tile *13*—returns it to (9)(a), so only the other three moves— namely, switching $\square$ with tiles *10*, *3*, or *15*—need to be considered. The resulting patterns for these moves are shown in (21), the tile distances from their destinations are shown in (22), and the total distances of each pattern from the target pattern are shown in (23).

(21)

$$
\text{(a)}\begin{bmatrix} 5 & 11 & 6 & 7 \\ 14 & 1 & \square & 4 \\ 9 & 13 & 10 & 3 \\ 8 & 2 & 15 & 12 \end{bmatrix}
\text{(b)}\begin{bmatrix} 5 & 11 & 6 & 7 \\ 14 & 1 & 10 & 4 \\ 9 & 13 & 3 & \square \\ 8 & 2 & 15 & 12 \end{bmatrix}
\text{(c)}\begin{bmatrix} 5 & 11 & 6 & 7 \\ 14 & 1 & 10 & 4 \\ 9 & 13 & 15 & 3 \\ 8 & 2 & \square & 12 \end{bmatrix}
$$

(22)

$$
\text{(a)}\begin{bmatrix} 1 & 3 & 2 & 2 \\ 3 & 2 & 3 & 1 \\ 0 & 2 & 1 & 3 \\ 5 & 3 & 0 & 1 \end{bmatrix}
\text{(b)}\begin{bmatrix} 1 & 3 & 2 & 2 \\ 3 & 2 & 2 & 1 \\ 0 & 2 & 2 & 1 \\ 5 & 3 & 0 & 1 \end{bmatrix}
\text{(c)}\begin{bmatrix} 1 & 3 & 2 & 2 \\ 3 & 2 & 2 & 1 \\ 0 & 2 & 1 & 3 \\ 5 & 3 & 1 & 1 \end{bmatrix}
$$

---

[69] *Suggested excursion:* Work out the next few levels of solution using the heuristic as it now stands, that is, city-block distance with tie breaking by fewest available moves. Does the situation improve? *(Hint:* Apply the evaluation function to all moves that don't return to the immediately preceding pattern.)

[70] *Suggested excursion:* Think of ways to refine the city-block distance function to work in a more local manner. *(Hint:* Try taking into account only the tiles that are immediately around the $\square$. Try taking into account only those tiles that have not yet been properly placed.)

(23)   (a)   32   (b)   30   (c)   32

This time there is an improvement, because (12)(c) has a distance of *32* from the target pattern, whereas (21)(b) has a distance of *30*. Switching ☐ with tile *3* has moved the puzzle closer to solution by moving each of ☐ and tile *3* one slot closer to its destination. We can now repeat the process with (21)(b) as the new starting point and hope that further progress will be made. In fact, switching ☐ with tile *12* in (21)(b) results in a pattern with an improved distance of *28* from its target pattern, because each of ☐ and tile *12* is brought one slot closer to where we want it to be.[71]

We can summarize what we have done thus far in the form of the *decision tree* shown in Figure 42.

---

[71] *Suggested excursion:* Verify this claim, that is, that switching ☐ with tile *12* results in a pattern whose distance is *28*. *(Hint:* Make the switch and compute the distance.)

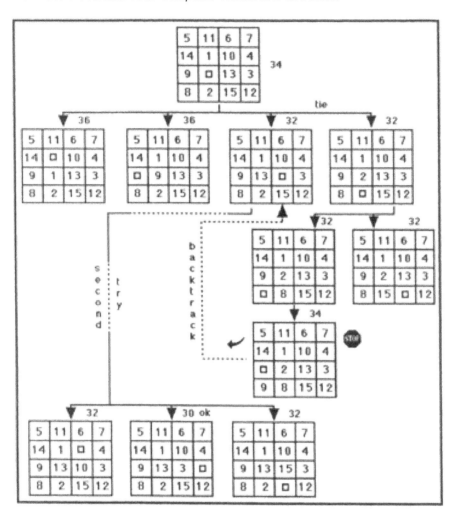

Fig. 42: Partial Decision Tree for the 15-Puzzle Problem Posed in Figure 36

The original source pattern appears at the root of the tree, level *0*, with all of the patterns that would result from possible moves at that level shown at level *1*. However, rather than generating at level *2* all of the patterns that would result from possible moves at level *1*—as an exhaustive algorithm would require—we generate at level *2* only those patterns that result from moves that are made from the best-valued pattern at level *1*. We then repeat the same for level *3* from the best-valued pattern at level *2*, with ties being broken by choosing the pattern with the fewest possible further moves. Since the distance value goes up at level *3*, we invoke a technique called *back-tracking*: moving back up the tree to the first *decision-point*, where a tie had to be broken, and choosing an alternate pattern from which to continue, as if we had used a different tie-breaking criterion. If we had originally decided to break a tie by choosing the pattern with the most, rather than the fewest possible further moves, then this alternate pattern would have already been the one chosen at that level, and we would not have needed this particular bit of back-tracking. However, we would have had no way of knowing this ahead of time; for a different source pattern, the first tie-breaking criterion might have worked perfectly well, with no need for back-tracking at all. If all goes well in generating and evaluating further moves, then a pattern will eventually appear that is identical to the target pattern and that therefore has a city-block distance of *0*, thereby solving the puzzle. However, it could also turn out that the computer enters an unending cycle, called an *infinite loop*, in which we repeatedly revisit the same sequence of patterns. If that happens, then we need to refine the heuristic further and begin the process again.[72]

A different sort of complication arises when we use heuristics to play *two-person games*, as contrasted with solving puzzles or playing one-person games: the opponent keeps getting in the way. Consider what it would take to get a computer to be able to play the simple game of *tic-tac-toe*. In this game two players alternately place an *X* or an *O* in the slots of a three-by-three game board with the aim of being the first to get three of one's own markers, *X* or *O*, in horizontal, vertical, or diagonal succession, as Figure 43 shows.

---

[72] *Suggested excursion:* Finish the game, that is, continue carrying out the described solution process until the target pattern is actually arrived at. Does the heuristic turn out to be in need of any further refinement? *(Hint:* Take excursion 71 first. Then repeat the steps as many times as necessary.)

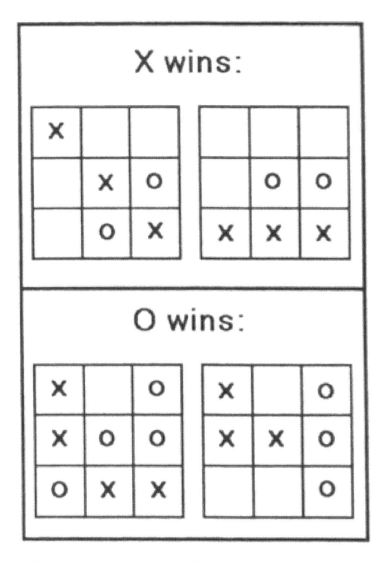

Fig. 43: Some Sample Winning Tic-Tac-Toe Patterns for X and O

Strategy in this game involves trying to prevent the opponent from reaching such a state while trying to get there oneself and can easily lead to a stalemate when applied with equal skill by both players, as the sample game in Figure 44 shows.

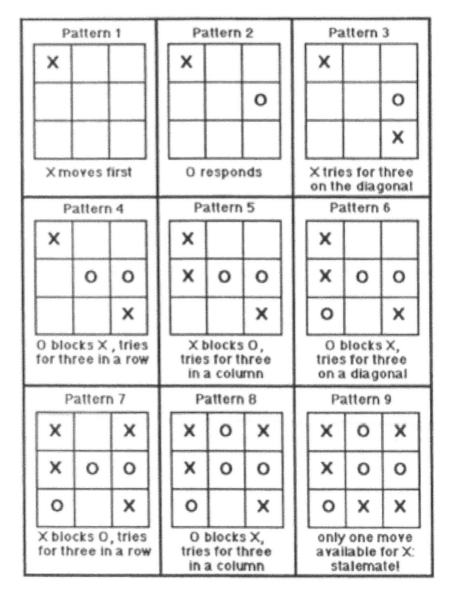

Fig. 44: A Sample Tic-Tac-Toe Game

Assume that the computer plays *X*, with a human opponent playing *O*, and that the computer moves first, as in Figure 44. As we saw in connection with the 15-puzzle, there are many possible ways to evaluate a game pattern in tic-toe-toe, from *X*'s point of view, and it is far from obvious which way is best. In contrast to the 15-puzzle, there is no single target pattern that the computer can aim for, because the opponent has the ability to block such an aim, so a measure such as city-block distance would be difficult to apply. A more promising approach would be to figure out what features make a pattern good or bad for X and to add in some measure of each good feature, while subtracting off some measure of each bad feature. The goal would then be to increase pattern values, rather than decrease them, in contrast to what we did for the 15-puzzle. In that case we were measuring a pattern's distance from a target pattern, rather than the "goodness" of a pattern itself.

It is good to have one's own markers in a row, a column, or a diagonal, but not if the opponent has markers there as well. It is bad to have some of the opponent's markers in a row, a column, or a diagonal without having any of one's own there to block them. To illustrate how we can formalize considerations of this sort—taking a cue from computer gamesman, David Levy—let us define a *1-line* to be any row, column, or diagonal that contains exactly one marker, X or O; a *2-line* to be any row, column, or diagonal that contains exactly two O's or exactly two X's, but nothing else; a *3-line* to be any row, column, or diagonal that contains exactly three X's or exactly three O's; and an *n-line* to be a 1-line, a 2-line, or a 3-line. It would be reasonable, as a first step in developing an evaluation function, to consider the value of a game pattern, from X's point of view, to be the number of n-lines that the pattern contains for X minus the number of n-lines that the pattern contains for O, since n-lines for X are good for X, while n-lines for O are bad for X. For example, as Figure 45(a) shows, Pattern 1 in Figure 44 has the value 3 by this measure, because it contains three 1-lines for X—a row, a column, and a diagonal—and no n-lines for O.

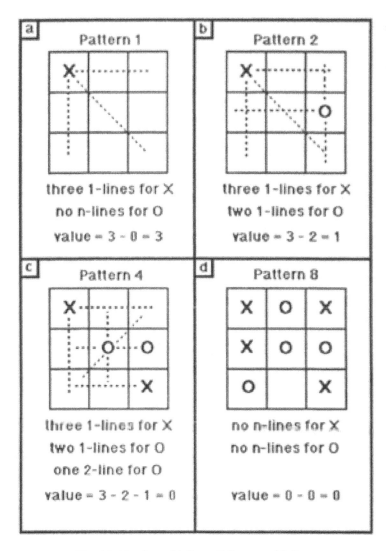

As Figure 45(b) shows, Pattern 2 is the same as Pattern 1 except that it also contains two 1-lines for *O*, so it has the value *1*, because we need to subtract the number of 1-lines for *O* from the number of 1-lines for *X*. As Figure 45(c) shows, Pattern 4 has three 1-lines for *X*, two 1-lines for *O*, and one 2-line for *O*, so it has a value of *0*. As Figure 45(d) shows, Pattern 8 also has a value of *0*, because it contains no n-lines at all, for either *X* or *O*. Figure 46 shows the number of n-lines in each of the patterns in Figure 44, along with each pattern's corresponding value.

Pattern 1

	X	O
1-lines	3	0
2-lines	0	0
3-lines	0	0

Value = 3

Pattern 2

	X	O
1-lines	3	2
2-lines	0	0
3-lines	0	0

Value = 3 - 2
= 1

Pattern 3

	X	O
1-lines	2	1
2-lines	1	0
3-lines	0	0

Value = 2 + 1 - 1
= 2

Pattern 4

	X	O
1-lines	2	2
2-lines	0	1
3-lines	0	0

Value = 2 - 2 - 1
= -1

Pattern 5

	X	O
1-lines	2	2
2-lines	1	0
3-lines	0	0

Value = 2 + 1 - 2
= 1

Pattern 6

	X	O
1-lines	1	1
2-lines	0	1
3-lines	0	0

Value = 1 - 1 - 1
= -1

Pattern 7

	X	O
1-lines	0	1
2-lines	1	0
3-lines	0	0

Value = 1 - 1
= 0

Pattern 8

	X	O
1-lines	0	0
2-lines	0	1
3-lines	0	0

Value = -1

Pattern 9

	X	O
1-lines	0	0
2-lines	0	0
3-lines	0	0

Value = 0

Fig. 46: Values of the Patterns in Figure 44

As the values in Figure 46 show, combining the numbers of n-lines in a game pattern is a good start on an evaluation function for tic-tac-toe. Pattern 1 is more highly valued than Pattern 9, as it should be, because in Pattern 1 the game is just beginning and X has many options open, whereas in Pattern 9, the game is over and X has no hope at all. However, the figure also shows that we need to refine the function further. The fact that Pattern 2 has the same value as Pattern 5 seems odd, because even though there are fewer options for X in Pattern 5, X is in a position to win in that pattern, but is not yet in such a position in Pattern 2. In effect, the transition from Pattern 2 to Pattern 5 in Figure 44 amounts to replacing a 1-line for X with a 2-line for X and replacing a 1-line for O with another 1-line for O, so the total numbers added and subtracted end up being the same. This evaluation function ignores the fact that n-lines differ in their usefulness for tic-tac-toe, because 2-lines are better than 1-lines and 3-lines are best of all, for each of the respective players. This fact can be accommodated by assigning different *weights* to the various sorts of n-lines and combining their weighted values, rather than simply counting how many of them there are.

Figuring out what those weights should be requires not only a careful analysis of the game itself to determine what values make sense for this game, but also experimentation to determine what values actually enable the computer to play the game most effectively. For example, one 3-line for X overcomes anything that O might have in the pattern, and the same also holds for O, if O gets a 3-line first. This is a fact about tic-tac-toe itself, regardless of who or what is playing it. A 3-line must therefore be weighted so as to more than compensate for any number of opposing 1-lines or 2-lines. However, even taking this fact into account, there is still a wide range of possible weight values for 3-lines, and the actual choice of value can make a significant difference in the efficiency of a particular program when it actually plays the game.

Since X moves first, the appearance of an O has the effect of depriving X of options that it previously had, so it is reasonable to assume that a 1-line for O should count more against X than a 1-line for X counts for X, and the same can be said about 2-lines. As already noted, a 2-line for either player should count more than a 1-line for either player, and a 3-line for either player should count more than a 2-line for either player and should also overwhelm anything the opponent might have in the pattern. One way of satisfying these requirements, just for illustration, would be to assume that a 3-line for either player counts at least three times as much as a 1-line for either player, that a 2-line for either player counts at least twice as much as a 1-line for either player, and that n-lines for O count at least twice as much against X as corresponding n-lines for X count in X's favor. Using X_1, X_2, and X_3 as parameters for the number of 1-lines, 2-lines, and 3-lines for X, respectively, using O_1, O_2, and O_3 as parameters for the number of 1-lines, 2-lines, and 3-lines for O, respectively, and using *value* as a parameter for the value of a pattern, the suggested evaluation function can be stated succinctly as in (24), where the operation symbols +, -, and * have their usual arithmetic meanings, that is, addition, subtraction, and multiplication, respectively.

$$(24) \quad value \quad = \quad (1 * X_1) + (4 * X_2) + (16 * X_3)$$
$$- (2 * O_1) - (8 * O_2) - (32 * O_3)$$

Figure 47 explicitly shows the weights that appear in (24).

weights	X	O
1-lines	1	2
2-lines	4	8
3-lines	16	32

Fig. 47: The Weights for n-lines that Are Used in (24)

It must be stressed again that these weights and (24) itself are just one way of satisfying one set of constraints that we can reasonably expect an evaluation function for tic-tac-toe to satisfy. They make sense, and they are useful for illustration. However, we would need to experiment extensively with programs using different weights and to carefully compare their results to obtain an evaluation function that would enable a particular computer system to play the game in the most efficient and effective way.

Using (24), the values in Figure 46 for the patterns in Figure 44 get replaced by those in Figure 48.

Pattern 1

	X	O
1-lines	3	0
2-lines	0	0
3-lines	0	0

Value = 3

Pattern 2

	X	O
1-lines	3	2
2-lines	0	0
3-lines	0	0

Value = 3 - 4
= -1

Pattern 3

	X	O
1-lines	2	1
2-lines	1	0
3-lines	0	0

Value = 2 + 4 - 2
= 4

Pattern 4

	X	O
1-lines	2	2
2-lines	0	1
3-lines	0	0

Value = 2 - 4 - 8
= -10

Pattern 5

	X	O
1-lines	2	2
2-lines	1	0
3-lines	0	0

Value = 2 + 4 - 4
= 2

Pattern 6

	X	O
1-lines	1	1
2-lines	0	1
3-lines	0	0

Value = 1 - 2 - 8
= -9

Pattern 7

	X	O
1-lines	0	1
2-lines	1	0
3-lines	0	0

Value = 4 - 2
= 2

Pattern 8

	X	O
1-lines	0	0
2-lines	0	1
3-lines	0	0

Value = -8

Pattern 9

	X	O
1-lines	0	0
2-lines	0	0
3-lines	0	0

Value = 0

Fig. 48: Revised Weighted Values of the Patterns in Figure 44

For example, Pattern 3 contains two 1-lines and one 2-line for X and one 1-line for O, while Pattern 6 contains one 1-line for X and one 1-line and one 2-line for O, so (24) becomes (25) for Pattern 3, and (26) for Pattern 6.

$$
\begin{aligned}
(25) \quad \text{value} \quad &= \quad (1 * 2) + (4 * 1) + (16 * 0) \\
&\quad - (2 * 1) - (8 * 0) - (32 * 0) \\
&= \quad 2 + 4 + 0 - 2 - 0 - 0 \\
&= \quad 4
\end{aligned}
$$

(26)   value   = $(1 * 1) + (4 * 0) + (16 * 0)$
$- (2 * 1) - (8 * 1) - (32 * 0)$
= $1 + 0 + 0 - 2 - 8 - 0$
= -9

The fact that fewer of the patterns in Figure 48 have the same value shows that the weighted evaluation function makes finer distinctions among the patterns than merely counting n-lines does. This is exactly what we want from the point of view of aiming to determine the best possible moves when actually playing the game. In Figure 46 Patterns 2 and 5 each have a value of *1*, Patterns 4, 6, and 8 each have a value of *-1*, and Patterns 7 and 9 each have a value of *0*, whereas in Figure 48 only Patterns 5 and 7 have the same value, namely, *2*. The weighted evaluation function also provides for a wider range of possible values, thereby giving us more perspective on the relative values of different patterns. The values in Figure 46 range from *-1* to *3*, while the values in Figure 48 range from *-10* to *4*. As the values that the two functions give for the winning patterns in Figure 43 show, this difference is even more substantial when 3-lines are taken into account. Figure 49 shows these values for the unweighted evaluation function, and Figure 50 shows them for the weighted one.

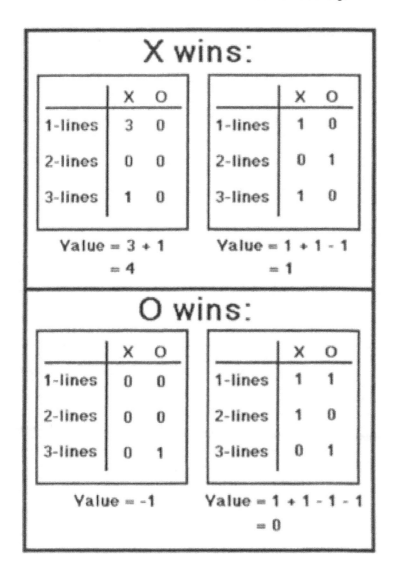

Fig. 49: Unweighted Values of the Winning Patterns in Figure 43

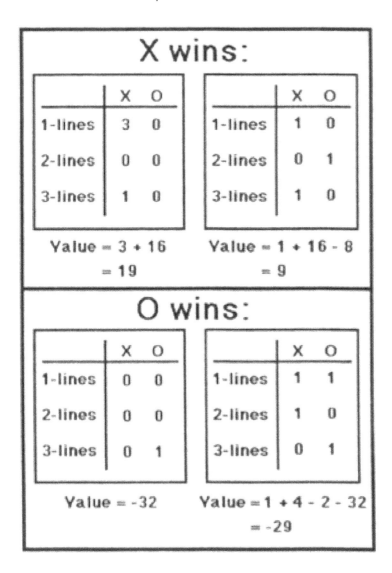

Fig. 50: Weighted Values of the Winning Patterns in Figure 43

In both Figures 49 and 50 the winning patterns for X get larger values than do the winning patterns for O—that is, the losing patterns for X— but in Figure 50 they are substantially larger. In Figure 49, the values range from *-1* to *4*, but in Figure *50* they range from *-32* to *19*.

Once we have provided it with a suitable evaluation function, the computer starts with the 3 X 3 square array in (27), in which every slot is blank, and examines each of its possible moves.

(27)

Since we can place an X in any one of nine slots, there are nine possible initial moves. However, we need to consider only three of those moves, because some of the moves are *symmetrically equivalent* to others. Each of the patterns in Figure 51(a) can be rotated around the center to match each of the other patterns in that figure, and the same is true of each of the patterns in Figure 51(b).

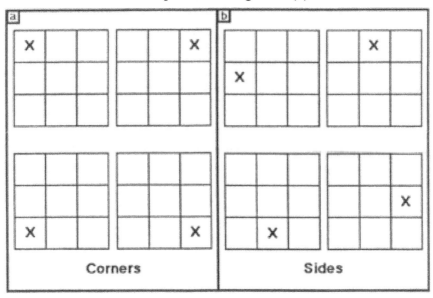

Fig. 51: Symmetrically Equivalent Patterns From Initial Moves by X

The patterns in each figure therefore have the same behavior in relation to this game, so we can take any one of them as representing them all. Mathematicians would say that the patterns in each figure comprise an *equivalence class* relative to the behavior of patterns in this game. The patterns that result from the first three moves for X from the initial pattern (27) are therefore those that result from placing an X in a corner, a side, or the middle, as (28) shows.

(28)

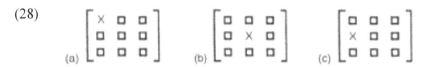

Since the only n-lines in these patterns are 1-lines for X, and since (28)(a),(b), and (c) have three, four, and two of these 1-lines, respectively, (24) gives these patterns the values shown in (29).

(29)   (a)   3   (b)   4   (c)   2

Since (24) measures a pattern's desirable features, from X's point of view, rather than a pattern's distance from a target, (29) tells us that (28)(b), the pattern with the largest value, is the best-valued pattern for X. However, we cannot conclude from this fact that (28)(b) is the move that X should make. It *might* be the best move for X to make, but (29), by itself, is not yet sufficient justification for us to draw that conclusion. In contrast to what we saw to be the case with the 15-puzzle, in this game there is an opponent to worry about, and we have not yet taken that fact sufficiently into account. We have incorporated O's *markers* into our formulation of the evaluation function, but we have not yet examined O's *moves* to determine what effect they might have on our *application* of the evaluation function. Even though moves by X yield the patterns in (28), those are not the actual results of these moves, because the opponent has a different goal from X in determining how to respond. To figure out what X needs to do in pattern (27) we need to look at how O might respond to the patterns in (28), because the patterns that result from those responses are really what X will be left with as a basis for deciding what to do next. X's goal is to win, but O's goal is to make X lose, so O will choose the move that yields the *worst* result for X. In other words, X needs to determine its move not on the basis of the values that (24) gives to the patterns in (28), but from the values that (24) gives to the patterns that O is willing to make available to X, *in response* to the patterns in (28). Since O wants X to lose, each of O's moves will result in the pattern that is the *least*-valued pattern for X. It is from these least values, not the values in (29), that X must choose the largest.

In (28)(a), we can place an O in an adjacent side, a near corner, the center, a far side, or the opposite corner, so the patterns that can result from O's moves in (28)(a) are those that (30) shows, along with three other patterns that are symmetrically equivalent to those and that we can therefore safely ignore.

(30)

$$
\text{(a)}\begin{bmatrix} \text{X} & \text{O} & \square \\ \square & \square & \square \\ \square & \square & \square \end{bmatrix}
\qquad
\text{(b)}\begin{bmatrix} \text{X} & \square & \text{O} \\ \square & \square & \square \\ \square & \square & \square \end{bmatrix}
\qquad
\text{(c)}\begin{bmatrix} \text{X} & \square & \square \\ \square & \text{O} & \square \\ \square & \square & \square \end{bmatrix}
$$

$$
\text{(d)}\begin{bmatrix} \text{X} & \square & \square \\ \square & \square & \text{O} \\ \square & \square & \square \end{bmatrix}
\qquad
\text{(e)}\begin{bmatrix} \text{X} & \square & \square \\ \square & \square & \square \\ \square & \square & \text{O} \end{bmatrix}
$$

The respective values that (24) gives to these patterns are shown in (31).

(31)   (a) 0   (b) -2   (c) -4   (d) -1   (e) -2

Since there are no 2-lines or 3-lines in these patterns, we obtain the value that (24) assigns in each case by subtracting twice the number of 1-lines for O from the number of 1-lines for X. Except in (30)(d), the O in each case has the effect of blocking exactly one of the 1-lines that X has in (28)(a)—though not the same one in each case—so the patterns all have the same number of 1-lines for X and differ at most in the number of 1-lines they have for O. For example, (30)(a) has two 1-lines for X—a column and a diagonal—and one 1-line for O—a column—so its value is two minus twice one, that is, 2 - (2 * 1), which is 0. Similarly, (30)(b) has two 1-lines for X—a column and a diagonal—and two 1-lines for O—again, a column and a diagonal—so its value is two minus twice two, that is, 2 - (2 * 2) = 2 - 4, which is -2. We can conclude that (30)(b) is worse for X and therefore better for O than (30)(a) is, at least as far as (24) is concerned as a way of measuring pattern values. Pattern (30)(c) has three 1-lines for O—a column, a row, and a diagonal—along with the two one-lines for X— so its value is 2 - (2 * 3) = 2 - 6 = -4, which is even worse for X than (30)(a) and (b) are. Similarly, (30)(e) has two 1-lines for O—a column and a row—which makes (24) give it the same value as the value it gives to (30)(b). In (30)(d), none of the 1-lines for X in (28)(a) gets blocked, so X still has three 1-lines; however, O now has two 1-lines of its own, so the value of the pattern is 3 - (2 * 2) = 3 - 4 = -1. This makes (30)(d) the second best pattern for X in (30), after (30)(a). Pattern (30)(d) has one more 1-line for X than (30)(a) has, but it also has one more 1-line for O. For the reason suggested earlier, (24) assumes that 1-lines for O are worse for X than 1-lines for X are good for X.

In (28)(b), we can place an O in either a corner or a side, so the patterns that can result from O's moves in (28)(b) are the ones that (32) shows, along with six other patterns that are symmetrically equivalent to those.

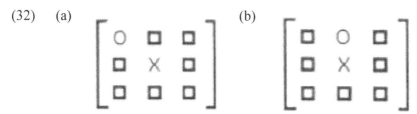

(32)   (a)   (b)

The respective values of these patterns are shown in (33).

(33)   (a)   -1   (b)   1

Each of these patterns contains three 1-lines for X, but (32)(a) contains two 1-lines for O, whereas (32)(b) contains only one, so the former is worse for X than the latter is. In (28)(c), we can place an O in an adjacent corner, a near side, a far corner, the center, or the opposite side, so the patterns that can result from O's moves in (28)(c) are those that (34) shows, along with three symmetrically equivalent patterns.

(34)

(a)   (b)   (c)

(d)   (e)

Their respective values are shown in (35).

(35)   (a)   -3   (b)   -2   (c)   -4   (d)   -5   (e)   -1

Patterns (34)(a), (d), and (e) each contain one 1-line for X, but (a) contains two 1-lines for O, (d) contains three, and (e) contains only one. The other patterns in (34) each contain two 1-lines for X, but (b) contains two 1-lines for O and (c) contains three so, of the patterns in

(34), (e) turns out to be the best pattern for X, and (d) turns out to be the worst.[73,74]

Of all the patterns in (30), (32), and (34), the best for X is (32)(b), and the worst for X is (34)(d). However, we still need to do further analysis to determine what X should do. X cannot access (32)(b), since O can block it by simply moving instead to (32)(a), and (34)(d) might still be avoidable despite O's interest in making that move.

- If X moves to (28)(a), then we can expect O to respond with (30)(c), since that is worst for X of all the options in (30), so the best result that X can reasonably expect to get from a move to (28)(a) is a pattern with the value (31)(c), namely, -4.

- If X moves to (28)(b), then we can expect O to respond with (32)(a), since that is worse for X than the other option in (32), so the best result that X can reasonably expect to get from a move to (28)(b) is a pattern with the value (33)(a), namely, -1.

- If X moves to (28)(c), then we can expect O to respond with (34)(d), since that is worst for X of all the options in (34), so the best result that X can reasonably expect to get from a move to (28)(c) is a pattern with the value (35)(d), namely, -5.

In other words, X must choose the best value not from the choices in (29), but from the choices in (36), because, even though these values are substantially worse for X than the values in (29), they are the best that we can expect O to allow X to choose from, since O wants X to lose.

(36)	(a)	-4	(b)	-1	(c)	-5
	[from (31)(c)		[from (33)(a)		[from (35)(d))	
	for (30)(c)		for (32)(a)		(for (34)(d))	
	in response to		in response to		in response to	

---

[73] *Suggested excursion:* Draw the symmetrically equivalent patterns for (30), (32), and (34) and figure out which of the shown patterns each of them is symmetrically equivalent to. *(Hint:* What happens when each of the patterns in (30) is folded over its left diagonal? What similar sort of thing has to be done to each of the patterns in (32) and (34) to reveal symmetric equivalence?)

[74] *Suggested excursion:* Verify the pattern values given in (32) through (35). *(Hint:* Just plug the number of 1-lines in each pattern for X and for 0 into the appropriate parameters in (24).)

(28)(a)]   (28)(b)]   (28)(c)]

Of the values in (36)—the only values that are accessible to *X*, after *O* has gotten in the way—(36)(b) is the largest and therefore represents the best move for *X* so, as its first move, *X* will choose (28)(b), the move that (36)(b) represents. This prevents *O* from being able to respond in any way that would yield a pattern that has a lesser value, such as (34)(d). In other words, the computer's first move is to put an *X* in the middle slot of the pattern, a result that should satisfy the gut intuitions of any experienced tic-tac-toe player. The decision tree in Figure 52 summarizes the process that led to this result.

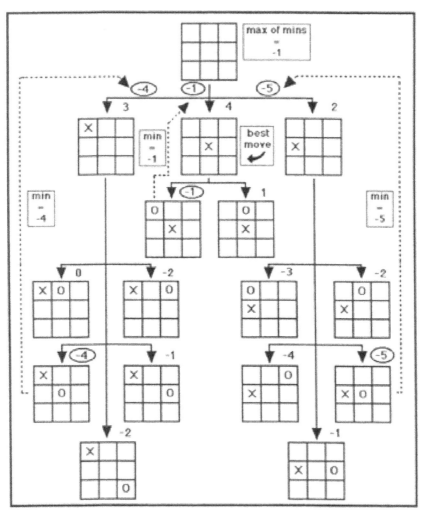

Fig. 52: Decision Tree for X's First Move in Tic-Tac-Toe

Once X has moved to (28)(b), we allow O to move, and the process begins again, repeating until a win or a stalemate occurs.[75] At each step of the game, we determine the worst of O's potential responses to each of X's potential moves, and we make the best of these worst responses the basis of X's actual move. Computer scientists call this process the *minimax strategy*, because the maximum value is chosen from a set of minimum values. The actual moves that O makes during the game may or may not be the ones that (24) predicts, even though we are using (24) to evaluate O's *potential* moves in figuring out what X should do. The reasoning behind the minimax strategy makes sense only if O is actually playing according to the evaluation function that X is using. However, since X has no access to O's mind, we have no choice—unless contrary evidence becomes available—but to assume that this is the case. In general, with no specific knowledge of the opponent, the best we can do is to develop, through reasoning and experimentation, the best evaluation function we can for the game and for the computer and then to assume that the opponent is as rational as we are. If some knowledge of a particular opponent's playing history, style, or strategic preferences is available, then we can use this knowledge to fine-tune an evaluation function specifically for that opponent's responses, just as human chess masters study their opponents' game-playing histories before embarking on major tournaments.

What about the enormous amount of computation that went into figuring out that (28)(b) is X's best first move? Do humans play this way? On a conscious level, they obviously do not; in fact, to play a game consciously in the way described here can be intolerably tedious for a human and can take an enormous amount of time, even though computers, ironically, can play much more rapidly and often better than humans by using precisely these methods. Humans play games primarily "by feel". Explicit step-by-step computation tends to get in the way and slow things down. However, just what is "feel", and how does it work? The sort of computation that we described on this expedition might very

---

[75] *Suggested excursion:* Do this. In other words, have someone place an O in response to X's first move, and then apply the same sort of reasoning to the resulting pattern to determine X's best next move. Redo this as many times as necessary to finish a complete game. *(Hint:* Be careful to check the symmetries at each step. They may change from move to move.)

well be what underlies what humans refer to as "feel" on a non-conscious neuronal level within the player's brain.[76]

---

[76] *Suggested excursion (difficult):* Having now seen several examples of heuristics for playing games, figure out some heuristics for getting a computer to be able to play Mastermind, and work through some sample games. *(Hint:* Formalize the three strategies we discussed in the text as evaluation functions, and then use them to evaluate moves that you generate in decision trees.)

5. Reasoning: Logic and Inference

I begin by telling the students that I will be playing Devil's advocate. I will try to prove something to them that they will not want to believe. Specifically, I will prove that all numbers are equal and, in particular, that the numbers one and zero are equal. They should try to find flaws in my argument until—if ever—I convince them I am right.

As usual, we begin with the number *1*. You can call something by any name you want, as long as you do not confuse it with something else, so we will give *1* the name *a*, as (1) states.

(1) $a = 1$

Since the two sides of (1) are equal, multiplying each side by *a* will give equal results. This is stated in (2), where "*" is used to indicate multiplication.

(2) $a * a = 1 * a$

Since *a * a* is the square of *a*, usually written as a^2, and since anything multiplied by *1* is itself, we can rewrite (2) as (3).

(3) $a^2 = a$

The two sides of (3) are equal, so the results we obtain by subtracting *1* from both sides of (3) will also be equal, as (4) states.

(4) $a^2 - 1 = a - 1$

Now, from algebra we know that (5) is a universal law of numbers.

(5) $x^2 - y^2 = (x + y) * (x - y)$

This law is often referred to as a *factoring rule*, because it states how a number described in general terms can be broken into *factors* that multiply to produce that number, much like the factorizations of particular numbers that we saw on Expedition 1. Rule (5) is true for any numbers at all. For example, if we take *x* to be *10* and *y* to be *5*, the left side of (5) and its right side both evaluate to *75*, as (6) shows.

(6)   (a) $10^2 - 5^2 = 100 - 25 = 75$

      (b) $(10 + 5) * (10 - 5) = 15 * 5 = 75$

Since (5) is true of all numbers, not just *10* and *5*, it is true, in particular, when we take *x* to be *a* and *y* to be *1*, as (7) states.

(7) $a^2 - 1^2 = (a + 1) * (a - 1)$

The square of *1* is *1*, so the left side of (4) equals the left side of (7); therefore, the right side of (7) equals the right side of (4), as stated, respectively, in (8), (9), and (10).

(8) $1^2 = 1$

(9) $a^2 - 1 = a^2 - 1^2$

(10) $(a + 1) * (a - 1) = a - 1$

Since the left and right sides of (10) are equal, the results of dividing each of them by the same quantity, *a - 1*, are equal, as (11) shows.

(11) $\dfrac{(a+1) * (a-1)}{a-1} = \dfrac{a-1}{a-1}$

The result of dividing *a - 1* by itself is *1*, as (12) states, so (11) becomes (13), when we perform that division.

(12) $\dfrac{a-1}{a-1} = 1$

(13) $(a + 1) * 1 = 1$

Then (13) becomes (14), because multiplying any number by *1* leaves that same number as the result.

(14) $a + 1 = 1$

Since the left and right sides of (14) are equal, we can subtract *1* from both sides, leaving *a* on the left and *0* on the right, as (15) states.

(15) $a = 0$

However, the letter "*a*" is just an alternate name that we decided to use for *1*, when we began this calculation, so we can replace *a* with *1* in (15), leaving (16) as the next result.

(16) $1 = 0$

If we add *1* to both sides of (16) and then repeat that addition again and again, we get the sequence of equations in (17).

(17) $1 = 0$

$2 = 1$

$3 = 2$

$4 = 3$

$5 = 4$

$6 = 5$

$7 = 6$

. . .

We have thereby shown that all numbers are equal, just as I promised at the beginning. Figure 53 summarizes the steps of the argument, along with some further points yet to be mentioned.

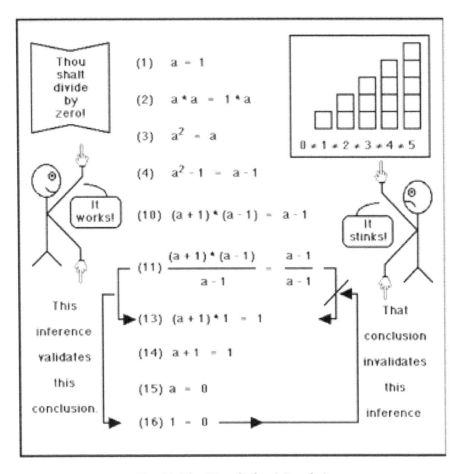

Fig. 53: The "Proof" that 1 Equals 0

At this point, most of the students are stunned but, inevitably, a few hands shoot up, accompanied by an eager chorus of "You can't divide by zero!" Indeed, since *a* and *1* are equal, the division step from (11) to (13) involves a division by zero, namely, *a - 1*, without which the argument would not go through. These students are sure they have me over a barrel, because somewhere along the way, someone has told them that division by *0* is "undefined". However, all fall silent, when I ask the obvious questions: *Why* is division by *0* undefined? Why don't we define it? If we just go ahead and define it, it won't be undefined.

The simple answer is that division by zero is not defined because, as we just saw, defining it leads to an absurd result, namely, that all numbers are equal. Since the result is absurd, there must be something wrong with the reasoning that led to it. All the other steps in the argument are valid, so it must be the division by zero that causes the problem. But is it really so clear that that result is absurd? Can a case, perhaps, be made, on grounds other than division by zero, to the effect that all numbers are equal? After all, as we saw on Expeditions 1 and 2, we can begin a recursion with either *1* or *0*. Might there be some good reason to think that *1* and *0* really are the same?

Many political or religious movements that have come and gone over the centuries have advocated the unity of mankind and the desirability of eliminating all national boundaries. What would the world be like if such a goal were ever to be achieved, and how would we describe it? In particular, how many countries would there be? On the one hand, since there would be no national boundaries separating one country from another, there would be no countries at all, just one "uncountried" planet. On the other hand, precisely for that reason, the entire planet could be considered one country, with no boundaries separating that country from any other. In other words, both (18)(a) and (18)(b) could reasonably be claimed to be true, if such a state of the world were ever to be achieved.

(18)　(a)　There is exactly one country on this planet.

　　　(b)　There are no countries on this planet.

Such a world would have both *1* and *0* countries at the same time, just as (16) suggests, so (16) turns out to be not so absurd after all. In fact, (17), which follows from (16), looks very much like recursion. What's so bad about that?[77]

There is value in pursuing this line a bit. What if you were to meet an adherent of a cult who insists that division by zero is possible because his leader says so? This is not far-fetched. Stranger things have happened. Pointing out that (16) is a consequence of the leader's claim would not suffice to refute the claim, but would simply identify a further belief that the adherent would be required–by logic–to hold. "That's just the way it goes," he might say. Since he is required to believe that division by zero is valid (because his leader says so), he also has to believe that all numbers are equal (because (16) follows

---

[77] *Suggested excursion:* Formulate a plausible response to this question. (*Hint:* The word *country* is being used in two different ways, that is, with two different meanings, in (18)(a) and (18)(b).)

logically from what his leader says). You could reply that a number system in which all numbers are equal is useless for doing anything practical, but that would be irrelevant, because *his* goal is to maintain his devotion to his leader, not to do anything that might be otherwise useful. *Your* desire to have a *useful* mathematics requires you to reject the conclusion (16), so the argument in Figure 53 forces you to reject the step from (11) to (13). However, since the cultist's need to obey his leader's edicts requires him to accept the step from (11) to (13), the same argument forces him to accept the conclusion (16). Since your goals are different, you draw different conclusions from the same piece of reasoning.

Examining a more substantial reason for the standard decision to leave division by zero "undefined" strengthens this point. Put zero aside for the moment, and consider what we mean by division in general. Saying that a number z is the result of dividing a number x by a number y is just an alternate way of saying that x is the result of multiplying y and z. We already know what that means from (28) of Expedition 1. In other words, (19) is just another way of expressing (20).

(19)
$$z = \frac{x}{y}$$

(20) $y * z = x$

Now consider what happens to (19) and (20), when we take y to be *0*, that is, if we divide some number x by *0*. If y is equal to *0*, then (19) becomes (21), which says simply that z is the result of dividing x by *0*.

(21)
$$z = \frac{x}{0}$$

As the cult adherent might well point out, this looks perfectly normal. However, at the same time, (20) becomes (22), which is—to say the least—a little peculiar.

(22) $0 * z = x$

What (22) says is that x is the result of multiplying *0* by z. This means that x has to be *0*, no matter what z is, because *0* times anything is *0*. In other words, the only number x that could ever possibly be divided by *0* is *0* itself: for x to be divided by *0*—as in (21)—is for (22) to be true, but (22) can be true only if x is *0*. So dividing a non-zero number by *0* is not just "undefined", but *impossible*, if we want to keep what we are doing consistent with the usual meanings of the words that we use—that is, that (20) is equivalent to (19).

Now, what about *0* itself? When *x* is *0*, (22) becomes (23).

(23) $0 * z = 0$

What values of *z* will make (23) true? As we just observed, *0* times anything is *0*, so (23) is true no matter what number *z* is. Any number will work for *z* in (23), so *z* is no particular number at all, and *0/0* cannot be said to have any particular value. In other words, relative to division by *0*, all numbers really are the same. No number will work for *z* in (21) if *x* is not *0*, and any number will work if *x* is *0*, so even (17) turns out to be not so absurd, after all.

For example, since (23) is true when *z* is *2*, we can take the equivalence of (19) and (20) as justifying the claim that (24) is true.

(24) $2 = \dfrac{0}{0}$

However, since (23) is just as true when *z* is *3*, we can also take the equivalence of (19) and (20) as justifying the claim that (25) is true at the same time.

(25) $3 = \dfrac{0}{0}$

From (24) and (25), it would *seem* to follow that (26) is true, since each of *2* and *3* is equal to the same thing, *0/0*, and similarly for the rest of (17).

(26) $2 = 3$

By this point, the cultist is throwing confetti. He can smugly claim to have been fully vindicated, and his faith in his leader remains unshaken.

This result illustrates a basic concept that logicians call *logical equivalence*. If we start with the assumption that division by zero is possible, then we can deduce that all numbers are the same. If we start with a willingness to treat all numbers as being the same, then we can deduce that division by zero is possible. The two concepts, *division by zero* and *the equality of all numbers*, are logically equivalent because each can be derived from the other through logically valid steps. If we accept either one, then we have to accept the other as well. If we reject either one, then we must also reject the other one.

More generally, this illustrates the basic fact that logic deals with relations between statements or concepts and not with what is factually true in the world. Logic can help us to understand the world, but only if we apply it to facts, and we always do that in relation to our goals. If our goal is to have a mathematics that is useful for doing calculations in science, business, or everyday life, then we had better not treat all numbers as being equal, so we must reject division by zero as a consequence, regardless of what some cult leader might say about it. However, if our goal is to defend a cultist dogma that insists that division by zero is possible, then we must be willing to accept a mathematics in which all numbers are considered equal, as well as the consequence that our cars will not move, our planes will not fly, and our bridges will collapse—if we ever manage to build them at all. Logic alone cannot tell us which goal we should choose, but only what consequences will follow from each available choice.

We can make reasoning of the sort illustrated in Figure 53 sufficiently precise for a computer to carry out by using a kind of formal logic called *predicate calculus*. This logic serves as the basis of many *expert systems*, computer programs that can deduce new knowledge from collections of facts known as *knowledge-bases*. Predicate calculus expresses the relations that hold among functions of two kinds—predicates and connectives—in terms of the boolean truth values *true* (*t*) and *false* (*f*), which we introduced at the end of Expedition 1.

A *predicate* is a function that tests whether or not some object has some property, characteristic, or attribute by generating one of the booleans based on some condition. For example, the functions (27)(a) and (27)(b) from Figure 15 are predicates that test whether a list is empty and whether a number is zero, respectively.

(27)   (a)   [=( )?]
               (is empty)
        (b)   [=0?]
               (equals 0)

The "*?*" in these predicates is simply a notational reminder that the predicates are testing for the presence or absence of the indicated property and, in that sense, are asking a question. Applying a predicate to a specific object expresses a *proposition*, a declarative statement that has *t* or *f* as a truth-value. For example, (28)(a) shows the application of the predicate (27)(b) to the number *0* to express the statement that *0* is equal to zero, which is true, while (28)(b) shows the application of (27)(b) to the number *3* to express the statement that *3* is equal to zero, which—protestations from the cult adherent not withstanding—is false.[78]

(28) (a)   [=0?](0)

(0 equals zero.)

(b)   [=0?](3)

(3 equals zero.)

In Figure 15, (27)(a) is applied to the list parameter *lst$_l$* to get the value of a boolean parameter that expresses the truth value of the proposition (29)(a), while (27)(b) is applied to the number parameter *num$_l$* to get the value of a boolean parameter that expresses the truth value of the statement (29)(b).

(29) (a)   [=( )?](lst$_1$)

(The indicated list is empty.)

(b)   [=0?](num$_1$)

(The indicated number equals 0.)

We can thus view a predicate as a device for distinguishing objects that have the property it expresses from those that do not have that property.

A *connective* is a function that has the effect of combining simpler propositions into more complex propositions by generating booleans from other booleans. The truth-values of the more complex propositions depend entirely on those of their component propositions. We defined the basic operations on booleans in (71) of Expedition 2, using prefix notation. The *truth tables* in Figure 54 summarize these operations using infix notation, with "+" overloaded to mean *or*, "*" overloaded to mean *and*, and "~" used to mean *not*.[79] The components

---

[78] *Suggested excursion:* Form some example propositions from (27)(a) and determine their truth-values. (*Hint:* Think of some example lists and apply (27)(a) to them.)

[79] *Suggested excursion:* Figure out why we overload " +" as *or* and "*" as *and*, rather than the other way around. (*Hint:* If there are *m* ways to do task *A* and *n* ways to do a different task *B*, then there are *m* + *n* ways to do either *A* or *B*, and there are *m* * *n* ways to do both *A* and *B* in succession.)

of a conjunction (*and*) are called its *conjuncts*, and the components of a disjunction (*or*) are called its *disjuncts*.

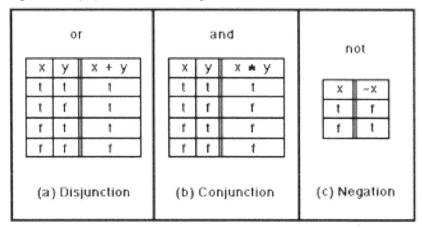

Fig. 54: Basic Operations of Boolean Algebra

In Figure 15, for example, the function *or* generates a value for a boolean parameter based on whether a particular list is empty or a particular number is zero. In effect, *or* combines the statements (29)(a) and (29)(b) to form the statement (30)(a), whose truth-value is entirely determined by those of its two disjuncts.

(30) (a) $[=(\ )?](lst_1) + [=0?](num_1)$

(Either the list is empty or the number is zero (or both).)

(b) $[=(\ )?](lst_1) * [=0?](num_1)$

(The list is empty and the number is zero.)

(c) $\sim [=(\ )?](lst_1)$

(The list is not empty.)

Statement (30)(a) is false only if both (29)(a) and (29)(b) are false, as Figure 54(a) says. Similarly, (30)(b) is true only if both (29)(a) and (29)(b) are true, as Figure 54(b) says. Statement (30)(c) is true only if (29)(a) is false, as Figure 54(c) says.

Logicians refer to the portion of predicate calculus that expresses the behavior of connectives as *propositional calculus*, because it deals with the relations between whole propositions, regardless of what predicates they are formed from. Mathematicians tend to call it *boolean algebra*, because it expresses the universal laws of booleans, just as ordinary algebra expresses the universal laws of numbers, as we saw on

Expedition 1. Different authors use different symbols for the boolean operations, but, as we saw on earlier expeditions, overloading "+" and "*" is useful for making comparisons. For example, boolean algebra satisfies many of the same laws as number algebra, such as the *commutative* laws, stated in (31), and the *associative* laws, stated in (32).

(31) (a) $x + y = y + x$

(b) $x * y = y * x$

(32) (a) $x + (y + z) = (x + y) + z$

(b) $x * (y * z) = (x * y) * z$

The commutative laws state that the order in which we operate on items has no effect on the result; whether we combine x with y or y with x, the final result is always the same, with either + or *. The associative laws say that how we group the items we operate on has no effect on the result; whether we combine x with the result of combining y with z or whether we first combine x with y and then combine that result with z, the final result is again the same, with either + or *. The associative laws enable us to omit parentheses from expressions that contain only occurrences of + or only occurrences or *, so we can confidently apply these operations to more than two objects at a time.[80]

In terms of the functions in Figure 15, (31)(a) amounts to saying that (33)(a) and (33)(b) always have the same truth-value, and (31)(b) amounts to saying that (34)(a) and (34)(b) always have the same truth-value.

(33) (a) $[=( )?](lst_1) + [=0?](num_1)$

(The list is empty or the number is zero.)

(b) $[=0?](num_1) + [=( )?](lst_1)$

(The number is zero or the list is empty.)

(34) (a) $[=( )?](lst_1) * [=0?](num_1)$

(The list is empty and the number is zero.)

(b) $[=0?](num_1) * [=( )?](lst_1)$

(The number is zero and the list is empty.)

---

[80] *Suggested excursion:* Verify that these laws work for numbers. (*Hint:* Choose values for x, y, and z, and then see what happens when you plug those values in.)

These are reasonable claims for an example of this sort. For example, if x is f and y is t, then the left-hand side of (31)(b) evaluates as (35)(a), and its right-hand side evaluates as (35)(b), which Figure 54(b) tells us has the same result.

(35)   (a)   f * t = f

          (b)   t * f = f

Similarly, we can introduce new predicates for *is even* and *is positive*, in which case (32)(a) amounts to saying that (36)(a) and (36)(b) always have the same truth-value, and (32)(b) amounts to saying that (37)(a) and (37)(b) always have the same truth-value, again reasonable claims.

(36)   (a)   [=( )?](lst$_1$) + ([=0?](num$_1$) + [>0?](num$_1$))

          (Either the list is empty, or the number is zero or positive.)

          (b)   ([=( )?](lst$_1$) + [=0?](num$_1$)) + [>0?](num$_1$)

          (Either the list is empty or the number is zero, or else the number is positive.)

(37)   (a)   [=( )?](lst$_1$) * ([>0?](num$_1$) * [even?](num$_1$))

          (The list is empty and the number is positive and even.)

          (b)   ([=( )?](lst$_1$) * [>0?](num$_1$)) * [even?](num$_1$)

          (The list is empty and the number is positive, and furthermore the number is even.)

For example, if x is f, y is t, and z is t, then the left-hand side of (32)(a) evaluates as (38)(a), and its right-hand side evaluates as (38)(b), again the same result, this time according to Figure 54(a).[81]

(38)   (a)   f + (t + t) = f + (t) = f + t = t

          (b)   (f + t) + t = (t) + t = t + t = t

Since parentheses serve merely to group items, we can remove them when we find that they group a single item, as is the case with two of the occurrences of t in (38).

---

[81] *Suggested excursion:* Prove the commutative and associative laws for booleans. (*Hint:* Just try all possible combinations of t and f in the operation tables.)

However, in contrast to what we saw on Expedition 1 was the case for addition and multiplication, disjunction and conjunction satisfy *both* of the *distributive* laws that we discussed there. These laws are restated here as (39).[82]

(39)   (a) $x * (y + z) = (x * y) + (x * z)$

     (b) $x + (y * z) = (x + y) * (x + z)$

Law (39)(a) is the distributive law of * over +, a law that we saw works for multiplication and addition. In terms of conjunction and disjunction, (39)(a) says that (40)(a) and (b) always have the same truth-value, which is a true claim for conjunction and disjunction.

(40)   (a) $[=( )?](lst_1) * ([=0?](num_1) + [>0?](num_1))$

        (The list is empty, and the number is zero or positive.)

     (b) $([=( )?](lst_1) * [=0?](num_1)) + ([=( )?](lst_1) * [>0?](num_1))$

        (Either the list is empty and the number is zero, or the list is empty and the number is positive.)

Law (39)(b) is the distributive law of + over *, a law that we saw does *not* work for addition and multiplication. However, in terms of conjunction and disjunction, (39)(b) says that (41)(a) and (b) always have the same truth-value, which again *is* a true claim for disjunction and conjunction.

(41)   (a) $[=( )?](lst_1) + ([>0?](num_1) * [even?](num_1))$

        Either the list is empty, or the number is positive and even.)

     (b) $([=( )?](lst_1) + [>0?](num_1)) * ([=( )?](lst_1) + [even?](num_1))$

        (Either the list is empty or the number is positive, and either the list is empty or the number is even.)

For example, if x is f, y is t, and z is t, then the left-hand side of (39)(a) evaluates as (42)(a), and its right-hand side evaluates as (42)(b), the same result, according to Figures 54(a) and (b), while the

---

[82] *Suggested excursion:* In (6) and (9) of Expedition 1, two versions were given for each of these distributive laws. Explain why that is not really necessary. (*Hint:* What do the commutative laws say about the two versions?)

left-hand side of (39)(b) evaluates as (43)(a) and its right-hand side evaluates as (43)(b), again the same result.[83]

(42)   (a) $f * (t + t) = f * (t) = f * t = f$
           (b) $(f * t) + (f * t) = (f) + (f) = f + f = f$

(43)   (a) $f + (t * t) = f + (t) = f + t = t$
           (b) $(f + t) * (f + t) = (t) * (t) = t * t = t$

In fact, *t* and *f* comprise a distributive lattice, one whose elements are booleans, rather than numbers, in contrast to those that we discussed on Expedition 1.[84] Figure 55 shows this lattice's very simple Hasse diagram.

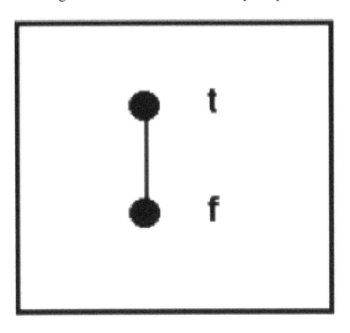

Fig. 55: The Hasse Diagram for the Boolean Distributive Lattice

We can use the basic boolean operations in Figure 54 to define further operations that are useful specifically for reasoning. In particular, there is the combination of *or* and *not* that we used in (21)

---

[83] *Suggested excursion:* Prove the distributive laws for booleans. (*Hint:* Just try all possible combinations of *t* and *f* in the operation tables.)

[84] *Suggested excursion:* Some books pretend that truth-values are numbers by using *0* for *f* and *1* for *t*. This might be fun for mathematicians, but is not a good idea for computer programming. Explain why. (*Hint:* Reread the last paragraph of Expedition 2.)

of Expedition 3 to bring about the effect of an *if...then* statement. In general, the statement *if x then y* can be written in the form (44), which expresses *if...then* through the infix operator ⊃.

(44)   x ⊃ y

This logical operation, called *material implication*, is defined in the table in Figure 56.

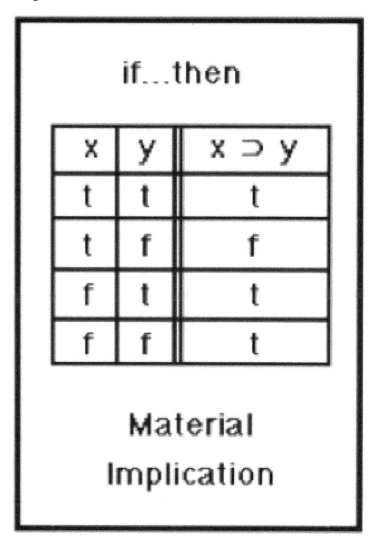

Fig. 56: A Further Boolean Operation

According to this definition, (44) is false only when x is true and y is false; otherwise (44) is true. For example, sentence (45) is false only when (29)(a) is true and (29)(b) is false.

(45) $[=(\ )?](lst_1) \supset [=0?](num_1)$

(If the list is empty, then the number is zero.)

If the list is empty and the number is zero, then (45) is true; if the list is empty and the number is not zero, then (45) is false; and if the list is not empty, then regardless of whether the number is zero or not, (45) is true.

Many students say they find this counterintuitive because they feel that the *consequent*, the statement after the $\supset$, should always have as much bearing on the truth-value of the entire statement as the *antecedent*, the part of the statement before the $\supset$, has on it. According to Figure 56, the consequent is irrelevant if the antecedent is false. I justify the definition to them by describing the following scenario. Suppose that you come to me near the end of the semester and tell me that you are worried about your grade. You failed the mid-term exam and got most of the homework exercises wrong. What if I respond to you with (46)?

(46)   If you ace the final exam, then you will pass the course.

Under what circumstances would you consider that I had lied to you, once the semester had ended? Figure 57 lists the possible results.

"If you ace the final exam, then you will pass the course."	
The student:	The professor:
aced the final and passed the course.	told the truth.
aced the final and failed the course.	LIED!!!!!
did not ace the final and passed the course.	is a nice guy.
did not ace the final and did not pass the course.	did what he said.

Fig. 57: An Example of Material Implication

If you aced the exam and then received a passing grade for the course, you would be pleased because you would consider that I had told you the truth; if you aced the exam and received a failing grade for the course, you would be angry, because you would consider that I had lied; if you failed to ace the exam, but still received a passing grade for the course, you would be surprised and figure that I was just a nice guy (or a wimp); and if you failed to ace the exam and got a failing grade for the course, you would shrug your shoulders and decide that this was just what you should have expected. In other words, the only case in which you would definitely consider me to have lied—that is, to have uttered (46) falsely—is exactly the one stated in Figure 56.

Now consider (47), which is what underlies the *if...then* effect of the disjunction of a negated statement with other statements in (21) of Expedition 3.

(47) $(\sim x) + y$

As Figure 58 shows, we can determine from Figures 54(a) and (c) what the truth-value of (47) is for the various choices of values for x and y.

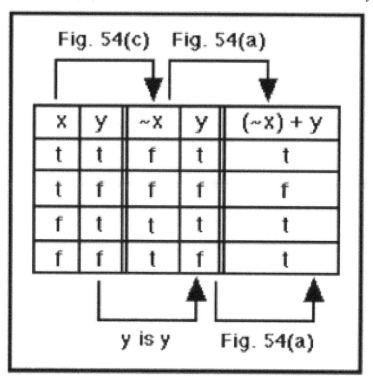

Fig. 58: The Truth Table of (47)

From the column of values for x we can get the column of values for $\sim x$ by using Figure 54(c). These values can then be combined with the column of values for y to get the column of values for $(\sim x) + y$ from Figure 54(a). If we compare that column to the column of values for

$x \supset y$ in Figure 56, we see that they are identical. Like (44), (47) is false only when x is true and y is false. In other words, the two statements are logically equivalent, in the sense that we discussed in connection with Figure 53: each statement always has the same truth-value as the other. In the case of Figure 53, we derived one statement from another through valid logical steps; in this case, we demonstrated the logical equivalence by looking directly at the statements' truth tables. Whichever of these routes we take, the result is the same. In circumstances in which either of the two statements is true, the other statement is also true, and in circumstances in which either is false, the other is also false. Rather than treating material implication as a separate operation, we can therefore consider it as being *defined* in terms of two of the three *basic* operations in Figure 54, as (48) states.

(48) $(x \supset y) = (\sim x) + y$

Figure 59 shows the very simple control structure for this definition, using *if...then* as the prefix notation for the name of the function that computes the truth-values of statements that contain $\supset$.[85,86,87]

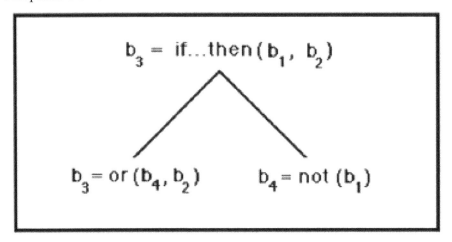

Fig. 59: Control Structure of Material Implication

---

[85] *Suggested excursion:* Draw the data dependency and data flow diagrams of material implication. (*Hint:* Review the latter part of Expedition 1.)

[86] *Suggested excursion:* Draw a more complete control structure tree for material implication in terms of the function *nor.* (*Hint:* Use your solution to excursion 25.)

[87] *Suggested excursion:* Reformulate (21) of Expedition 3 as an *if...then* statement in two ways, using the $\supset$ operation of Figure 56, and using the *if...then* function of Figure 59. (*Hint:* Use (48).)

We can also use boolean operations to formulate and prove *rules of inference* that justify the valid steps in arguments like the one in Figure 53. Consider the statement in (49) and its truth table in Figure 60.

(49) $(x * (x \supset y)) \supset y$

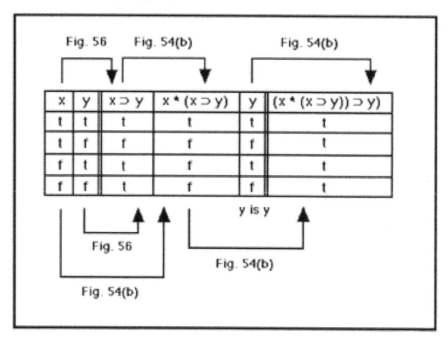

Fig. 60: The Truth Table of (49)

As the column for $(x * (x \supset y)) \supset y$ shows, this statement is never false, regardless of the values of x and y. Logicians call such a statement a *tautology*. The $x \supset y$ column contains f only on the second row, because the x column contains t and the y column contains f only on that row. The $x * (x \supset y)$ column contains t only on the first row because it is only on that row that both the x column and the $x \supset y$ column contain t. The f's in the second through fourth rows of the $x * (x \supset y)$ column yield t's in the corresponding rows of the $(x * (x \supset y)) \supset y$ column regardless of the values of the y column, for the reasons we discussed in connection with Figure 57. The t's in the first row of both the $x * (x \supset y)$ column and the y column yield t also in the first row of the $(x * (x \supset y)) \supset y$ column, so the latter column turns out to have t on every row. In other words, it never happens that (50)(a) is true and (50)(b) is false, the only case that could ever falsify (49).

(50)   (a) $x * (x \supset y)$

(b)   y

So it cannot be that (50)(a) is true without (50)(b) being true as well. Another way of saying that is to state the formal rule of inference (51) to the effect that we can validly infer (50)(b) whenever the two conjuncts of (50)(a) have already been established.

(51)   Premise 1:   x

Premise 2: $x \supset y$

∴ Conclusion: y

Given that the *premises* x and $x \supset y$ are true, the *conclusion* y is therefore also true—where ∴ is the traditional symbol for *therefore*. Medieval logicians, who wrote in Latin, named this rule *modus ponens*. Modern logicians still use that name, but they tend to prefer to call (51) *detachment*, since it gives us a way to "detach" y from $x \supset y$. Figure 61 gives some other valid boolean rules of inference.[88]

---

[88] *Suggested excursion:* Prove the rules of inference in Figure 61. (Hint: For each rule of the form (i), use truth tables to prove that the statement (ii) is a tautology.)

(i)   Premise 1

Premise 2

∴ Conclusion

(ii) $((\text{Premise 1}) * (\text{Premise 2})) \supset \text{Conclusion}$

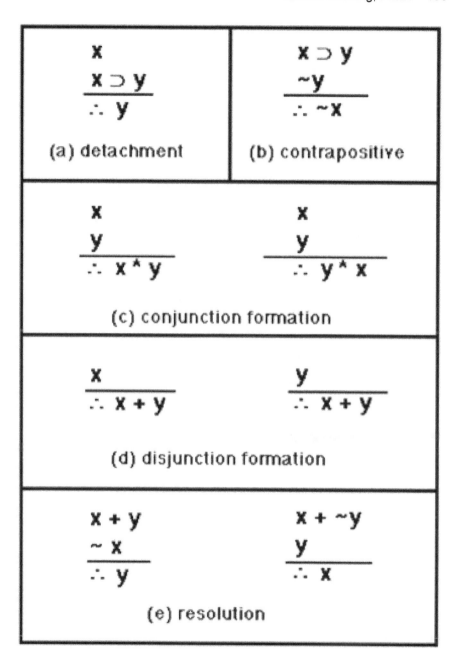

Fig. 61: Some Valid Boolean Rules of Inference

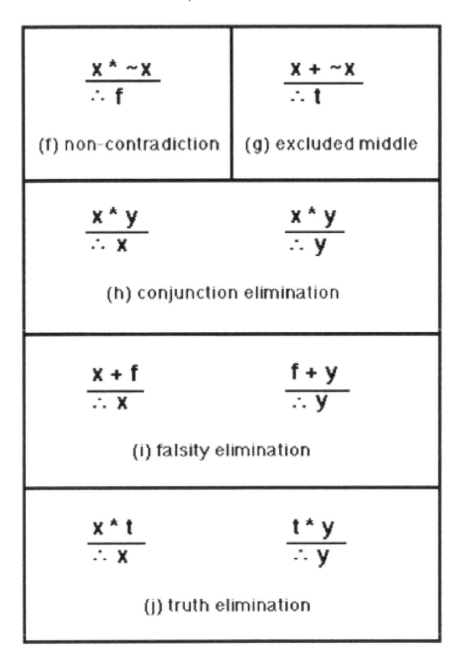

Fig. 61 (cont.): Some Valid Boolean Rules of Inference

We can also formulate rules of inference for predicates, but we cannot derive such rules from tautologies provable through truth tables, as we can for the rules for connectives.[89] In particular, there is the fact that universal laws for a kind of object apply to *every* object of that kind. This is the content of the rule of *universal instantiation*, given in (52), in which P is any predicate or boolean combination of predicates.

(52) Premise: P(general parameter of some type)
      ∴ Conclusion: P(specific object of the same type)

In other words, once we have shown that a *general* statement is true for *any* object at all of some data type, we can validly infer that the statement is true of some *particular* object of that type, no matter which object of that type it might be.

For example, we know that (53)(a) is true of any number at all, so (52) justifies our inferring from it the specific facts (53)(b) and (53)(c) about the respective particular numbers *0* and *7*.[90]

(53) (a)   [<0?](num) + [=0?](num) + [>0?](num)

            (A number, in general, is either less than zero, equal to zero, or greater than zero.)

      (b)   [<0?](0) + [=0?](0) + [>0?](0)

            (The particular number 0 is either less than zero, equal to zero, or greater than zero.)

      (c)   [<0?](7) + [=0?](7) + [>0?](7)

            (The particular number 7 is either less than zero, equal to zero, or greater than zero.)

According to Figure 54(a), together with the relevant associative law, (53)(b) is true because its middle disjunct is true, and (53)(c) is true because its right-most disjunct is true, so—just as (52) says—the inference from (53)(a) to each of these conclusions is, in fact, valid.[91]

---

[89] *Suggested excursion:* Explain why this is so. (*Hint:* Connectives are defined entirely in terms of truth tables. Predicates are not.)

[90] *Suggested excursion:* Is the left-most disjunct really necessary in (53)? (*Hint:* See excursion 31.)

[91] *Suggested excursion:* Figure 54(a) defines disjunction for pairs of propositions, but the statements (53)(b) and (53)(c) each contains three propositions as disjuncts. Why

As a further example, we can express the principle of mathematical induction—which we noted informally on Expedition 1 as the basis of recursion—more formally as a predicate-based rule of inference, namely, (54).

(54)	Premise 1:	P(1)
	Premise 2:	$P(num) \supset P(num + 1)$
	∴ Conclusion:	P(any particular number)

We can understand this rule as abbreviating an infinite sequence of repeated applications of (51) and (52), together with the associative law. If we know that both *Premise 1* and *Premise 2* of (54) are true for some predicate *P*, then (54) essentially summarizes the reasoning in (55).

(55)   1.   P(1)
             [Premise 1 of (54)]

       2. $P(1) \supset P(1 + 1)$
             [from Premise 2 of (54) and (52)]

       3.   P(1 + 1)
             [from 1., 2., and (51)]

       4. $P(1 + 1) \supset P(1 + 1 + 1)$
             [from Premise 2 of (54), (32)(a), and (52)]

       5.   P(1 + 1 + 1)
             [from 3., 4., and (51)]

       6.   6. $P(1 + 1 + 1) \supset P(1 + 1 + 1 + 1)$
             [from Premise 2 of (54), (32)(a), and (52)]

       7.   P(1 + 1 + 1 + 1)
             [from 5., 6., and (51)]

       8. $P(1 + 1 + 1 + 1) \supset P(1 + 1 + 1 + 1 + 1)$
             [from Premise 2 of (54), (32)(a), and (52)]

       9.   P(1 + 1 + 1 + 1 + 1)
             [from 7., 8., and (51)]

                •

                •

                •

---

is this okay? (*Hint:* What does the associative law say about the two ways of grouping three disjuncts?)

Since *1 + 1* is *2*, *2 + 1* is *3*, *3 + 1* is *4*, *4 + 1* is *5*, and so on, statements 1., 3., 5., 7., 9., and so on, become the statements in (56), which attribute *P* to all of the numbers in Figure 4.

(56)   P(1)

P(2)

P(3)

P(4)

P(5)

•

•

•

In other words, once we have established that a particular predicate produces a true statement when applied to the particular number *1,* and also that the predicate produces a true statement when applied to the successor of any number for which the predicate produces a true statement, we can validly infer that the predicate produces a true statement when applied to any number at all. This rule just makes more precise the informal notion of eventually reaching every number by starting at *1* and climbing one step at a time up the lattice in Figure 4. Number theorists use it extensively to prove theorems expressing interesting and useful general truths about all numbers.

With (51), (52), and the rules in Figure 61, we can now make sense of the reasoning in Figure 53 in a form that a computer can process—from either the cultist's or the scientist's point of view. Analysis of this reasoning requires extensive use of laws involving $=$. To make the analysis as clear as possible, we will formulate these laws in terms of the infix notation (57)(a), rather than the equivalent—but less familiar—prefix notation (57)(b).

(57)   (a) $x = y$ (x is in the equals relation to y.)

       (b) $[=?](x, y)$ (The equals relation holds for x and y.)

For example, the step from (15) to (16) is based on the law (58), which says that two numbers that are each equal to a third number are equal to each other.

(58) $((x = y) * (x = z)) \supset (z = y)$

This is not only a law of numbers, but is part of the *meaning* of = for any kind of object at all, as one version of the *transitive law*. The equivalent of (58), using prefix notation for =, is shown in (59).

(59) $([=?](x,y) * [=?](x,z)) \supset [=?](z,y)$

Since = is a predicate with two parameters, we can instantiate it for specific objects by applying (52) twice. In general, we can instantiate a law for specific objects by applying (52) as many times as there are parameters in the law—for example, three times in the case of (59).

Formally, the argument from (15) to (16) works as (60) shows.

(60)   The reasoning from (15) to (16):

    1. $a = 0$
        [from (15)]

    2. $a = 1$
        [from (1)]

    3. $(a = 0) * (a = 1)$
        [from 1., 2., and Fig. 61(c)]

    4. $((a = 0) * (a = 1)) \supset (1 = 0)$
        [from (58) and (52), with $x = a$, $y = 0$, and $z = 1$]

    5. $1 = 0$
        [from 3., 4., and (51)]

Clearly, this is a valid argument: statement 3. follows from statements 1. and 2. by conjunction formation, statement 4. follows from the universal law (58) by universal instantiation, and statement 5. follows from statements 3. and 4. by detachment. If statement 5. seems strange, then we must therefore attribute its strangeness to whatever the source of statements 1. and 2. might have been. Since statement 2. was simply a stipulation (in (1)) of what we were choosing to mean by *a*, the problem—if there is one, as the cult adherent will remind us—can only be in whatever was the source of statement 1., that is, in whatever it was that led to (15).

The step from (13) to (14) is also based on (58), together with the further law (61), which says that multiplying any number by *1* results in the same number.

(61) $x * 1 = x$

This is part of the definition of multiplication, as (28) of Expedition 1 states.[92] Formally, the argument from (13) to (14) works as (62) shows.

(62) The reasoning from (13) to (14):

1. $(a + 1) * 1 = 1$

[from (13)]

2. $(a + 1) * 1 = a + 1$

[from (61) and (52), with $x = a + 1$]

3. $((a + 1) * 1 = 1) * ((a + 1) * 1 = a + 1)$

[from 1., 2., and Fig. 61(c)]

4. $(((a + 1) * 1 = 1) * ((a + 1) * 1 = a + 1)) \supset (a + 1 = 1)$

[from (58) and (52), with $x = (a + 1) * 1$, $y = 1$, and $z = a + 1$]

5. $a + 1 = 1$

[from 3., 4., and (51)]

Be careful not to get confused by the overloading here. The left- and right-most instances of "*" in statement 3. express multiplication on numbers—namely, $a + 1$ and 1—while the middle instance expresses conjunction on booleans—namely, the truth-values of statements 1. and 2.

As (63) shows, (60) and (62) have identical *deductive structures*, even though they have very different contents.

(63) The deductive structure of (60) and (62):

1.   Premise 1

[from some source]

2.   Premise 2

[from some source]

3.   Premise 1 * Premise 2

[from 1., 2., and Fig. 61(c)]

4.   (Premise 1 * Premise 2) $\supset$ Conclusion

[from (58) and (52)]

---

[92] *Suggested excursion:* This statement is not quite correct in relation to the present argument. Explain why and figure out how to fix it. (*Hint:* See excursion 7.)

5.   Conclusion

[from 3., 4., and (51)]

We can see from the justifications under the statements, that the reasoning in (62) is identical to that of (60), except for the sources of the first two statements. In each case, the first two statements are conjoined, and their conjunction is then used as the antecedent of a material implication, thereby enabling the consequent of that implication to be detached as a conclusion in its own right. In both cases, the respective material implications are instances of the law (58).

Studying a deductive structure such as (63) is a good way to develop a sense of how to go about constructing a formal argument. Clues can be obtained by reading the deductive structure in reverse. First, decide what conclusion you would like to try to prove. Then examine the available laws or previously inferred statements to see whether there are any that are material implications with consequents that match the conclusion you want. This would enable (51) to apply. If there is such a law or inferred statement, then examine its antecedent to see how that can be obtained via any of the laws in Figure 61 and, perhaps, (52). In (63), for example, the conclusion matches the consequent of a material implication that has a conjunction as its antecedent, so the two conjuncts must first be established individually and then conjoined by Figure 61(c). There is nothing circular about proceeding in reverse or deciding in advance what you want to try to prove, as long as you do this simply as a matter of strategy in looking for a possible proof. There may turn out to be no statements that lead to the conclusions you want, in which case there will be no proof, and you will not be entitled to infer those conclusions.

The step from (2) to (3) is based not on (58), but on the related law (64) instead.

(64) $((y = x) * (x = z)) \supset (y = z)$

This law says that one number that is equal to a second number that is equal to a third number is itself equal to the third number. This is another variant of the transitive law; it is logically equivalent to (58), but more convenient for what we are now looking at.[93] This step does use (61) again, together with the commutative law (31)(b) and (65), which says that the square of a number is the result of multiplying the number by itself.

(65) $x^2 = x * x$

Since (65) just provides an alternate way of writing $x * x$, it is really a definition—just as (1) is—but it functions in arguments in the same way as any other premise does.

Formally, the argument from (2) to (3) works as (66) shows.

(66)   The reasoning from (2) to (3):

   1. $a * a = 1 * a$
         [from (2)]

   2. $a^2 = a * a$
         [from (65) and (52), with $x = a$]

   3. $(a^2 = a * a) * (a * a = 1 * a)$
         [from 1., 2., and Fig. 61(c)]

   4. $((a^2 = a * a) * (a * a = 1 * a)) \supset (a^2 = 1 * a)$
         [from (64) and (52), with $x = a * a$, $y = a^2$, and $z = 1 * a$]

   5. $a^2 = 1 * a$
         [from 3., 4., and (51)]

   6. $a * 1 = a$
         [from (61) and (52), with $x = a$]

   7. $1 * a = a * 1$
         [from (31)(b) and (52), with $x = 1$ and $y = a$]

   8. $(1 * a = a * 1) * (a * 1 = a)$
         [from 6., 7., and Fig. 61(c)]

   9. $((1 * a = a * 1) * (a * 1 = a)) \supset (1 * a = a)$
         [from (64) and (52), with $x = a * 1$, $y = 1 * a$, and $z = a$]

   10. $1 * a = a$

---

[93] *Suggested excursion:* Justify the claim that (58) and (64) are logically equivalent. (*Hint:* What can you say about the relation between $x = y$ and $y = x$ and between $y = z$ and $z = y$?)

[from 8., 9., and (51)]

11. $(a^2 = 1 * a) * (1 * a = a)$

[from 5., 10., and Fig. 61(c)]

12. $((a^2 = 1 * a) * (1 * a = a)) \supset (a^2 = a)$

[from (64) and (52), with $x = 1 * a$, $y = a^2$, and $z = a$]

13. $a^2 = a$

[from 11., 12., and (51)]

This argument is longer than (60) or (62), because it requires three uses of detachment, rather than just one. The third of these uses—comprising statement 5. and statements 10. through 13.—is identical in structure to (63), except for the fact that (64) rather than (58) is used as the justification for the material implication in the fourth statement. Each of the first two uses—comprising statements 1. through 5. and statements 6. through 10—also differs from (63) in having (67)(a), rather than (67)(b), as its respective third statement and as the antecedent of its respective fourth statement.[94]

(67)   (a)   Premise 2 * Premise 1

         (b)   Premise 1 * Premise 2

Each of the first two uses of detachment in (66) is self-contained and thus consists of five statements, just as (63) does. However, the argument as a whole contains only thirteen statements, rather than fifteen, because the third use of detachment overlaps with the first two uses by taking their conclusions as its premises, rather than getting its premises from an external source.

The step from (4) to (10) is based on both (58) and (64), together with the factoring law (5), the particular fact (8), and the law (68).[95]

(68) $(y = z) \supset (x - y = x - z)$

This law says that subtracting two equal numbers from the same number yields equal results, and it follows from the fact that subtraction is the *inverse* of addition, in the same sense in which (19)

---

[94] *Suggested excursion:* Write out this deductive structure explicitly. (*Hint:* Just interchange *Premise 1* and *Premise 2* in statements 3. and 4., and replace (58) in (63) with (64).)

[95] *Suggested excursion:* Prove (8). (*Hint:* Use (65) together with (28) of Expedition 1.)

and (20) state that division is the inverse of multiplication.[96] Strictly speaking, we should have a further conjunct in the antecedent of (68) to the effect that the equal numbers must be less than or equal to the number we are subtracting them from, unless we choose to allow negative numbers. However, we can omit this detail, because in this case that condition is satisfied anyway.[97]

Formally, the argument from (4) to (10) works as in (69).

(69)   The reasoning from (4) to (10):

1. $a^2 - 1 = a - 1$
     [from (4)]

2. $1^2 = 1$
     [from (8)]

3. $((1^2 = 1)) \supset (a^2 - 1^2 = a^2 - 1)$
     [from (68) and (52), with $x = a^2$, $y = 1^2$, and $z = 1$]

4. $a^2 - 1^2 = a^2 - 1$
     [from 2., 3., and (51)]

5. $(a^2 - 1^2 = a^2 - 1) * (a^2 - 1 = a - 1)$
     [from 1., 4., and Fig. 61(c)]

6. $((a^2 - 1^2 = a^2 - 1) * (a^2 - 1 = a - 1)) \supset (a^2 - 1^2 = a - 1)$
     [from (64) and (52), with $x = a^2 - 1$, $y - a^2 - 1^2$, and $z - a - 1$]

7. $a^2 - 1^2 = a - 1$
     [from 5., 6., and (51)]

8. $a^2 - 1^2 = (a + 1) * (a - 1)$
     [from (5) and (52), with $x = a$ and $y = 1$]

9. $(a^2 - 1^2 = a - 1) * (a^2 - 1^2 = (a + 1) * (a - 1))$
     [from 7., 8., and Fig. 61(c)]

10. $((a^2 - 1^2 = a - 1) * (a^2 - 1^2 = (a + 1) * (a - 1)))$
     $\supset ((a + 1) * (a - 1) = a - 1)$

---

[96] *Suggested excursion:* Prove that (68) follows from the fact that subtraction is the inverse of addition. (*Hint:* $x - y$ is the number that, when added to y, yields x. $x - z$ is the number that, when added to z, yields x.)

[97] *Suggested excursion:* Figure out where in the argument the condition would be relevant in this case. (*Hint:* Look at statement 3.)

[from (58) and (52), with $x = a^2 - 1^2$, $y = a - 1$, and $z = (a + 1) * (a - 1)$]

11. $(a + 1) * (a - 1) = a - 1$

[from 9., 10., and (51)]

Statements 7. through 11. comprise a sub-argument of (69) that has exactly the deductive structure (63). Statement 1. and statements 4. through 7. comprise a sub-argument that has as its deductive structure the variant of (63) that we discussed in connection with (67). Statements 2. through 4. comprise a sub-argument that has the different deductive structure (70).

(70)   The deductive structure of the first sub-argument of (69):

1.   Premise

[from some source]

2.   Premise $\supset$ Conclusion

[from (68) and (52)]

3.   Conclusion

[from 1., 2., and (51)]

Since there is only one premise here, there is no need for the conjunction rule and a simple detachment suffices for the inference.[98]

All of the other steps in the argument in Figure 53 depend on laws that say that doing the same thing to both sides of a true equation always results in a true equation. For example, the step from (1) to (2) is based on the law (71), which states that fact for multiplication.

(71) $(x = y) \supset ((x * z) = (y * z))$

Formally, the argument from (1) to (2) works as (72) shows.

(72)   The reasoning from (1) to (2):

1. $a = 1$

[from (1)]

2. $(a = 1) \supset ((a * a) = (1 * a))$

---

[98] *Suggested excursion:* Rework (69) and (70) to include the condition of excursion 97. (*Hint:* Use $((y = z) * ((y < x) + (y = x)))$ instead of $(y = z)$ as the antecedent of (63).)

[from (71) and (52), with $x = a$, $y = 1$, and $z = a$]

3. $a * a = 1 * a$

[from 1., 2., and (51)]

This is a straightforward application of detachment with the deductive structure (70), except that (71), rather than (68), serves as the justification for statement 2.

The step from (3) to (4) is based on the law (73), along with (64) and the *symmetric law* (74), which says that $=$ is reversible.

(73) $((x = y) * ((z < x) + (z = x))) \supset (x - z = y - z)$

(74) $(y = x) \supset (x = y)$

Again, note the overloading of "*" and "+" to mean *and* and *or*, respectively. What (73) says is that subtracting the same smaller or equal number from both sides of a true equation results in a true equation. As we noted earlier, in connection with (68), we can remove the restriction that z is less than or equal to x from (73), if we choose to permit negative numbers.

Formally, the argument from (3) to (4) works as in (75).

(75)   The reasoning from (3) to (4):

1. $a^2 = a$

[from (3)]

2. $a = 1$

[from (1)]

3. $(a^2 = a) * (a = 1)$

[from 1., 2., and Fig. 61(c)]

4. $((a^2 = a) * (a = 1)) \supset (a^2 = 1)$

[from (64) and (52), with $x = a$, $y = a^2$, and $z = 1$]

5. $a^2 = 1$

[from 3., 4., and (51)]

6. $(a^2 = 1) \supset (1 = a^2)$

[from (74) and (52), with $x = 1$ and $y = a^2$]

7. $1 = a^2$

[from 5., 6., and (51)]

8. $(1 < a^2) + (1 = a^2)$

[from 7. and Fig. 61(d)]

9.   9. $((a^2 = a) * ((1 < a^2) + (1 = a^2)))$

[from 1., 8., and Fig. 61(c)]

10. $((a^2 = a) * ((1 < a^2) + (1 = a^2))) \supset (a^2 - 1 = a - 1)$

[from (73) and (52), with $x = a^2$, $y = a$, and $z = 1$]

11. $a^2 - 1 = a - 1$

[from 9., 10., and (51)]

The role of statements 2. through 9. in (75) is solely to establish that the number we are subtracting is less than or equal to the number we are subtracting it from. If we remove that restriction from (73), then (75) reduces to the three statements 1., 10. (suitably modified), and 11., and thus has the deductive structure (70), with (73) as a justification instead of (68).[99] As it stands (75) contains three sub-arguments, one to get statement 5., one to get statement 7., and one that uses those two statements to get statement 11., which is the conclusion (4).[100]

With laws (64) and (74), together with the *reflexive law* (76), we can derive all of the essential properties of = for any sort of object.[101]

(76) $y = y$

More precisely, these three laws define a kind of predicate that expresses what mathematicians call an *equivalence relation*, of which = is the most basic and familiar instance. For example, *has the same remainder as, when divided by three*, is an equivalence relation for numbers and *has the same birthday as* is an equivalence relation for people.[102] Many students jump to

---

[99] *Suggested excursion:* Rework (75) without the condition that z is less than or equal to x. (*Hint:* Use $(x = y)$ instead of $((x = y) * ((z < x) + (z = x)))$ as the antecedent of (73).)

[100] *Suggested excursion:* Explicitly write out the sub-arguments of (75) and their deductive structures. (*Hint:* Look for where the detachments take place and the statements that lead up to them.)

[101] *Suggested excursion:* Prove (58) from (64) and (74). (*Hint:* What does (74) say about the relation between (58) and (64)? See excursion 93.)

[102] *Suggested excursion:* Prove that *has the same remainder as, when divided by three*, is an equivalence relation for numbers, and that *has the same birthday as* is an equivalence relation for people. (*Hint:* Form the respective analogues of (64), (74),

the conclusion that we do not really need (76) on the grounds that we can prove it (via (52)) from (64) and (74) by plugging y in for z in (64) to get an argument like the one in (77).

(77)   The purported reasoning from (64) and (74) to (76):

    1. $(y = x) \supset (x = y)$

        [from (74)]

    2. $((y = x) * (x = z)) \supset (y = z)$

        [from (64)]

    3. $((y = x) * (x = y)) \supset (y = y)$

        [from 2. and (52), with $z = y$]

    4. $y = y$

        [from 1., 3., and (51)]

However, this is incorrect. The desired detachment that purportedly results in statement 4. does not go through, because statement 1. contains $\supset$, rather than *, so it does not match the antecedent of statement 3., as (51) requires. In fact, for many predicates other than $=$, the analogue of each of (64), (74), and (76) can be true in situations where the analogues of the other two are not. Therefore, they are independent laws; all of them really are necessary to enable us to define predicates of the same kind as $=$.[103]

---

and (76) for each of these predicates. For example, the analogues for *has the same birthday as* are (i), (ii), and (iii).

(i)   ((y has the same birthday as x) * (x has the same birthday as z)) $\supset$ (y has the same birthday as z)

(ii)   (y has the same birthday as x) $\supset$ (x has the same birthday as y)

(iii)   y has the same birthday as y

Show that these statements are true.)

[103] *Suggested excursion (difficult):* Prove that (64), (74), and (76) are independent laws. (*Hint:* Consider the respective analogues, (i), (ii), and (iii), of these three laws, for predicates R other than $=$.

(i) $((y \, R \, x) * (x \, R \, z)) \supset (y \, R \, z)$

(ii) $(y \, R \, x) \supset (x \, R \, y)$

(iii) $y \, R \, y$

The step from (14) to (15) is also based on (73), together with (58), (64), (74), the law (78), and the fact (79).

(78) $(x + 1) - 1 = x$

(79) $1 - 1 = 0$

Law (78) says that the predecessor of the successor of a number is the number itself, in the sense in which we used the terms *predecessor* and *successor* on Expedition 1; in other words, moving one step up and then one step down in the lattice in Figure 4 leaves you back where you started. Since subtraction is the inverse of addition, (78) follows from the definition of addition in (18) of Expedition 1. The fact (79) also follows from the definition of addition, once we extend that definition to include 0.[104,105]

Formally, the argument from (14) to (15) works as (80) shows.

(80)   The reasoning from (14) to (15):

1. $a + 1 = 1$
        [from (14)]

2. $(a + 1 = 1) \supset (1 = a + 1)$
        [from (74) and (52), with $x = 1$ and $y = a + 1$]

3. $1 = a + 1$
        [from 1., 2., and (51)]

4. $(1 < a + 1) + (1 = a + 1)$
        [from 3. and Fig. 61(d)]

5. $(a + 1 = 1) * ((1 < a + 1) + (1 = a + 1))$
        [from 1., 4., and Fig. 61(c)]

6. $((a + 1 = 1) * ((1 < a + 1) + (1 = a + 1))) \supset ((a + 1) - 1 = 1 - 1)$
        [from (73) and (52), with $x = a + 1$, $y = 1$, and $z = 1$]

7. $(a + 1) - 1 = 1 - 1$

_____

Think of situations in which each of these analogues can be true, for some predicate *R*, without the others being true.)

[104] *Suggested excursion:* Prove (78). (*Hint:* See excursion 96.)
[105] *Suggested excursion:* Prove (79). (*Hint:* See excursions 7 and 96.)

[from 5., 6., and (51)]

8. $1 - 1 = 0$

[from (79)]

9. $((a + 1) - 1 = 1 - 1) * (1 - 1 = 0)$

[from 7., 8., and Fig. 61(c)]

10. $(((a + 1) - 1 = 1 - 1) * (1 - 1 = 0)) \supset ((a + 1) - 1 = 0)$

[from (64) and (52), with $x = 1 - 1$, $y = (a + 1) - 1$, and $z = 0$]

11. $(a + 1) - 1 = 0$

[from 9., 10., and (51)]

12   $(a + 1) - 1 = a$

[from (78) and (52), with $x = a$]

13   $((a + 1) - 1 = 0) * ((a + 1) - 1 = a)$

[from 11., 12., and Fig. 61(c)]

14   14. $(((a + 1) - 1 = 0) * ((a + 1) - 1 = a)) \supset (a = 0)$

[from (58) and (52), with $x = (a + 1) - 1$, $y = 0$, and $z = a$]

15   $a = 0$

[from 13., 14., and (51)]

The complexity of this argument stands in stark contrast to the simplicity of its content. A human looking at (80) immediately sees "short-cuts": *of course a + 1 = 1* can be reversed in statement 1. to get statement 3; *obviously 1 - 1* can be replaced by *0* in statement 7. to get statement 11. However, a computer does not have this bird's-eye view. When we try to make explicit just what it is that makes these facts obvious, so we can give that to a computer to use in its processing, we inevitably come up with some equivalent—in one form or another—of statements like 2. and 8. through 10.

As we noted in the last paragraph of Expedition 4, it is likely that people are doing something very much like this in their brains on some *non-conscious* level. Athletes, musicians, and other accomplished experts all know that they have really mastered a skill only when they can do it without consciously thinking about all the details. Even an act as simple as walking down the street would become an impossibility, if we needed to be aware of the movement of every one of our muscles at every moment. A species whose members need to be constantly aware of every step they take while walking—or of every step in an argument like (80)—would have a significant survival disadvantage in comparison to humans, who can do all of this automatically "behind the scenes." We become conscious only of the meaningful facts we need for whatever particular task is at hand.[106]

Somewhere in the reasoning from (10) to (13) is the lynchpin of the argument in Figure 53. The step from (10) to (11) is again based on a "do the same thing on both sides" law, namely, (81), which says that dividing both sides of a true equation by the same number results in a true equation.

(81)
$$(x = y) \supset (\frac{x}{z} = \frac{y}{z})$$

The step from (11) to (13) is based on the law (82), together with the two *cancellation laws* (83) and (84).

(82) $(x = y) \supset ((z * y) = (z * x))$

(83)
$$\frac{x}{x} = 1$$

(84)
$$\frac{x * y}{z} = x * \frac{y}{z}$$

Law (82) is logically equivalent to (71), because of the commutative and symmetric laws.[107] The first cancellation law (83) says that dividing any number by itself results in *1*; this follows directly from (19), (20), and (61)—as long as we do not have *0*.[108] The second cancellation law (84) says that dividing a number into a product is equivalent to dividing that number into one of its factors; this follows directly from (19) and (20), together with the commutative and associative laws.[109]

---

[106] *Suggested excursion:* Explicitly write out the sub-arguments of (80) and their deductive structures. (*Hint:* See excursion 100.)

[107] *Suggested excursion:* Prove (82). (*Hint:* What does the commutative law say about $x * z$ and $z * x$? What does the symmetric law say?)

[108] *Suggested excursion:* Prove the claim that (83) follows directly from (19), (20), and (61). (*Hint:* Let y be x in (19) and (20).)

[109] *Suggested excursion:* Prove the claim that (84) follows directly from (19) and (20), together with the commutative and associative laws. (*Hint:* First, $\frac{x * y}{z}$ is the

Formally, the argument from (10) to (11) works as (85) shows, and the argument from (11) to (13) works as (86) shows.

(85) The reasoning from (10) to (11):
1. $(a + 1) * (a - 1) = a - 1$
   [from (10)]

2. $$((a+1)*(a-1)=a-1) \supset (\frac{(a+1)*(a-1)}{a-1} = \frac{a-1}{a-1})$$
   [from (81) and (52), with $x = (a +1) * (a - 1)$, $y = a - 1$, and $z = a - 1$]

3. $$\frac{(a+1)*(a-1)}{a-1} = \frac{a-1}{a-1}$$
   [from 1., 2., and (51)]

(86) The reasoning from (11) to (13):
1. $$\frac{(a+1)*(a-1)}{a-1} = \frac{a-1}{a-1}$$
   [from (11)]

2. $$\frac{a-1}{a-1} = 1$$
   [from (83) and (52), with $x = a - 1$]

3. $$(\frac{(a+1)*(a-1)}{a-1} = \frac{a-1}{a-1}) * (\frac{a-1}{a-1} = 1)$$
   [from 1., 2., and Fig. 61(c)]

4. $$((\frac{(a+1)*(a-1)}{a-1} = \frac{a-1}{a-1}) * (\frac{a-1}{a-1} = 1)) \supset (\frac{(a+1)*(a-1)}{a-1} = 1)$$
   [from (64) and (52), with $x = \frac{a-1}{a-1}$, $y = \frac{(a+1)*(a-1)}{a-1}$, and $z = 1$]

---

number that yields $x * y$ when multiplied by z. Then, $\frac{y}{z}$ is the number that yields y when multiplied by z.)

5. $$\frac{(a+1)*(a-1)}{a-1}=1$$
    [from 3., 4., and (51)]

6. $$\frac{(a+1)*(a-1)}{a-1}=(a+1)*\frac{a-1}{a-1}$$
    [from (84) and (52), with $x = a + 1$, $y = a - 1$, and $z = a - 1$]

7. $$((\frac{(a+1)*(a-1)}{a-1}=1)*(\frac{(a+1)*(a-1)}{a-1}=(a+1)*\frac{a-1}{a-1}))$$
    [from 5., 6., and Fig. 61(c)]

8. $$((\frac{(a+1)*(a-1)}{a-1}=1)*(\frac{(a+1)*(a-1)}{a-1}=(a+1)*\frac{a-1}{a-1}))$$
    $$\supset ((a+1)*\frac{a-1}{a-1}=1)$$
    [from (58) and (52), with $x = \frac{(a+1)*(a-1)}{a-1}$, $y = 1$, and
    $z = (a+1)*\frac{a-1}{a-1}$]

9. $$(a+1)*\frac{a-1}{a-1}=1$$
    [from 7., 8., and (51)]

10. $$(\frac{a-1}{a-1}=1) \supset ((a+1)*1=(a+1)*\frac{a-1}{a-1})$$
    [from (82) and (52), with $x = \frac{a-1}{a-1}$, $y = 1$, and $z = a + 1$]

11. $$(a+1)*1=(a+1)*\frac{a-1}{a-1}$$
    [from 2., 10., and (51)]

12. $$((a+1)*1=(a+1)*\frac{a-1}{a-1})*((a+1)*\frac{a-1}{a-1}=1)$$
    [from 9., 11, and Fig. 61(c)]

13. $$(((a+1)*1=(a+1)*\frac{a-1}{a-1})*((a+1)*\frac{a-1}{a-1}=1)) \supset ((a+1)*1=1)$$
    [from (64) and (52), with $x = (a+1)*\frac{a-1}{a-1}$, $y = (a+1)*1$,
    and $z = 1$]

14. $$(a+1)*1=1$$
    [from 12., 13., and (51)]

The argument in (85) has essentially the deductive structure (70),[110] while (86) is only a little more complex than (80).[111]

Statement 2. in (86) provides the crux of what is going on in Figure 53. Statement 2 is an instantiation of the purported "universal law" (83), via (52). It is used twice in (86), first to derive statement 5. from statement 1., via statements 3. and 4., and then to derive statement 11. directly from statement 10. Those are the places in (86) where (87) gets replaced by *1*, thereby implementing (83).

(87) $\dfrac{a-1}{a-1}$

The cult adherent "knows" that (83) is an inviolable law because his leader tells him so. For the rest of us, however—since we want our mathematics to be interesting and useful—this purported "law" is defective because it fails to mention *0* as an exception. The proper formulation of this cancellation law is (88), which makes the replacement of (87) by *1* conditional on *a* itself not being *1*, by requiring that *a* - *1* not be *0*.

(88) $(x \neq 0) \supset (\dfrac{x}{x} = 1)$

Using (88), instead of (83), in (86) invalidates the justification for the inferences from statement 1. to statement 5. and from statement 10. to statement 11., because there is no way to infer (89)(a), the required antecedent for the instance of (88) that would be required for those inferences to work.

(89)   (a) $a - 1 \neq 0$

        (b) $a - 1 = 0$

In other words, for the inferences to work, statement 2. would have to be (90), whose own antecedent, (89)(a), has not been derived and, in

---

[110] *Suggested excursion:* Explain what *essentially* means in that sentence. (*Hint:* What about the justifications?)

[111] *Suggested excursion:* Explicitly write out the sub-arguments of (86) and their deductive structures. (*Hint:* See excursions 100 and 106.)

fact, cannot be derived, without some equivalent misstep, precisely because (89)(b) is true.[112]

(90) $$(a - 1 \neq 0) \supset (\frac{a-1}{a-1} = 1)$$

The problem here is not that (90) is false; on the contrary, in accordance with the truth table for $\supset$, (90) is true because of the falsity of its antecedent, (89)(a). However, the falsity of the antecedent—while it makes (90) itself true—prevents (51) from applying, so the detachment of the consequent of (90)—namely, statement 2. of (86)—cannot occur.

In contrast to (83), the statements (81) and (84)—where we might also have expected to find problems—really are valid laws—if we interpret them appropriately for a computational context. In relation to computation, the most natural way to interpret (81) is to take it as saying that dividing two equal numbers by the same number *always produces the same result*. Since dividing zero by zero results in no particular number, as we saw in connection with (23), and since dividing any non-zero number by zero results in no number at all, as we saw in connection with (22), (81) remains true under this interpretation, whether z is 0 or not. The reasoning in (85), which makes use of (81), thus works perfectly well, just as it stands. The situation is similar in regard to (84).[113]

We can make this way of interpreting our laws work by expressing the *result* of division by zero in terms of the *error* element that we introduced in connection with the data structures of Expedition 2. More specifically, we can supplement (88) with the further law (91), which generates *error* for the case that (88) does not cover.

(91) $$(x = 0) \supset (\frac{x}{x} = error)$$

When a computer that is executing a statement that instantiates (91) generates *error* as its result, it typically triggers an *error message* to

---

[112] *Suggested excursion:* Prove (89)(b). (*Hint:* Start with (1) and use (79).)

[113] *Suggested excursion:* Is this true? Work it out explicitly. (*Hint:* Carefully examine what happens when each of the parameters in (84) is or is not 0.)

that effect—sometimes in a *dialog box* such as the one in Figure 62—and the calculation comes to a halt.

Fig. 62: Error Message Dialog Box for Division by Zero

The human user can then decide how to proceed next by clicking one of the available choices or by typing something at the keyboard, without having to worry that something strange might happen, such as the system shutting down or proving that all numbers are equal. In particular, *error* works perfectly well with (81) and (84).[114] Even though the falsity of (89)(a) prevents statement 2. in (86) from being validly derived, the truth of (89)(b) enables the correct law (91) to be used instead.[115] Of course, the result is very different.

Formally, the argument works as (92) shows.

---

[114] *Suggested excursion:* Is this true? Work it out explicitly. (*Hint:* See excursion 113.)

[115] *Suggested excursion:* Prove (91) from the more general statement (i).

(i) $\dfrac{x}{0} = \text{error}$

(*Hint:* Examine the truth table for $\supset$.)

(92)   Valid reasoning from (11):

1. $\dfrac{(a+1)*(a-1)}{a-1} = \dfrac{a-1}{a-1}$

[from (11)]

2. $a - 1 = 0$

[from (89)(b)]

3. $(a-1=0) \supset (\dfrac{a-1}{a-1} = \text{error})$

[from (91) and (52), with x = a - 1]

4. $\dfrac{a-1}{a-1} = \text{error}$

[from 2., 3., and (51)]

5. $(\dfrac{(a+1)*(a-1)}{a-1} = \dfrac{a-1}{a-1}) * (\dfrac{a-1}{a-1} = \text{error})$

[from 1., 4., and Fig. 61(c)]

6. $((\dfrac{(a+1)*(a-1)}{a-1} = \dfrac{a-1}{a-1}) * (\dfrac{a-1}{a-1} = \text{error})) \supset (\dfrac{(a+1)*(a-1)}{a-1} = \text{error})$

[from (64) and (52), with $x = \dfrac{a-1}{a-1}$,

$y = \dfrac{(a+1)*(a-1)}{a-1}$, and z = *error*]

7. $\dfrac{(a+1)*(a-1)}{a-1} = \text{error}$

[from 5., 6., and (51)]

8. $\dfrac{(a+1)*(a-1)}{a-1} = (a+1) * \dfrac{a-1}{a-1}$

[from (84) and (52), with x = *a +1*, y = *a - 1*, and z = *a - 1*]

9. $(\dfrac{(a+1)*(a-1)}{a-1} = \text{error}) * (\dfrac{(a+1)*(a-1)}{a-1} = (a+1) * \dfrac{a-1}{a-1})$

[from 7., 8., and Fig. 61(c)]

10. $$((\frac{(a+1)*(a-1)}{a-1} = error)*(\frac{(a+1)*(a-1)}{a-1} = (a+1)*\frac{a-1}{a-1}))$$

$$\supset ((a+1)*\frac{a-1}{a-1} = error)$$

[from (58) and (52), with $x = \dfrac{(a+1)*(a-1)}{a-1}$, $y = error$,

and $z = (a+1)*\dfrac{a-1)}{a-1}$]

11. $$(a+1)*\frac{a-1}{a-1} = error$$

[from 9., 10., and (51)]

12. $$(\frac{a-1}{a-1} = error) \supset ((a+1)*error = (a+1)*\frac{a-1}{a-1})$$

[from (82) and (52), $x = \dfrac{a-1}{a-1}$, $y = error$, and $z = a+1$]

13. $$(a+1)*error = (a+1)*\frac{a-1}{a-1}$$

[from 4., 12., and (51)]

14. $$((a+1)*error = (a+1)*\frac{a-1}{a-1})*((a+1)*\frac{a-1}{a-1} = error)$$

[from 11., 13., and Fig. 61(c)]

15. $$(((a+1)*error = (a+1)*\frac{a-1}{a-1})*((a+1)*\frac{a-1}{a-1} = error)) \supset ((a+1)*error = error)$$

[from (64) and (52), with $x = (a+1)*\dfrac{a-1}{a-1}$, $y = (a+1)$

* error, and $z = error$]

16. $(a+1)*error = error$

[from 14., 15., and (51)]

In other words, *error* propagates through (92) in the same way that *1* propagates through (86), presenting no problems for (84). The conclusion, statement 16., provides no new knowledge, since any numerical operation, when actually applied to *error*, always results in *error*. In particular, it provides no basis for the rest of the argument in Fig. 53, so (13) through (16) simply disappear.

Without prior knowledge that division by zero is impossible, we could take Figure 53 itself as a proof of that fact, given that we know that all numbers are not equal and thus that the conclusion (16) is false. We would base the argument on the fact that a false conclusion can be validly derived only from a false premise. Reasoning that leads to a false conclusion must have something wrong with it; since all the other steps in Figure 53 are valid, it must be the division by zero that is wrong.

The formal argument would run roughly as follows. Take all of the statements in the arguments (60), (62), (66), (69), (72), (75), (80), (85), and (86), except the conclusion (16), and form their conjunction. Call that statement s. Claiming that the argument in Figure 53 is valid amounts to saying that s cannot be true without (16) being true as well and thus that (93) is true, by Figure 56.

(93) $s \supset (16)$

In effect, the assumption that s is true, combined with (93) and detachment, is precisely what the cult adherent takes as justifying (16) in Figure 53. However, since (16) is known to be false, (94) is true instead.

(94) $\sim(16)$

Together with (93) and the rule of contrapositive in Figure 61(b), (94) justifies the inference that s itself is false. However, s is a conjunction of many statements and so, by Figure 54(b) and the associative law, s can be false only if one (or more) of its conjuncts is false. Since all the other steps have been shown to be valid, it must be the division by zero (namely, statement 2. of (86)) that is wrong.

The argument is summarized in (95).

(95)   Sketch of the reasoning from (16):

    1. $s \supset (16)$
          [from (60), (62), (66), (69), (72), (75), (80), (85), (86), and Fig. 56]

    2. $\sim(16)$
          [from reality]

    3. $\sim s$
          [from Fig. 61(b)]

    4. $\sim((\text{clearly true statements}) * (\text{division by zero}))$

[from 3. and what *s* is]

5.   ~(division by zero)

[from 4., (32)(b), and Fig. 54(b)]

There are two sub-arguments consisting of statements 1. through 3. and statements 4. and 5. Statement 4. is simply a more explicit rewriting of statement 3. The respective deductive structures are shown in (96) and (97).[116]

(96)   The deductive structure of the first sub-argument of (95):

1.   Premise $\supset$ Conclusion

[from some source]

2.   ~Conclusion

[from some source]

3.   ~Premise

[from 1., 2., and Fig. 61(b)]

(97)   The deductive structure of the second sub-argument of (95):

1.   ~((Validated conjuncts) * (Questionable conjunct))

[from some source]

2.   ~(Questionable conjunct)

[from 1. and Fig. 54(b)]

In sum, logical reasoning is a two-edged sword. We can trust valid reasoning methods to result in true conclusions, when we apply them to true premises. However, we must always test the truth of the conclusions independently of the reasoning that we used to reach them. A reasoning method applied to true premises can result in false conclusions. When that happens, the reasoning method itself is faulty and must be examined to determine the source of the error.

We can build all of the universal laws and rules of inference that we have used here to analyze Figure 53 into a computer's hardware or provide it to a computer in program form; either way, we can then use

---

[116] *Suggested excursion:* Formulate and prove an explicit rule that justifies the inferences from statement 4. to statement 5. of (95), and from statement 2. to statement 3. of (97). (*Hint:* Show that $(\sim(t * y)) \supset \sim y$ is a tautology).

it as the basis of an *expert system*. The laws and rules provide the basis for an expert system's *inference engine*, which the computer uses in conjunction with one or more stored *knowledge bases* to derive new knowledge from what we already know. For example, the statements shown in (98) comprise a very (!) simple medical knowledge base that we can use to derive prescriptions in response to presented symptoms and medical histories.

(98)　(a)　[is sneezing](x) ⊃ ([has a cold](x) + [has allergy](x))

　　　(b)　[is fatigued](x) ⊃ ([has a cold](x) + [has flu](x))

　　　(c)　[has been vaccinated](x) ⊃ ~[has flu](x)

　　　(d)　[has a cold](x) ⊃ [needs chicken soup](x)

　　　(e)　[has allergy](x) ⊃ [needs antihistamine](x)

　　　(f)　[has flu](x) ⊃ [needs lots of sleep](x)

The system tests for two symptoms, sneezing and fatigue, and for one aspect of medical history, namely, whether or not the patient has been vaccinated. If the patient is sneezing, the system diagnoses cold or allergy. If the patient is fatigued, it diagnoses cold or flu. If the patient has been vaccinated, it rules out flu. As prescriptions, the system recommends chicken soup for a cold, antihistamines for an allergy, and sleep for the flu.

　　　The system derives these prescriptions through the process of *forward chaining*. This involves first matching a fact to the antecedent of a material implication, via (52), and then inferring that implication's consequent, via (51). The system then takes this consequent as a further fact to be matched with the antecedent of some other material implication and continues the process as long as it can. For example, if Joe shows signs of fatigue, the human user enters the fact (99) into the computer as a *query* and the inference engine then compares that fact with each of the statements in (98) until it gets a match, or until it reaches the end of the list without finding one.

(99)　[is fatigued](joe)

　　　(Joe is fatigued.)

As it happens, (99) matches the antecedent of (100), the *joe*-instance of (98)(b), via (52), so the inference engine infers (101), via (51).

(100)   [is fatigued](joe) ⊃ ([has a cold](joe) + [has flu](joe))

(If Joe is fatigued, then either Joe has a cold or Joe has the flu (or both).)

(101)   [has a cold](joe) + [has flu](joe)

(Either Joe has a cold or Joe has the flu (or both).)

If Joe is not sneezing, then no fact is entered into the computer that matches the antecedent of an instance of (98)(a), so the system infers nothing from (98)(a). However, if Joe's medical record shows that he has been vaccinated, then that fact is entered as (102), which matches the antecedent of (103), the *joe*-instance of (98)(c), via (52), so the inference engine infers the new fact (104), via (51).

(102)   [has been vaccinated](joe)

(Joe has been vaccinated.)

(103)   [has been vaccinated](joe) ⊃ ~[has flu](joe)

(If Joe has been vaccinated, then Joe does not have the flu.)

(104)   ~[has flu](joe)

(Joe does not have the flu.)

This new fact is then compared to each of the statements in the knowledge base (98) and to each previously inferred fact and is thereby found, together with (101) and the commutative law, to match the rule of inference in Figure 61(e), so the inference engine infers the further fact (105).

(105)   [has a cold](joe)

(Joe has a cold.)

This fact matches the antecedent of (106), the *joe*-instance of (98)(d), so the inference engine infers the fact (107).

(106)   [has a cold](joe) ⊃ [needs chicken soup](joe)

(If Joe has a cold, then Joe needs chicken soup.)

(107)   [needs chicken-soup](joe)

(Joe needs chicken soup.)

Since there are no further matches, the inference engine concludes that Joe needs chicken soup, and the computer prints a prescription to that effect.

A more sophisticated system would have a more extensive knowledge base and might also have the ability to report back intermediate results, rather than waiting until it reaches a predicate for which it finds no further match. For example, we might design a system to stop matching as soon as it reaches a predicate that the computer has been programmed to recognize as a prescription, rather than a symptom or an item of medical history, even if a further match is possible. The human user can then decide whether further inquiry is necessary.

We can program an expert system to work in either a closed-world or an open-world way. A *closed-world* expert system will report back and remember that a query for which it finds no match is false, while an *open-world* expert system will report back and remember that it does not know the answer to such a query. For example, because nothing in (98) matches (108), the inference engine of an open-world system based on (98) will respond to (108) with some equivalent of (109)(a), while the inference engine of a closed-world system based on (98) will respond to (108) with some equivalent of (109)(b).

(108)   [is coughing](joe)
         (Joe is coughing.)

(109)   (a)   Don't know.
         (b)   No.

This difference matters because a *No* answer to (108) counts as a *Yes* answer to (110), as the computer seeks further matches, but a *Don't know* answer does not.

(110)   ~[is coughing](joe)
         (Joe is not coughing.)

In effect, a *No* answer to (108) adds (110) to the knowledge base as a previously inferred fact, relative to the current query, whereas a *Don't know* answer leaves the knowledge base unchanged. Closed-world systems are simpler than open-world systems and their reasoning is easier to follow, because every tested fact adds knowledge to the knowledge base, whether a match is found or not. However, such systems require us to exercise extra care in ensuring the completeness of their knowledge bases in order to prevent insufficient data from generating otherwise unwarranted *No* answers.[117]

We can also organize a knowledge base in such a way as to permit the inference engine to derive conclusions through *backward chaining*. This operates in the opposite direction, matching queries against consequents, rather than antecedents. Note that backward chaining cannot be an outright reversal of forward chaining, because $\supset$ is not reversible; in contrast to $+$ and $*$, it does not satisfy a symmetric law. In other words, (111)(a) is not logically equivalent to (111)(b),[118] and (112) is not a valid rule of inference.[119]

(111) (a) $x \supset y$

(b) $y \supset x$

(112) Premise 1: y

Premise 2: $x \supset y$

∴ Conclusion: x

To see how backward chaining does work, consider the very simple zoological knowledge base (113).

(113) (a)   [is a dog](x) $\supset$ [barks](x)

(b)   [is a dog](x) $\supset$ [buries bones](x)

(c)   [is a dog](x) $\supset$ [chases cats](x)

(d)   [is a cat](x) $\supset$ [meows](x)

(e)   [is a cat](x) $\supset$ [climbs trees](x)

(f)   [is a cat](x) $\supset$ [chases mice](x)

(g)   [is a lion](x) $\supset$ [growls](x)

(h)   [is a lion](x) $\supset$ [hunts antelope](x)

(i)   [is a lion](x) $\supset$ [hunts elephants](x)

---

[117] *Suggested excursion:* Investigate what happens to the story-guessing game that begins Expedition 3, if you play it in an open-world way, rather than a closed-world way. (*Hint:* Tell the guessers that you will answer their questions with *yes, no,* or *irrelevant,* and then base your answers on some three-way division of the alphabet, rather than on consonants vs. vowels.)

[118] *Suggested excursion:* Prove that (111)(a) is not logically equivalent to (111)(b). (*Hint:* Construct their truth tables.)

[119] *Suggested excursion:* Prove that (112) is not a valid rule of inference. (*Hint:* Use truth tables to prove that the statement $(y * (x \supset y)) \supset x$ is not a tautology.)

(j)   [is a wolf](x) ⊃ [howls](x)

(k)   [is a wolf](x) ⊃ [chases rabbits](x)

(l)   [is a wolf](x) ⊃ [catches rabbits](x)

(m)   [is a seal](x) ⊃ [barks](x)

(n)   [is a seal](x) ⊃ [eats fish](x)

(o)   [is a seal](x) ⊃ [likes to swim](x)

(p)   [is a tiger](x) ⊃ [growls](x)

(q)   [is a tiger](x) ⊃ [hunts antelope](x)

(r)   [is a tiger](x) ⊃ [has stripes](x)

(s)   [is a walrus](x) ⊃ [growls](x)

(t)   [is a walrus](x) ⊃ [eats fish](x)

(u)   [is a walrus](x) ⊃ [likes to swim](x)

(v)   [is a walrus](x) ⊃ [howls](x)

(w)   [is a hyena](x) ⊃ [hunts antelope](x)

(x)   [is a hyena](x) ⊃ [eats carrion](x)

(y)   [buries bones](x) ⊃ [lives in city](x)

(z)   [hunts antelope](x) ⊃ [lives in jungle](x)

(aa)   [likes to swim](x) ⊃ [lives in water](x)

(bb)   [chases rabbits](x) ⊃ [lives in forest](x)

Suppose that you see an animal of a kind that you do not recognize burying a bone at some distance, and that you hear some person running after it calling it Fido. If you present the fact (114) to a backward-chaining inference engine associated with (113), the computer will try to match (114) with the consequent of each of the statements in (113).

(114)   [buries bones](fido)

(Fido buries bones.)

It will find that (114) matches the consequent of (115), the *fido-*instance of (113)(b), and no such instance of any of the other statements in (113).

(115)   [is a dog](fido) ⊃ [buries bones](fido)

(If Fido is a dog, then Fido buries bones.)

It will therefore conclude that, *according to the information contained in this knowledge base,* Fido can be taken to be a dog and it will report back the fact (116).

(116)   [is a dog](fido)

                     (Fido is a dog.)

Clearly, this could be wrong, if there are other bone-burying animals we have inadvertently omitted from the knowledge base. It is up to the person who constructs the knowledge base to ensure that the information it contains is complete enough to justify the computer's conclusions.

Suppose that you have difficulty sleeping, because one of your neighbors has brought home a new pet, which barks incessantly all night through your bedroom wall. You hear your neighbor calling the animal Waldo, and you wonder, "What sort of animal is this Waldo?" If you present the query (117) to a backward-chaining inference engine associated with (113), the computer will find that it matches the consequent of (118)(a), the *waldo*-instance of (113)(a), and that it also matches (118)(b), the *waldo*-instance of (113)(m), but no such instance of any of the other statements in (113).

(117)   [barks](waldo)

        (Waldo barks.)

(118)   (a)   [is a dog](waldo) ⊃ [barks](waldo)

                (If Waldo is a dog, then Waldo barks.)

        (b)   [is a seal](waldo) ⊃ [barks](waldo)

                (If Waldo is a seal, then Waldo barks.)

The computer can therefore report back the disjunctive fact (119), that is, that—according to the information in this knowledge base—Waldo is either a dog or a seal.

(119)   [is a dog](waldo) + [is a seal](waldo)

        (Either Waldo is a dog or Waldo is a seal (or both).)

Again, it is up to the person who builds the knowledge base to ensure that its information is as complete as possible.

Some backward-chaining systems, such as those written in the programming language PROLOG, may not give a disjunctive result such as (119), but will report each disjunct as it is found, and ask the user whether it should seek further results. In other words, such a system will first report (120)(a), then (120)(b), and then (120)(c), when further instances are asked for.

(120) (a)   [is a dog](waldo)

(Waldo is a dog.)

(b)   [is a seal](waldo)

(Waldo is a seal.)

(c)   no

However, the effect is the same. The human user knows that each response prior to the occurrence of a *no* response is only one of the possible alternatives, and that the full answer is the disjunction of all those alternatives. In particular, in this instance, (119) is the disjunction of (120)(a) and (120)(b).

If you are disturbed not only by Waldo's barking, but also by a stench of rotting fish that began soon after Waldo's arrival, then you might surmise that the fish were brought in for Waldo's benefit. You might therefore present not only (117), but also (121), to your backward-chaining expert system.

(121)   [eats fish](waldo)

(Waldo eats fish.)

The inference engine will find that (121) matches the consequents of (122)(a) and (122)(b), the respective *waldo*-instances of (113)(n) and (113)(t), but no such instance of any of the other statements, so the computer will report the disjunctive fact (123) (either all at once or individually by disjunct, as in PROLOG).

(122) (a)   [is a seal](waldo) ⊃ [eats fish](waldo)

(If Waldo is a seal, then Waldo eats fish.)

(b)   [is a walrus](waldo) ⊃ [eats fish](waldo)

(If Waldo is a walrus, then Waldo eats fish.)

(123)   [is a seal](waldo) + [is a walrus](waldo)

(Either Waldo is a seal or Waldo is a walrus (or both).)

If you have programmed the inference engine with the capacity to do further processing, and if you ask it to do so, then it will combine (119) and (123) by Figure 61(c) to get the conjunctive fact (124).

(124)   ([is a dog](waldo) + [is a seal](waldo))
       * ([is a seal](waldo) + [is a walrus](waldo))

(Waldo is either a dog or a seal (or both) and is either a seal or a walrus (or both).)

This, in turn, is found to be logically equivalent, first, to (125) and, then, to (126) by the distributive, commutative, and associative laws.[120]

(125)   ((([is a dog](waldo) + [is a seal](waldo))
       * [is a seal](waldo))
       + ((([is a dog](waldo) + [is a seal](waldo))
       * [is a walrus](waldo))

(Either Waldo is either a dog or a seal (or both) and is a seal, or Waldo is either a dog or a seal (or both) and is a walrus (or both).)

(126)   ([is a dog](waldo) * [is a seal](waldo))
       + ([is a seal](waldo) * [is a seal](waldo))
       + ([is a dog](waldo) * [is a walrus](waldo))
       + ([is a seal](waldo) * [is a walrus](waldo))

(Waldo is either a dog and a seal, a seal and a seal, a dog and a walrus, or a seal and a walrus (or some combination thereof).)

If you have incorporated into your inference engine (or have extended (113) with) information to the effect that one animal cannot be of two different species (for example, through some equivalent of rules such as those in (127)), then—via (51), (52), and several uses of Figure

---

[120] *Suggested excursion:* Work out the details of deriving (125) and then (126) from (124). (*Hint:* First, take x, y, and z to be (i), (ii), and (iii), respectively, in (39)(a) to get (125).

(i)   ([is a dog](waldo) + [is a seal](waldo))

(ii)   [is a seal](waldo)

(iii)   [is a walrus](waldo)

(iv)   [is a dog](waldo)

Then use two applications of the commutative reversal of (39)(a), first, with x, y, and z as (ii), (iv), and (ii), respectively, and then with x, y, and z as (iii), (iv), and (ii), respectively, to get (126).)

61—the inference engine will be able to infer that all but the second of the disjuncts in (126) are false.

(127) (a)   [is a dog](x) ⊃ ~[is a seal](x)

(A dog is not a seal.)

(b)   [is a dog](x) ⊃ ~[is a walrus](x)

(A dog is not a walrus.)

(c)   [is a seal](x) ⊃ ~[is a walrus](x)

(A seal is not a walrus.)

For example, taking the disjuncts separately, the first disjunct of (126) is (128).

(128)   [is a dog](waldo) * [is a seal](waldo)

(Waldo is a dog and a seal.)

From (128) the inference engine will infer each of (129)(a) and (129)(b), via two uses of Figure 61(h).

(129) (a)   [is a dog](waldo)

(Waldo is a dog.)

(b)   [is a seal](waldo)

(Waldo is a seal.)

From (129)(a) and (127)(a) it will infer (130), via (51) and (52).

(130)   ~[is a seal](waldo)

(Waldo is a not seal.)

However, from (130), (129)(b), and Fig. 61(c), it will infer (131), which is false by Figure 61(f).

(131)   [is a seal](waldo) * ~[is a seal](waldo)

(Waldo is a seal and Waldo is not a seal.)

The same animal cannot both be a seal and not be a seal. Similar reasoning also shows that the third and fourth disjuncts of (126) are false, so (126) justifies an inference to (132)[121] and therefore to (133), by Figure 61(i) and the associative law.

(132)   f + ([is a seal](waldo) * [is a seal](waldo)) + f + f

(133)   [is a seal](waldo) * [is a seal](waldo)

(Waldo is a seal and Waldo is a seal.)

This enables the inference engine, finally, to infer (134) by Figure 61(h).

(134)   [is a seal](waldo)

(Waldo is a seal.)

In other words, insofar as we can determine on the basis of the information in this knowledge base, Waldo is a seal.[122]

Since each of the *specific* facts in (127) is an instance of the *general* fact that one animal cannot belong to more than one species, it is tempting to try to abbreviate them all in terms of *general predicates*—that is, variables whose values are predicates—for example, as the statement (135).

(135) $(P \neq R) \supset (P(x) \supset {\sim}R(x))$

---

[121] *Suggested excursion:* Show that this step is justified, that is, that the disjuncts can be treated separately in this way. (*Hint:* Formulate a rule of *disjunctive detachment* (i).

(i)	Premise 1:	$x + z$
	Premise 2:	$x \supset y$
	∴ Conclusion:	$y + z$

Prove the rule is valid by examining the truth table of $((x + z) * (x \supset y)) \supset (y + z)$. Show how it applies to (126).)

[122] *Suggested excursion:* Suppose that you tell the inference engine that Leo lives in the jungle and growls. Show in detail how it would infer that Leo is a lion or a tiger. (*Hint:* Start with (i) and use it to infer (ii).)

(i)   [lives in jungle](leo) * [growls](leo)

(ii)   [is a lion](leo) + [is a tiger](leo)

This statement says that if P and R are different predicates, then an object that P is true of is an object that R is false of; in other words, anything that is an instance of P is not an instance of R. For example, if P is instantiated as *[is a dog]* and R is instantiated as *[is a seal]*, then (135) justifies an inference to (127)(a); similarly, if P is instantiated as *[is a seal]* and R is instantiated as *[is a walrus]*, then (135) justifies an inference to (127)(c).[123]

However, (135), as it stands, is much too general, because it immediately conflicts with every statement in (113). For example, if P is instantiated as *[is a dog]* and R is instantiated as *[barks]*, then (135) conflicts with (113)(a); similarly if P is instantiated as *[is a seal]* and R is instantiated as *[eats fish]*, then (135) conflicts with (113)(n).[124] To abbreviate (127) accurately in general terms we need to restrict (135) specifically to predicates that identify species, for example, as in (136).

(136) $(S \neq T) \supset ([is\ a\ S](x) \supset \sim[is\ a\ T](x))$

This statement is compatible with (113) but, as it stands, is again too general, because it would rule out the possibility of predicates for units larger than species. For example, (136) conflicts immediately with (137), the very simple claim that dogs are mammals.[125]

(137) $[is\ a\ dog](x) \supset [is\ a\ mammal](x)$

Bringing (136) more into line with what we would need for a proper abbreviation of (127) would require us to complicate it still further.

Now that we have introduced general predicates into our knowledge base, we might also be tempted to try to use them to develop an analogy between our boolean and predicate rules of

---

[123] *Suggested excursion:* Figure out what else we would really need to justify these conclusions. (*Hint:* Try (51). What about (52)?)

[124] *Suggested excursion:* Work out the details of these conflicts. (*Hint:* Use Figure 61 to infer f (i.e., *false*) from (i), (ii), and (iii).

(i) $[is\ a\ dog](x)$
(ii) $[is\ a\ dog](x) \supset [barks](x)$
(iii) $[is\ a\ dog](x) \supset \sim[barks](x)$

In other words, (ii) and (iii) together imply that there are no dogs.)

[125] *Suggested excursion:* Work out the details of this conflict. (*Hint:* See excursion 124.)

inference. Just as the boolean rules of inference in Figure 61 contain parameters, x and y, for general unspecified propositions, the predicate rules of inference (52) and (54) contain a parameter, P, for a general unspecified predicate. The boolean rules apply to any propositions at all, the predicate rules apply to any predicates at all, and the two sorts of rules can be used together in any combination. Since the boolean rules are based on statements of material implication that we can show to be tautologies and that can themselves be used in arguments—such as (49) for detachment, for example—it would be natural to want to have statements with those same characteristics for the predicate rules as well. For example, (52) and (54) would correspond to the respective statements (138) and (139).

(138)   P(parameter of some type)
⊃ P(specific object of the same type)
(If P is an attribute, in general, of objects of some type, then it is an attribute, in particular, of some specific object of that type.)

(139)   (P(1) * (P(num) ⊃ P(num + 1)))
⊃ P(any particular number)
(If P is an attribute of the particular number 1 and is also an attribute, in general, of the successor of whatever number already has it as an attribute, then it is an attribute of any particular number at all.)

We could then introduce further rules of inference to reason validly about statements of this more general sort.

Logicians call reasoning systems that incorporate general predicates *higher-order logics* and have, in fact, developed and used them for various kinds of theoretical investigations, such as the explication of mathematical induction in (55). However, the use of general predicates is tricky in practice, because it increases the power of the inference engine to such an extent that the well-known *incompleteness theorem* that was proven by the logician Kurt Gödel in the 1930's becomes operative. As long as the statements in a knowledge base do not contain general predicates, we can be sure that the inference engine can derive all true statements about the knowledge base's subject matter and no false ones. However, if we allow statements that contain general predicates into the knowledge base, then one of those conditions must fail: either there will be true statements about the subject matter that the inference engine cannot derive, or there will be false statements about the subject matter that the inference engine can derive. In the former case, the knowledge base is *incomplete*; in the latter case, the knowledge base is *inconsistent*. Since the goal of an expert system is to get as accurate an account of the subject matter as possible—for example, in a more extensive and realistic medical knowledge base than the one shown in (98)—it is therefore prudent to avoid statements that contain general predicates—or, at least, to provide very tight constraints on how they can be used. Some versions of PROLOG, for example, take the latter course.

Epilogue: Further Exploration

There are many good books available at every level of difficulty, if you'd like to learn more about the topics you've explored here. Browse the shelves of bookstores and libraries—or, if you prefer, the web—to find books that suit your temperament and learning style. If you're ambitious, and you want to dive really deeply, you would do well to look at the following classics:

Number Theory, Helmut Hasse. Springer-Verlag.

The Design and Analysis of Computer Algorithms. Alfred V. Aho, John E. Hopcroft, Jeffrey D. Ullman. Addison-Wesley.

System Design from Provably Correct Constructs. James Martin. Prentice-Hall.

Systems Analysis and Design. Gary B. Shelly, Thomas J. Cashman, Harry J. Rosenblatt. Course Technology.

Data Structures and Algorithms. Alfred V. Aho, Jeffrey D. Ullman, John E. Hopcroft. Addison-Wesley.

Introduction to Automata Theory, Languages, and Computation. John E. Hopcroft and Jeffrey D. Ullman. Addison-Wesley.

Computer Gamesmanship: The Complete Guide to Creating and Structuring Intelligent Games Programs. David N. L. Levy. Simon & Schuster.

Introduction to Mathematical Logic. Elliott Mendelson. CRC Press.